SINS OF THE FATHERS

A STUDY OF INIQUITY

By

Ricki Goral

Copyright © 2011 by Ricki Goral

Sins Of The Fathers
A Study Of Iniquity
by Ricki Goral

Printed in the United States of America

ISBN 9781612157832

All rights reserved solely by the author. The author guarantees all contents are original and do not infringe upon the legal rights of any other person or work. No part of this book may be reproduced in any form without the permission of the author. The views expressed in this book are not necessarily those of the publisher.

Unless otherwise indicated, Bible quotations are taken from The King James Version of the Bible. Copyright © 1972 BY THOMAS NELSON INC.; The ESV Study Bible™, English Standard Version® (ESV®). Copyright © 2008 by Crossway Bibles, a publishing ministry of Good News Publishers; and The Holy Bible, English Standard Version ® (ESV®). Copyright © 2001 by Crossway Bibles, a publishing ministry of Good News Publishers. ESV Text Edition: 2007.

www.xulonpress.com

April 2011

Dear Berwicks

I hope you will enjoy my new book. Perhaps God will show you something you have not known or understood. That is the sole purpose of this book. I love you all very much

Love
Ricki

A study of iniquity;

Generational sin, curses and attending spirits.

TABLE OF CONTENTS

Chapter 1 – Without Understanding 15

Chapter 2 – What Exactly Is A Stronghold? 30

Chapter 3 – Sin, Transgression And Iniquity 44

Chapter 4 – Self Fulfilling Prophesy 54

Chapter 5 – Angels And Demons 62

Chapter 6 – Angels, Angels Everywhere 74

Chapter 7 – Chastisement Or A Curse? 101

Chapter 8 – The Curse Causeless 119

Chapter 9 – Stronghold Or A Curse? 130

Chapter 10 – My Childhood 141

Chapter 11 – Generation to Generation 158

Chapter 12 – Death To Life 171

Chapter 13 – The Spirit Of Death 180

Sins Of The Fathers

Chapter 14 – Spirit Ties...199

Chapter 15 – Let's Talk About Deliverance...........................213

Chapter 16 – What Are Some of The Biblical Curses?...........225

Chapter 17 – Witchcraft And The Occult...............................235

Chapter 18 – You Shall Not Suffer A Witch To Live...............253

Chapter 19 – A Fortress Inside Of Me 269

Chapter 20 – Mental Illness And Attending Spirits................275

Chapter 21 – Help Me! There Are Giants In My Land 286

Chapter 22 – What Kind Of Spirit Is It? 303

Chapter 23 – Jezebel Is In the House 326

Chapter 24 – Tearing Down Strongholds And Breaking
  Curses...341

INTRODUCTION

Some time around 1983 God began to speak to me about generational sin and generational curses. One day He simply said, "You are living out the life of your Mother."

I began to think about that and wondered what He was talking about. When He said the word Mother, I knew He meant my birthmother. As I prayed and waited before Him regarding this matter, He began to show me how generational sin and curses come down the family line. He began to point out particular people in my family line and their behavior patterns along with some other things that I had never noticed before. Although I saw most of these things myself as an actual eye witness while I was a child growing up, and heard about certain other family events during that time, I just never gave it much thought. When I would think or remember some of these things as an adult, it never occurred to me that it was anything more than a matter of personality and character or family traits and issues.

Over the years I studied this subject and God revealed so much more to me each time I came before Him with it. God has allowed me to teach extensively on this subject. I am always amazed at what God shows the people I am teaching about their own generational sin and the curses that are operating in their own family line. And these same people are always very surprised and even shocked by what He shows them as well.

So we are going to take a little bit of time to examine our past generations to see exactly what has been transferred down into our lives and the lives of our children. We will look individually at our mothers, fathers, grandparents, great-grandparents, aunts, uncles, brothers, sisters, and cousins. We want to see what is really happening in our family line and as a result, in our own personal life as well.

We will see that each one of us have a spiritual heritage which we are already walking in. Where did it come from? Did it come from God? Or are we still living out of the sins and habits of our dead relatives from past generations?

We will also see that we have a spiritual heritage which we will pass on to our children and our future generations. What is this heritage? Is it a godly heritage? Or is it something left over from the curses and sins of those who went before us?

We will see that spirits can dominate whole families for generations, and even have control over whole areas geographically. The Prince of Persia is an example of a geographic demonic spirit or power having dominion over a physical area. Michael the Archangel is another example of an angel of God having power and dominion over a physical area and people.

Luke 11:24; "When the unclean spirit has gone out of a person, it passes through waterless places seeking rest, and finding none it says, 'I will return to my house from which I came.' And when it comes, it finds the house swept and put in order. Then it goes and brings seven other spirits more evil than itself, and they enter and dwell there. And the last state of that person is worse than the first."

Demonic spirits want a permanent home. They search out a place of habitation. Please notice in the above Scripture that the demonic being calls the person "my house." He has set up a habitation within that human being. He considers it **HIS HOUSE!** That is why Scripture says after a place is swept clean and adorned or decorated, the evil spirit goes about looking for another place to inhabit, and (in this case it is seeking another person to inhabit). Finding none, he returns to the place (or the person – the house) he left behind. If he finds this person (this house) cleaned out but empty, (not filled with the Word of God and the presence of God), this same demonic spirit comes back in and brings with him seven other spirits more powerful than himself. Then they inhabit the same place again together with each other. The last state of this person is now far worse than it was in the past because now more spirits are operating in this person's life than ever before. To clarify, once we

xi

receive deliverance we feel clean and refreshed and new in a sense. But we must also take care to fill that place where the demonic had exerted control in the past through our thought life or actions. This house must not be found deserted and empty, devoid of the life of God within. We are to be a dwelling place for the Holy Spirit. We must be careful to fill **THIS HOUSE** with the Word of God and a strong relationship with the Father, Son and Holy Ghost. We must not neglect this work.

DOWN THROUGH THE GENERATIONS

After any type of unclean spirit enters in and takes control over a portion of a person's life, the actions and influence of that particular spirit will become a permanent manifestation of the person's thought life and actions. Once a spirit gains control over a certain area of a person's thought life (which is called BONDAGE), this same spirit begins to work and manifest its traits and characteristics throughout the person's personality and character. This person now begins to take on the traits and distinctive persona of this demonic spirit.

If any particular evil spirit can set up a stronghold he has already gained access to that person's life. If that stronghold is not broken through repentance and drawing near to God, then that spirit can continue on down through the family line until the bondage is broken and destroyed, and the person is set free. If the person is not set free but remains in bondage to this demonic spirit, then when they die

Sins Of The Fathers

the evil spirit finds itself without a home or a host on which he can exert continued influence. The unclean spirit is always much more comfortable when it has invaded a person's life where it can take up permanent residence and pass this same influence on down through the family line, one member after another for generations.

I believe God has given every believer the ministry of deliverance. God does show me things in the spirit realm and when I lay hands on others I do often see what kind of spirit is operating. Perhaps this is so because I have needed so much deliverance myself because of past bondage and generational sin.

In any case, over the years God has shown and taught me many things in regard to strongholds, bondage, generational sin, curses, and deliverance. God has allowed me to see in the spirit realm in order to identify particular spirits which are in operation. He has also made me acutely aware of various actions and behaviors enabling me to discern when a person is motivated or activated by demonic spirits. In other words God has made me very aware of demonic activities or behaviors which might be overlooked or even possibly seem quite normal to others. This is of course, simply discernment, which is something we should all have operating in our life. He has placed within me a great desire to see the Body set free from bondages. I feel very frustrated when I see believers who are held in bondage when they could be free, especially when they have been saved for many years and sit in church every Sunday without ever finding change or release. Every child of the Great King deserves to

xiii

Sins Of The Fathers

be freed completely because Jesus already purchased their freedom and paid for it with His own precious blood. As children of the Great King of the entire universe, it is the inherited right of every believer to walk out their life on this earth in complete freedom in the name of Jesus Christ!

Psalm 51:9-12, 17; Hide your face from my sins, and blot out all my iniquities. Create in me a clean heart, O God, and renew a right spirit within me. Cast me not away from your presence, and take not your Holy Spirit from me. Restore to me the joy of your salvation, and uphold me with a willing spirit. The sacrifices of God are a broken spirit; a broken and contrite heart, O God, you will not despise.

I do hope you will enjoy this book and gain revelation and insight into your own family history.

CHAPTER ONE

WITHOUT UNDERSTANDING

So many believers sit in their churches receiving teaching about salvation and the baptism of the Holy Spirit week after week. That is good! But it is not enough! Scripture tells us that we are to move on past the elementary (beginning) teachings of Christ and move into the depth of Christ to gain understanding of all that He purchased for us on Calvary.

Hebrews 6:1; Therefore leaving the principles of the doctrine of Christ, let us go on unto perfection; not laying again the foundation of repentance from dead works, and of faith toward God.

We are told that it is our responsibility to learn and grow in our faith. Each one of us is required to walk out our own salvation with fear and trembling.

Philippians 2:12-13; Therefore, my beloved, as you have always obeyed, so now, not only as in my presence but much more in my

absence, work out your own salvation with fear and trembling, for it is God who works in you, both to will and to work for his good pleasure.

What does it mean to say work out your own salvation? It means we are to pick up our own gifts which we received through the Baptism of the Holy Spirit and we are to begin to responsibly walk out the call on our life, in faith before God, while we are on this earth. Too many believers think, "Well, I got saved, that's all there is!"

No! That's not all there is! That is just the very beginning. That is the first stage of re-birth. But after one is born, that child must learn to sit up, to crawl, to stand up, to walk, to run and then eventually, to function as an adult. This is true in the natural realm and in the spiritual realm as well. We are to take hold of what is ours by faith, to lay hold of our spiritual *inheritance* through Christ, and thereby prosper in our salvation and fulfill our purpose in this life.

Acts 26:18; To open their eyes, and to turn them from darkness to light, and from the power of Satan unto God, that they may receive forgiveness of sins, and *inheritance* among them which are sanctified by faith that is in me. (Italics added for emphasis).

SOZO:

We see by this verse that each one of us already have an inheritance in Christ. First of all, it is most important that we recognize the fact that Jesus Christ not only purchased salvation for each one of us, but also to understand exactly what that salvation includes. Our inheritance begins with our salvation. It is a complete inheritance. It is a spiritual inheritance, a physical inheritance and a material inheritance that Christ purchased for each individual person when He gave His life on Calvary. Our salvation also includes healing and deliverance. One of the words used for salvation is SOZO. This word is used to describe our all encompassing salvation. It tells us that Jesus provided salvation for your soul through the forgiveness of all sin, iniquity and transgression, as well as deliverance from all demonic spirits or beings and their attacks against you. It also includes healing of every type or kind that might be necessary for you. SOZO includes provision for every need both current and future. It includes a solution for every problem that comes your way. Everything that we as an individual believer will ever need during our lifetime on this earth is already laid up for us in heavenly places. We pull it into our life through faith and prayer. This means that everything we will ever need for our life and our godliness is already secured for us individually. SOZO also includes as a covering for us, a mantle of His righteousness because we cannot stand in our own righteousness. We are covered over and clothed in His robes of righteousness. What does that mean for you and me? It means we no longer have to struggle under the staggering burden of trying to have our own righteousness, virtue or goodness before God, which will not happen. No man can stand before God in his own righteousness. All our righteousness is as filthy rags before Him. (See Isaiah 64:6). Scripture clearly tells us that He has provided our sanctification through the sinless life of Jesus Christ. SOZO includes all that you or I as a human being will ever need on this earth for our life and godliness.

Isaiah 48:18; O that thou hadst hearkened to my commandments! then had thy peace been as a river and thy righteousness as the waves of the sea.

God said, "If you had listened to Me and obeyed Me, right now you would have great peace flowing through your life like a river, and righteousness would overtake you as great blessing. You would have a great spiritual prosperity."

Isaiah 51:1; Hearken to me, ye that follow after righteousness, ye that seek the Lord: look unto the rock whence ye are hewn, and to the hole of the pit whence ye are digged.

Seek your Creator for your righteousness. Look at Abraham who obtained righteousness by faith, whereas the Israelites tried to obtain their own righteousness by the works of the law. Jesus already lived a righteous life in your behalf, so you can stand in His stead, covered over in His righteousness. It is free! It is your blessing! It is bequeathed to you! It is your inheritance in Him!

II Peter 1:3; His divine power has granted to us all things that pertain to life and godliness, through the knowledge of him who called us to his own glory and excellence.

The word "godliness" here means holiness. God is saying that in SOZO (in salvation), He has provided for each one of us through Christ's substitutionary death on Calvary, everything that we would ever need to live a life of godly relationship with Him, a holy and sanctified life on this earth. Then it says He has called us to glory and virtue. We read these things but don't really mediate on them. What is this glory and virtue as it pertains to us individually? The word "glory" in this verse is translated to mean that God has called us to dignity, honor and praise. Virtue in this instance signifies excellence or manliness. It means that He has called us to grow up, to be strong for battle, and to walk out our walk in excellence. Of course we are completely unable to do that apart from His grace, mercy, strength and wisdom. But that is the thing; He has provided all that for us already, it is a part of SOZO. It includes deliverance from evil, freedom from the guilt of sin, rescue from the bondage of the devil, deliverance from the curse of generational sin and from every other kind of curse possible. That is why Jesus wore the crown of thorns on His head at Calvary. He wore it for you and He wore it for me. The crown of thorns is a symbol of the curse. He wore it plainly on His head for all to see so that all these generations later, you and I could look at it and we would know and understand that we do NOT have to labor under the curse. He paid the price, He took the curse and we can be free.

Unfortunately, many Christians have not had good in-depth teaching in their churches. As a result they are unaware of the tactics of the devil. But that will not be an excuse for them because the devil will continue to take advantage of them. He will not look on them with pity and decide not to destroy them because they just do not understand what is theirs by right of inheritance. He will continue to plot and plan against them regardless of their ignorance or innocence, and perhaps even more so because they will be easier to destroy than someone who is able to stand up and do battle for what is spiritually, mentally, emotionally, physically and financially his. The whole and continued effort of the enemy of our soul is to destroy man in one way or another. I don't think he is real particular about just how he destroys a believer, just as long as the believer is destroyed, his faith is shipwrecked and he gives up on God and backslides into perdition. If he cannot destroy man by some ravaging disease, he will find some other open door in the person's life and come in that way. There are so very many ways the powers of darkness work against each person, especially those of the household of faith. His whole desire is to destroy each believer so God cannot have that person with Him throughout eternity. His plot is against you, but even more so, it is against God to cripple or completely destroy God's plans for each individual person. The devil will work endlessly to destroy you so God cannot enjoy you; His creation, throughout eternity. When he destroys or shipwrecks a believer, he wounds the very heart of God.

Very often the devil will use the sins of the parents or the generations past as an open door to invade a person's life. He can even invade a tiny, helpless, child in the womb, especially if the parents do not want the child. But even sometimes if they both want the child, the enemy of our soul can enter into a child in the womb through the past unrepented sins of the parents or the generations past.

For that reason we need to be aware of his tactics. When we see an iniquitous pattern in our own personal life we need to search out the open doors and then repent for the sins, whether they are our own personal sins or the sins of past generations. We must make every effort to close those spiritual doors once and for all.

I have heard stories of loving families who desperately wanted children, so they chose adoption. They embraced the child with open arms and open hearts pouring their life and love out to the new member of their family. But as time went on things began to surface, certain behaviors or personality problems that were foreign to the new parents. Without a clue as to what was going on, the new parents tried everything in their power to monitor behavior, to bring healthy correction, reinforce love and acceptance in the home and bring about change. But nothing availed. All their hopes were dashed as time went on and before long the adoptive parents were heartbroken and sure that somehow they had failed to love enough or provide enough. They were so certain that it was their own fault, not recognizing that the child or children had been invaded in the spirit realm by unseen forces due to their birth parentage or the generations past. All along it was not a matter of not having enough love to give or enough money or things. It was a matter of generational sin and the attending spirits that invade one's life. What was most needed was recognition of what was at work, and effectual prayer to break the generational curses off of these little lives, as well as a cutting off of the activity of the familiar spirits which were at work bringing destruction to the child, hopelessness and the agony of helplessness to the parents.

IDENTIFICATIONAL REPENTANCE:

When we repent of the sins of our generations past, that is called "identificational repentance." This is a Biblical concept. David did it. The prophets throughout the Bible identified with the sins of the people who were currently alive and repented for their sins, asking God's forgiveness and mercy. They also identified with the past generations and repented for those sins as well. Moses stood in the gap and repented for the sins of the people. There can be identificational repentance for an individual person, a family, a city, a state, or a nation. When we do this we are personally identifying with the specific sins of a person or group of people and asking God to forgive those sins. We can identify with our generations past; our parents, grandparents, great-grandparents, and even those beyond that time. We can repent for their personal sin which opened the doors to spirits of darkness and ultimate curses that have come upon us, our children and our children's children, or our city, our state, and our nation.

A Christian cannot be possessed by the devil. However a Christian can certainly be harassed, oppressed, afflicted and tormented by the enemy and a true believer can still have a stronghold or many strongholds and bondages of sin in their life.

HOW IS A DOOR IN THE SPIRIT REALM OPENED TO THE DEVIL?

A door is opened to us in the spirit realm when we or someone in our past continues in a certain sin without repentance. At some point this continued sin develops into a stronghold in their life. That stronghold, if not broken through repentance becomes a bondage to that particular sin pattern. Doors have now been opened into the spirit realm for attending spirits to begin to harass and oppress this person and often even control this area of the person's life. If there is still no repentance then these attending spirits continue on into the next generation bringing other family members into bondage. These spirits are called "familiar spirits" because they travel down through family lines and are very familiar with the traits, talents, abilities, qualities, failures and sin of members of the same family.

I have had personal encounters with familiar spirits from my own family line. One spirit in particular, a spirit of death hounded me for many years. How? There were diagnosis' of odd sicknesses and diseases; random, strange maladies that came out of nowhere with a vengeance; an invasion into my life without rhyme or reason. These were things that puzzled the doctors, generally illnesses without cause or cure. I will talk more about this in another chapter, but I want to relay one incident I recall at this time. One night I was asleep in my bed. I awoke to a night vision. Standing beside my bed and more or less hovering over me was a figure of a woman. She looked very much like me. I was very frightened at the sight of her. She had chains wrapped around her face, around her mouth in particular. She spoke to me. She told me I needed to die. I pushed through the fear and rebuked her in the name of Jesus telling her that she absolutely must leave. She did. I was still shaken and prayed until I fell back to sleep again. Not too long after that, within several weeks, I had another night vision. This time I was kneeling in what appeared to be a park like setting. The grass was very green and groomed beautifully. There was a woman kneeling next to me. I thought we were going to pray together about something. Instead she bent forward and patted the ground beneath her with both of her hands. She spoke to me and said, "This is where you belong, in this grave."

Until that moment I had no idea who she was but when she said that to me I looked at her and saw that she looked exactly like me. It was like I was looking in a mirror. Obviously this was a familiar spirit. My birth-mother was ill on and off all of her life with various illnesses of unknown origin. This same demonic spirit was trying to find entrance in order to take control over this area of my life and exert its influence over me. Again, I came out of that vision quite shaken and praying in the spirit demanding this demon leave me immediately in Jesus' name.

But I want you to notice something here. In the second vision, kneeling next to the woman at the cemetery; initially I felt no fear, nothing odd. I didn't even know it was an unclean spirit. I felt kind of happy in the vision, thinking I was kneeling down with a friend to pray on the beautiful green grass. What is interesting about this is that I believe it shows us that there can be things at work in our life and we have no sense of it. We are not afraid or wary of it in any way because we are so used to having it there. We have come to the place where we think it is a normal part of our life, when it is anything but that. So it is very important for us to become aware of what is operating in our life. If I had gone into the vision knowing in advance that it was a spirit of death, an unclean spirit, I would not have felt friendly and obliging toward it. I would have been more prepared spiritually and rebuked it immediately. Does this make sense to you?

Just as a side note because this seems like the place to say it in order to give clear understanding, demonic spirits can appear in varied forms. They can appear as angels of light, or as human beings, and as either male or female. They can appear as someone you know very well or even as an enemy. They can appear as "you" as they did in both of these visions which I had. They can appear as animals as well. I have had dreams, vision, appearances, when demons appeared as many different people I know, friends and enemies alike. Just because you have a dream about someone and see them doing something they should not in the dream, BE CAREFUL! You better check with God on this one. It may not at all be what you think. The devil comes to DECEIVE. We will talk more about this in the chapter about angels.

When I used to go to minister in the jails and prisons, I met countless men and women who had many family members who had served time in jail or prison as well. One after another, it was like sort of ritual or right of passage. Family members were or had been in jail so often that many times the rest of the family thought little of it. It was just a part of life.

Many would say this is a learned behavior and crime is simply due to social issues; environment, poverty or a lack of education. Of course it is often a learned behavior because children model what they see in the home and that in itself is a part of generational sin and bondage. We also know that circumstances can and often do contribute to the problems. I would say however that these types of problems are not solely due to poverty or lack of education as some would try to make us believe. These problems will not be solved by building newer, bigger and better schools, paying more wages, giving more benefits, or any other type of external help. These problems cannot and will not be solved by doling out more welfare. This has already been evidenced by our past record. There are many underprivileged people who have taken hold of their gifting and responsibly pursue a lifestyle that brings honor to themself and those around them. What then is the difference? Is it simply a matter of will power? No, it is not. These problems must be destroyed at the root. It is imperative that we as believers begin to recognize the validity of generational sin and the attending familiar spirits. Often it is the generational sin and spirits that drive one to crime and poverty. We must begin to recognize their role in carrying on the perpetuation of certain sin patterns and bondages throughout any particular family line. The impetus comes from familiar spirits who carry the same sinful behavior and bondage from one generation to the next.

What can we do? Sound Biblical teaching in local churches is a good beginning. Moving on from salvation to bring the people into a depth of relationship with God is required. We are to raise up the body and prepare them for ministry. We need to become responsible prayer warriors who know our authority in Christ and are not afraid to cast out demons and to loose the prisoners. We need those who are not afraid to stand up and teach the congregations exactly what Christ purchased for them and to speak plainly about sin. So many believers do not even know what is theirs in salvation. They often do not really know or believe that they can be free. We need to train our people to stand up, put on the armor of God and go to battle for those around them, especially their own family. War! Exposing the works of darkness and opening the prison doors by cutting off the sins of the past and casting out those spirits that carry out their assignments over us by bringing sickness, disease and spiritual death at every turn.

Poverty and alcoholism are bondages that we often see carried down through family lines. Another is uncleanness and sexual perversion. Molestation, rape, prostitution, incest and homosexuality travel down family lines at breakneck speed until at last someone gets saved and repents of their own sin. Then, recognizing what is theirs in Christ they stand up and take hold of it by faith. It only takes one person to be saved and then begin to war against what they see going on in their own family. For just one to take hold of what Christ promised in His Word and begin to break the curses and the power of the assignments written against their family in ongoing generational sin is a major breakthrough.

It is God's sincere desire to restore to each one all the years the locusts have eaten, even all the years of pain and misery due to the destruction of sin. God's heart is to pour out His love and His healing oil, the balm of Gilead, all over those broken hearts and devastated lives. It is His heart to restore all. But we have a responsibility in this matter. It is ours to open our eyes and ears, to begin to recognize, to clearly see what is hindering our life and the lives of those we love, even the lives of those around us. It is ours to take up the battle cry, wave the banner of freedom, take the sword in both hands and swing it high over our head with all our might, and war for the deliverance and healing of our families.

SPIRITS GAIN ENTERANCE THROUGH A VARIETY OF CIRCUMSTANCES:

- Spirits can enter into a child in the womb.
- Spirits can enter into a person's life during a time of trauma, crisis or great loss.
- Spirits can enter in any area of our life through our own personal sin and iniquity.
- Spirits can gain entrance into a person's life through sexual contact because the two separate individuals become one flesh during sexual intercourse.
- Spirit ties with another person can open doors.
- Curses can come on us because of our own unrepented sin and rebellion against God.
- We can speak curses over our own lives and they will come to pass. This is called self fulfilling prophecy.
- Curses can enter through the partaking or practice of mysticism, witchcraft or the occult which includes new age practices. This can be sin on the part of the person who is seeking freedom or because of past generations which were involved in these practices.
- Curses can be put on us or spoken over us by someone else.

CHAPTER TWO

WHAT EXACTLY IS A STRONGHOLD?

In the Bible one of the Hebrew words for "heart" is leb or lebab. This word is used to indicate feelings, including the will of man and his intellect. It means his inner being, his mind, will and emotions.

In Greek and Latin, the word for heart is kardia or cor. It means the heart and mind which are made up of our thoughts, feelings and will power. So in both the Old and New Testament, when referring to our inner man we are speaking of our mind, will and emotions. I may use these words interchangeably.

THE CHAIN OF SIN:

Sin is at first just a sin which can be repented of. The word "sin" in Hebrew is chata' or chatta'ah and it means to commit an offence. The Greek rendering of the word sin is hamartano and it means to miss the mark. It is a fault.

Here is how it works. We commit a particular sin. If we do not repent of that sin but continue to commit the same sin, it becomes a habit. If we continue on in this newly established habit of sin it now takes another form and becomes a stronghold in our life. If we do not repent and ask God to break this stronghold in our life, it penetrates into our life on a deeper level and becomes bondage. We are now in bondage to this particular sin. If we continue in this bondage the devil has free reign and can exert control of our life in that area. We all know people who are in bondage in some way.

IT LOOKS LIKE THIS:

- Sin is Sin. It means missing the mark.
- Continued sin which is not repented of becomes habitual sin. We now have a habit that is sinful.
- Unrepented habitual sin which is continued becomes a stronghold in our life. It becomes a defended area protected by demonic forces.
- An unrepented stronghold which is continued becomes bondage. Bondage demonstrates a strong demonic influence over this area of life.
- Bondage without repentance and finding freedom in Christ opens the door to demonic possession.

The word bondage means to become a bondservant or a slave. It means to be enslaved and become a servant to sin, a servant of the powers of darkness. This happens when a person continues to entertain sin and refuses to turn from it. We become the servants of whatever or whoever we give ourself to.

Romans 6:16; Do you not know that if you present yourselves to anyone as obedient slaves, you are the slaves of the one whom you obey, either of sin, which leads to death, or of obedience, which leads to righteousness?

In this section I am going to use the words heart, soul, mind and thought life, interchangeably at times.

SIN IS A TEMPTATION RECEIVED AND ACTED ON:

- A stronghold is very simply a pattern of thinking that has been engrained in a person's mind because of repeated and unrepented sin.
- It is a set of thought patterns that have been established in a person's life and now the person begins to act out of those established patterns of thinking.
- A stronghold is a determined and established way of thinking much like a fortress or a fortified area.
- Think of it like a defended thought pattern in a person's life, like a garrisoned place in the mind.
- A stronghold produces a vice grip on a particular part of our life which affects our character and personality.
- It is a place where the devil wields his power over a person.

- A stronghold is a fortification constructed within our heart and soul (mind) and will.

We can say a stronghold in our life is constructed by our arch-enemy Satan, however, in most cases it is built up by our cooperation with him. It is a joint effort. One thing you can be certain of is that it is definitely defended by the devil and his cohorts. Once a stronghold exists in someone's thought life, it is a safe place for the powers of darkness to work from. That is the whole point of inhabiting, oppressing or afflicting a human being, so that these powers can accomplish their intended work against God through the individual with the purpose and full intent of completely destroying and negating the plans and purposes of God in that individual life.

A stronghold is first set up or established in our heart and mind by our continued desire toward this sin. Then a bastion is built in our mind and thought life by a continual reverting or relapsing again and again into this same sin. Now in bondage to this sin because of our own heart and mind, we find we are filled with a constant, nagging, desire for this sin. Our mind is tugged on with temptation toward this sin and every time the opportunity presents itself we revert back to the same sinful behavior. This only exacerbates the problem because whatever the sin is, it cannot be satisfied by our giving in to it. It simply entrenches the bondage deeper into our soul. Our continued appetite for this specific sin is now satisfied only when we commit this sin again and again. A longing is actually activated within us that will draw us repeatedly into the very same sin.

I think of it as compared to someone whose appetite is out of control. They have a constant craving for food. Their body does not really need the food and as a matter of fact they would be healthier without it. However, their body now responds on its own to the thought processes in the brain, because this pattern of thinking has been established. The appetite is no longer controlled by the body's need to survive, but the appetite is now controlled by the desire in the thought life. It becomes a constant craving. So it is with any sin we practice. We build a fortress of sin in our mind by a constant practice of that sin and create a nagging desire within us for that sin. We actually become addicted to that particular sin. Now we have a stronghold of sin in our life.

For many years I had a pinched nerve that bothered me after being rear-ended in a motor vehicle accident. The doctors simply said it was a bad whiplash. I have no medical training or special knowledge of any sort; I only know what I experienced during this time. That nerve would lock in place and cause me months of excruciating pain. It would be months of torture before that nerve would unlock and release again. Then without any warning the simplest thing like turning around or bending over or rolling over in bed, would snap it right back into that vice-grip hold of pain again. It would bring me right back into many more months of agony. It would always seem to snap right back into the same place over and over again as though a path had been created.

I compare this to being in bondage because once the stronghold is developed in our thought life (heart); we live it out in our behavior. At that point a path has been created. We seem to revert constantly back to the same old behavior patterns time and time again, even though it causes us pain, even though we know it is wrong, and even though it is crippling to our personality and character. Even when we finally come to the place that we want to be free, it just keeps snapping back into the same place. We revert back to the same old behavior pattern.

The easiest way to explain this is to take as an example a man who decided one day to buy a pornographic magazine or encountered pornographic pictures over the internet. The pictures were enticing, stimulating, and thrilling to look at. This man received a particular pleasing satisfaction while looking at these pictures as his passions were stirred. After finishing with the magazine or the internet these images kept coming back to his mind, again and again, and along with the images reoccurring in his mind there was a desire for more.

This man first indulged the temptation when he gave in and purchased the book or studied the images on the internet. The fascination held him when he should have looked away and repented immediately, but he didn't. He nurtured his desire by enjoying the temptation which was now full blown sin. Now the temptation comes to his thoughts over and over again. He cannot seem to get these pictures out of his mind. They pop into his head at the worst times. He did not sincerely repent at the onset and so now, instead of repenting of his sin and crying out to God to strengthen him against this sin and set him free, he indulges this same sin over and over again. He continues to look at pornography. The hook has been set in his jaw and now he finds he is in a strong bondage that seems to be impossible for him to break. He must sincerely repent and receive God's deliverance and healing. He has been taken hostage by the enemy of his soul and is completely miserable, secured under the bondage of sin!

The enemy of our soul, the devil, is able to create a stronghold in a person's mind (heart), because the individual does not resist temptation but entertains it. This can be true of any sin, not just pornography. We must control our passions and we must conquer our thought-life. We are supposed to die to self and resist the devil. We are told by James to flee youthful lust. Unfortunately, it is not just the youthful that lust, especially in our current culture. Our society seems to be embroiled with lust, consumed and completely given over to a licentious and idolatrous spirit.

The King James Bible often also uses the word "reins" which means our inner being, the inner man, or the heart and soul of man. In Old Testament times people believed that the inner being of man was in the kidney area or the bowels of man, meaning the inner recesses of the human being.

The word reins in Hebrew is kilyah, which is pronounced as kil-yaw'. It literally means the kidney or the mind, the inner being

36

of man, the seat of his thought life, and his will and emotions. In the Bible the words "heart and soul" are often used interchangeably.

Matthew 22:37; Jesus said unto him, Thou shalt love the Lord thy God with all thy heart, and with all thy soul, and with all thy mind.

So in other words, everything we do is created and released from within our heart (soul). All our actions are motivated, set into action, and proceed from the thoughts that are lodged within our own heart. Our character and our personality are the product of our heart (our inner man). Our heart or inner man is what defines us. We can speak, but our actions will always speak louder than our words. Therefore, Scripture warns us that we are to guard our heart carefully.

Proverbs 4:23; Keep thy heart with all diligence; for out of it are the issues of life.

We see that the heart and soul is the center of all human activity. Every thought and action comes out of our heart or our inner being. We are controlled and motivated out of our heart and inner being. If these thoughts (temptations) are not dealt with, then the temptation will continue to come. With each successive temptation that one gives into, the tempter gains more strength. He is empowered more and more, thus enabling him to gain more ground in the person's heart (soul - inner being). This is an assault against the individual, so it must be dealt with. Scripture tells us to flee temptation. God has also given us very specific weapons for our warfare. However, if temptation is not dealt with it soon becomes a major stronghold.

Our heart is also the seat of our conscience. If we continue to allow temptation without taking our thoughts captive, of course we will act out the temptation. When we continue in this way, our heart (soul) becomes hardened by our continued sin and we are no longer bothered by our sin. The Bible says our conscience becomes seared. By not resisting temptation we make our heart insensitive to the Holy Spirit and we can come to the place where we no longer hear His voice at all. That is a very dangerous place to be. There are many examples of those in the Bible who hardened their heart against God, against His prophets, and against His people. Pharaoh is an example of a man who hardened his own heart against the will of God.

The Word tells us we can combat the powers of darkness with the power of God's Word and that if we will just resist the devil he will run from us. Why is this so important? Because it is out of our own heart that we will draw forth whatever is within us. We will be and continue to become more and more of whatever is buried in the depth of our heart. It is out of our heart that we live. That is why, when we come to a salvation experience, God will begin a work deep within our heart (inner being), and soul (mind, will and emotions), to bring about a complete change within us. When we are truly saved we will have heart surgery performed by the Holy Spirit. We will become a new man who can no longer operate out of a cold, hard heart. As we continue to yield to God and allow the work of the

Holy Spirit in our life, our heart will be changed. When our heart is changed, our thoughts, words and actions will follow suit.

Ezekiel 36:26; A new heart also will I give you, and a new spirit will I put within you: and I will take away the stony heart out of your flesh, and I will give you an heart of flesh.

The Word says our own heart is wicked and deceitful. (See Jeremiah 17:9). We can have mixture in our heart, a mixture of good and evil. That is why God is looking for a change of heart. He wants to create in us a pure heart, and we are to concentrate on those things that are pure, lovely, and of a good report. (See Philippians 4:8). We are to think about good and positive things so that our heart and mind are renewed and changed. This change will come about as we spend time in His Word and in His presence and it will surely bear fruit upward out of our heart, into our mouth, through our actions, saturating our character and our personality. We are to draw living water out of the wells of salvation.

So we see that strongholds are created by thought patterns which are first launched in the individual's mind, will and emotions in the form of temptation. The tempter sees an inner weakness and comes with his assault against our mind. He carefully inserts his thoughts into our mind. If we listen carefully we will take notice that the voice sounds exactly like our own. These thoughts (temptations) come to us in a voice that sounds like our voice inside our own head.

We think and believe that these are our thoughts, not immediately recognizing it as the devil bringing temptation.

We need to learn to pay attention and take our thoughts captive. When we realize the temptations come to us sounding like our own voice inside our head, we will be quicker to act upon them. It will not sound like some strange voice coming at us. A big scary voice sounding like a devil would be too easy. Temptation will come in the sound of our own voice, in the same kind of words, tones and inflections we would use if we were speaking. It will sound just like you sound. If the devil came to us in any other way, we would immediately recognize and reject him. He comes to us with an appealing invitation from darkness to enter into a particular type of sin. Temptation comes to everyone, we are all tempted by the devil, we must learn to take control of our thought life and submit our thoughts to Christ.

When I first began to be aware of certain temptations that were coming to me through the tapes playing in my head, I would immediately call to mind the Scripture that says I am to take my thoughts captive. At that point I would remind the enemy that I have the mind of Christ. I would have to say it out loud and then take authority over my own thoughts. I would pray something like this; "Lord, forgive me for allowing those thoughts in my mind and heart. Forgive me for any part I have in this temptation, anything I have done or any thoughts I have allowed to remain in my mind and heart. I take my thoughts captive and I submit all my thoughts to Jesus Christ.

I thank You, Father, that You have said I have the mind of Christ. I refuse all temptation and anything that is not of You. I command the devil upon the authority of Your Word to flee from me right now! You have given me this authority and power in Your name and I take hold of it right now as my right by inheritance through the death of Jesus Christ in my behalf. I command the devil or demon(s) to depart from me immediately in the name of Jesus."

That would pretty much end it for the time being. But it would take this for me to begin to have the strongholds in my thought life broken down. Each time the same temptation came to me I would pray out loud and submit my thoughts to Christ, taking authority over my own thought life. Eventually I became so aware of this temptation that the prayers became automatic and that part of my thought life was cleansed, that stronghold broken down and I was free.

Generally, at the first entrance of temptation, we feel a certain delight with the temptation. If this were not so, the devil would come to us in another way, one that he knows would be more appealing to us. He already knows all our weaknesses and foibles. So we relate to the temptation and begin to bathe it with our thoughts. We start by nursing it in our mind. Now we are fully cooperating with the devil. Our cooperation through our thoughts feed the sin thereby establishing the stronghold and entrenching it in our mind (heart). The stronghold continues to gain force and power within us because we do not cut off the thoughts of temptation, but we allow them to continue. At first it is mere temptation, but very quickly it becomes sin, which then grows into bondage and brings death into our heart and spirit. Because God is a just God, our sin must be judged one way or another unless we repent.

If we do not learn to take our thoughts captive and submit our mind to Christ, the strongholds which are our sinful thought patterns will not be broken down and we will continue to strengthen them by cooperating with or entertaining them. We empower the devil by our cooperation and that is all he needs. At the point that we do not resist him, it is already sin. Our joint effort with the devil is what establishes the stronghold at first and then the bondage which allows the devil to gain strength in any area of our life. Remember? The man who lusts in his heart has already sinned even though he has not acted out physically in that particular sin.

Matthew 5:28; But I say to you that everyone who looks at a woman with lustful intent has already committed adultery with her in his heart.

I am not certain why, but this analogy always comes to mind whenever I think of or see someone trapped in bondage. The Romans, when they ruled most of the world, were masters of torture. They devised and invented some of the cruelest tortures known to man at that time. One of the tortures they employed was perpetrated against someone who had been accused and found guilty of murder. Often they would take the body of the murder victim and tie it to the back of the accused murderer. The accused was then allowed to go free, but every place he went he had this dead and rotting corpse tied onto his back. Under penalty of death, no one was allowed to help him or set him free and no one was allowed to kill him to put him out of his misery. This man found no place of rest or refuge. The stench of death drove everyone far from him. Anyone previously compassionate enough to speak to him or try to comfort him in any way fled far away from him. Flies and worms consumed the rotting flesh tied on his back. Rats nibbled by night and birds followed him by day attacking the putrid decaying flesh fixed on his back, and eventually attacking his own flesh. It was only a matter of days before the corpse tied securely onto his back began to fester and putrefy. His own body quickly fused with the collective oozing flesh and now the two bodies became one as the murderer struggled beneath the rancid decaying weight of his murdered victim.

Bondage is much like that. When we refuse to resist temptation and continue to give in to it, we come into bondage which is like having this terrible weight tied to us. It is a weight we cannot free ourselves from and we are helpless under its burden. We are being consumed by it and yet we are unable to get free of it. We are in bondage and under the sentence of death because of our sin.

James 1:15; Then desire when it has conceived gives birth to sin, and sin when it is fully grown brings forth death.

CHAPTER THREE

SIN, TRANSGRESSION AND INIQUITY

Exodus 34:7; Keeping mercy for thousands, forgiving iniquity and transgression and sin, and that will by no means clear the guilty; visiting the iniquity of the fathers upon the children, and upon the children's children, unto the third and to the fourth generation.

Notice God uses three separate words here to describe our failure and faults. He says He forgives our iniquity, our transgression and our sin. So then our question is, "what is the difference?"

SIN:

Hebrew is chata' or chatt'ah pronounced khat-taw-aw'. It simply means an offence against God. This can be either a voluntary act or it can be a voluntary neglect of God's command. So it can be either action or neglect of action, a sin of commission or a sin of omission. Any sin can be in the form of actions or neglect of actions, words, thoughts, desires, imaginations, purposes, or anything that is contrary to God's will and desire. We are each born with an inherent sin nature. This is often called the carnal man or our old nature or our Adamic nature. It is that bent to sin that is within each one of us when we are born - because in Adam we were all sold into sin.

Romans 3:23; For all have sinned, and come short of the glory of God.

TRANSGRESSION:

In Hebrew one of the words for transgression is pesha' or pasha. It means to break away from righteous authority, to rebel or revolt. It means to apostatize and surpass all set limits. It is knowingly breaching all authority. It is a willful violation of law or moral principles with full knowledge of what is right or wrong.

Another word in Hebrew is ma'al which means to commit treachery. It means a betrayal or an act of treason against God. One who is without law or considers themself to be above the law.

Sin comes to us in seed form. The thought injected into our mind (heart), is like a tiny seed at first. This seed of sin holds within it the potential to grow and become a powerful force, even a great stronghold in our life. The sin in seed form actually carries within it the potential for a full harvest. Every seed carries the fruit of its own nature. In the natural realm a tiny seed planted can bring forth a huge tree, roots and all. It is the same in the spiritual realm. Whatever is planted in the soil of our heart will grow. That is why Jesus talked about the seed being planted in good soil or being planted in hard unprepared soil. The harvest of sin is the consequence or end result built into that sin. The consequence can be anything from a loss of peace, a guilty conscience, a loss of self worth, poverty, failure or even a particular sickness or disease, as is clearly outlined in Scripture.

THE HARVEST OF SIN:

The Word tells us that there is a harvest of sin. We cannot take fire into our bosom and not be burned. When we sow to the wind we reap the whirlwind. (See Jeremiah 51:33, Joel 3:13). We could call this reaping judgment, or we could call it a curse, or the harvest of sin. But whatever we would choose to call it, we can clearly see from Scripture that whatever we sow in our life, we shall also reap unless we repent of our sins.

Hosea 6:11; For you also, O Judah, a harvest is appointed, when I restore the fortunes of my people.

Job 4:8; Even as I have seen, they that plow iniquity, and sow wickedness, reap the same.

Continued sin is iniquity, it is a moral unrighteousness and depravity. Scripture tells us that if we sow iniquity we will reap vanity. The word iniquity in the Hebrew is 'aven. It simply means to exert oneself and go to extremes in rebellious unrighteousness or injustice. Iniquity is something that is completely useless, nothingness, and false. It brings forth emptiness and vanity, leading one away from God. In choosing our iniquity by continuing in the sins of our past generations, we choose vanity and we forsake God's mercy.

As we live out our lives, our path is often determined by the smallest daily choices. By our own free will we can choose to walk in the righteousness God has provided for us through Jesus Christ, or we can choose to go our own way, which is rebellion against God. But whatever our choices are, in the end there will be an outcome. There will be a harvest. We will either reap the blessings of God or we will reap curses into our life. We will sow to life and reap abundant life or we will sow to the flesh and reap death.

Psalm 31:10; For my life is spent with grief, and my years with sighing: my strength faileth because of mine iniquity, and my bones are consumed.

INIQUITY:

There are several words in Hebrew for iniquity, on is avon, pronounced aw-vone'. It means unrighteousness, perversity or a moral evil. It also means a wickedness and vanity, something that will come to nothing.

Proverbs 22:8; He that soweth iniquity shall reap vanity: and the rod of his anger shall fail.

The judgment of God will either bring death to the sin or death to the sinner. The choice belongs to the one who is under the judgment or curse.

INIQUITOUS PATTERNS BRING A CURSE INTO OUR LIFE:

There are many curses and judgments pronounced against individuals, peoples, tribes, and even against whole nations because of particular sin patterns. These are listed, declared, pronounced and remembered throughout the whole Bible. (See Genesis 49:7, Exodus 21:17, Exodus 22:28, Deuteronomy 27:15, Leviticus 19:14, Leviticus 24:10-16, Matthew 15:4, Mark 7:10). For example, scripture lists a multitude of curses for blasphemy and idolatry.

Judgments and curses can be passed down through the generations, from one generation to the next bringing with them a moral deterioration which increases with each successive generation, and most often includes a physical, mental, and/or emotional component of the same. It manifests as a corruption within the heart of man affecting his moral nature, character and personality.

There was a proverb that was spoken in Israel saying that the father would eat the sour grapes and his children's teeth were set on edge by the bitterness of the fruit. A modern translation of that proverb might be; "The apple doesn't fall far from the tree." It simply means that the patterns of sin and iniquity of the fathers became the same sin patterns of the sons born to them. The sons learned the sin habits of their past generations and those sins have taken root and brought forth the same kind of fruit in their own lives as they brought forth into their parents lives. Then these behaviors and habit patterns were passed on to the next generation as well. In other words, "like father – like son."

Now here is where people say to me, "But Jesus died for our sin. This was cut off when I got saved, wasn't it?"

You tell me! Is your life free of the iniquitous patterns of your past generations? Do you have and practice some of the same sins that your father or your mother did? Perhaps the same sins as your grandfather or your grandmother? Maybe you are not even aware of it. Look back over your family tree and begin to examine it carefully. Sit before the Lord and ask Him to show you what is hidden in the leaves of that tree. I think you will begin to see some things you have not been aware of in the past.

Are you walking out the curses or judgments that have come from the sins of your past generations? Just as you had to reach out and receive salvation through faith, you must also reach out and receive the Baptism of the Holy Spirit by faith. Also, if you want healing you must take hold of healing by faith. If you need deliverance you must reach out and appropriate deliverance by faith just as

49

you receive everything else that Christ purchased for you. Yes, it is yours but you must reach out and take it.

Ezekiel 18:1-3; The word of the Lord came to me: "What do you mean by repeating this proverb concerning the land of Israel, 'The fathers have eaten sour grapes, and the children's teeth are set on edge?' "As I live, declares the Lord God, this proverb shall no more be used by you in Israel. Behold, all souls are mine; the soul of the father as well as the soul of the son is mine: the soul who sins shall die."

Jeremiah 31:29-30; In those days they shall no longer say: "The fathers have eaten sour grapes, and the children's teeth are set on edge. But everyone shall die for his own sin. Each man who eats sour grapes, his teeth shall be set on edge."

Why will God's people no longer have an opportunity to use this proverb? Because Jeremiah and Ezekial spoke of a future time when the Messiah would come to Calvary and take all of the sin of all mankind upon Himself. He would bear all the sin of all mankind on Calvary. All the individual sin of every man woman and child was paid in full so that each one might be made free and not stagger under the burden of sin and the heavy yoke of bondage. The cost of the sin of the whole world was paid in a bloody barter. But in order to take advantage of that barter, His life for ours, His death for our sin, we must reach out and take hold of it by faith. We must appropriate what He already purchased in our behalf.

God knew that as a Son, Jesus would free the sons of the world so that they would no longer have to bear the iniquity of their fathers and the past generations, but from then on each one would die for their own unrepented sin.

Sin that is sincerely repented of will not bring a curse because God is the Just Judge of all the earth. He is the Faithful One and He states in His own Word that if we confess our sin, He is faithful and just to forgive us our sin and will not attribute or impute iniquity to us. In other words, God said that He will hold us guiltless of the sins of the generations past and He will not ascribe or credit their wickedness or their crimes to us. But if we fail to sincerely confess our sin there is a harvest that awaits us and possibly our succeeding generations.

I John 1:9; If we confess our sins, he is faithful and just to forgive us our sins, and to cleanse us from all unrighteousness.

One day shortly after I was saved I was driving my car down the road when the Father spoke to me. He said, "You are perverted."

I almost went off the road. I pulled off the road and to be quite honest I was not only very surprised but I really was very upset and offended to hear Him say this to me because as far as I knew there was no sexual sin in my life. Most of us equate the word "perverted" to mean sexually perverted. I said, "God, how can You say that to me? There is no sexual sin in my life that I am aware of. What have I done that You would say that to me?"

Then I had a vision. I saw two hands held out to me. In one hand was a pathway to life. It was a straight and even path. In the other hand there was also a pathway to life but it was twisted and tangled and hedged up in places with rubble. He said, "I created your life to be this," as He held out one hand showing me the straight path. "But because of sin; your sin, the sins of generations past, and the sins of others against you, your life has become this." He held out the other hand to me showing me the twisted and tangled path that had become my life.

That day on the road I got a good look at the effect of generational sin and how it perverts a life from God's original intent and purpose. But He already knew that would happen and so He made provision for us on Calvary.

Psalm 32:1-2; Blessed is he whose transgression is forgiven, whose sin is covered. Blessed is the man unto whom the Lord imputeth not iniquity, and in whose spirit there is no guile.

Iniquity is a willful ignorance of God and His ways. It is a willful lack of understanding or caring about what God requires or desires, and a willful choosing of sin. And by the way, what exactly is guile? Guile is deceit. It means acting false or deceitfully, or acting in a manner which is less than full hearted. It is a half hearted attitude or an attitude of spiritual laziness. Being slack and not giving your self over fully to God and His purposes.

There are two kingdoms, the kingdoms of light and darkness. There are two rulers, they are God and Satan. There are two dominions which are liberty in Christ or bondage to Satan. There are two results or effects, they are blessing or cursing. We are free to choose according to our own desire. He will never force us or determine the outcome for us. It is ours to freely choose.

Deuteronomy 30:19; I call heaven and earth to record this day against you, that I have set before you life and death, blessing and cursing: therefore choose life, that both thou and thy seed may life.

CHAPTER FOUR

SELF FULFILLING PROPHESY

Many people are guilty of opening doors to the powers of darkness with their own words. We are cautioned to be careful of the words we speak not only about others, but we must also be careful of the words we speak over our own lives.

Do you know someone who is extremely negative? Almost every word that comes out of their mouth is complaining, critical, condemning, or accusing. I find it very difficult to be around someone like that. One would say they have a poor self image. That may be so, but I believe it is much more than that. After all, where does our self image come from? We are made in the image of God. We are to be conformed into the image of Christ. If our image comes from any other source we have a false image, an image created by our own vanity. That would indeed be a poor self image because it will not stand the test of time.

The negative person described has no idea who they are in Christ. They are lost in some time and space continuum that does not include God. They have for some reason or another locked their radar onto the devil's words over their life and the devil's words regarding others. They see themselves as less than God ever created or intended them to be and they see others through dark glasses, not giving God any glory for His creation.

Sometimes you will hear someone say things like this; "I am always so clumsy." "I am so stupid." "Why can't I ever do anything right?" "I will never get married, no one will want me," or things along these lines.

Once we begin to understand who we are in Christ we see that our heavenly Father is the One Who establishes our worth and value by the mere fact that He created us. Then, after we made such a mess of everything, He did not stop there, but He gave His only Son to die for us. Jesus gave His life as a forfeit for our life and therein is the secret of our significance. He surrendered to death so we could have life. His death made us heirs of our heavenly Father, heirs of heaven, heirs of eternal life, and part of the heavenly bride company. With His own life, He purchased our life. What more could anyone have done that would bring worth and value to any human being?

When Jesus bled and died for us He high jacked us from the kingdom of darkness and transported us into the kingdom of light. We have been taken from the orphanage of the world and brought into the family of the Great King. We have escaped the flames of hell and we have been washed in the blood of the Lamb of God. We have been rescued from sin and degradation and conveyed into the realm of God's purpose and intent.

There used to be an old saying that God didn't create any junk! That is so true. He created each and every person with distinct and divine purpose and He buried an individual destiny deep inside of each one of us. There is no one who ever lived on this earth and no human being who ever will live on this earth that is or was here by happenstance or coincidence. Before the very foundations of the earth, God knew each and every one and I believe He rejoiced the day each one was born, even knowing that not each one would be welcomed into the world. Even while knowing this in advance, He kept His plans and His purposes in tact and watched carefully to bring His intended design into place by utilizing every single thing that comes into our life whether intended by Him or not. He promises that He will use everything for our good and our benefit. No matter what, he will turn it around if we just trust Him.

Romans 8:28; And we know that all things work together for good to them that love God, to them who are called according to his purpose.

If we do not understand who we are in Christ, we do not have a clear understanding of who we are at all. Without knowing who we are in Christ we have a total misconception of the purposes and the significance of our life. Without knowing who we are in Christ we have absolutely no understanding of our own value or worth as a human being on this earth. I am not talking about pride or lifting ourself up above others, I am speaking of having a clear perception of our tremendous value and worth because God Himself gave His only Son that we should live and not die and share eternity with Him. We must have a clear understanding that our time on this earth is valuable and with great intent and purpose designed by God. This is of the utmost importance.

When we do not have the understanding of who we are in Christ we raise up our own standard and try to measure up to it in our own strength. We lift up our personal measuring stick and raise it up high enough over our head to make us look bigger, better and taller than others. All the while we are expecting that this will somehow give us some footing, that extra oomph we need to be accepted. This is why people build so many walls, have so many facades, wear so many masks, and try to live under the pretense of self importance. They act as if they are someone they are not in order to assuage their beat up self image. In their inadequacies they try to grab any fig leaf they can to cover themself. Some blindly pursue ambition in an effort to become someone of significance. They do not understand that their significance as a human being is not held in titles, degrees or accolades, but their significance as a human being is held in the very hand and heart of God.

One who does not know who they are in Christ will either begin to expect so much from themselves that they will beat themself up for the smallest things, or they swing the other way and expect nothing from themself and give nothing of themself. In this case it is because they do not believe they have anything worthwhile to give. Neither of these people have any understanding that it is God's heart to bless each one of them and give them a square and solid footing on the Rock, Christ Jesus. His desire is to raise them up in high places before Him.

When we discount ourselves in either of these manners, we declare that we are unworthy of His blessings and we negate His goodness to us by the very words that come out of our own mouth. There is no need for anyone else to curse us because we so often do it ourself. The devil stands close by to feed these words into our mind and heart in the form of temptation, and as we receive them there is a strong reinforcement of the words to make sure they come to pass. Remember that we live out of the abundance of our heart, so whatever is in our heart is what will come out when we open our mouth. Whatever is in our heart will not only come out of our mouth, but it will be displayed in our actions and attitudes.

I remember when I was a new believer I used to put myself down all the time because while growing up I was put down all the time. It was a learned behavior. I had taken up the banner that was placed over my head by those in authority and I began to run with it. I decided somehow that I would be the one who would openly declare that I was all the things others said about me. I was just a little girl and I did not fully understand a lot of what was said about me and I could not understand why I was so different, but I did know the things that were said were not good. I had been labeled with many labels, none of which were what God had in mind for me. But when you hear something demeaning about yourself day after day and year after year you begin to accept it as truth. The humiliation wears you down. The words get into your heart and mind and become a part of your being. You chew them up and swallow them and begin to live off of them. You just accept and believe all the words. So I picked up the banner of self fulfilling prophesy that had been placed over me and I waved it heartily along with the others. Over and over I heard others declaring me to be so much less than God ever meant for me to be or become and I received it as absolute truth. I learned that in order not to be humiliated it was easier for me to declare the odious words over myself before anyone else did. I would be the first one to speak and declare my total inadequacies. In this way I would not have to bear the shame and humiliation of having others speak it over me and feel put down. So I took up my mantra of self deprecating words and began to declare them over my own life not understanding the ramifications of such action. I learned how to beat myself up for the smallest infraction. Living in this prison you soon find there is no escape because no matter how hard you try, you are helpless to change what others think of you or to transform the hatred they feel toward you into anything else. Only God can change a heart.

One day shortly after salvation I was driving my car and made an incorrect turn. I began to pound on the steering wheel declaring myself to be useless, stupid, inept, and who knows what else. I was furious with myself for making a wrong turn on the highway. Suddenly God spoke to me and told me that I was sinning against Him by declaring these hate filled words over my own life. I was shocked to hear this. God began to deal with me about my words regarding my own life. He told me that He loved me and He had plans for me, but in order for me to come into what He had for me I would have to stop belittling and criticizing myself. He gave me understanding that day that the words I spoke over myself were not what was in His mind regarding me. It was false and it was sin. He told me that I needed to repent and treat myself with respect because I belonged to Him. That was such a tremendous revelation to me.

A wrong turn on the highway that day was the beginning of a renewal of my mind and a change of heart. From then on whenever something self depreciating came to my lips the Holy Spirit would caution me to stop immediately, think of what I was saying, repent and speak right words about myself. At first I felt kind of silly speaking nice things over myself out loud, but I continued to do so until it became an automatic thinking and speaking process. I no longer go around speaking out loud over myself because I have been freed from that terrible prison. God also showed me that I am not to allow others to speak in such a manner over me. I am to speak and hear truth.

When we speak demeaning or derogatory words over our own life or allow others to do so we are cutting off the blood supply

Sins Of The Fathers

of Jesus Christ. This is the healing blood, the cleansing blood, the blood that restores our own heart and soul. We are cutting off the very gift He gave us in His desire to bring wholeness to us. Without blood we die. We must have the blood of Jesus Christ and all that His blood purchased for us in order to regain all that was lost to us by our sin and fallen condition.

So we must be very careful to begin to line up our thoughts and our words with His thoughts and His words over us. Our mouth needs to speak out clearly what He says about us, not what others say or even the words we may have spoken over our own life in the past. Our mind must be renewed and our mouth must be renewed at the same time. It is a sin to defame ourself. When we do so, we speak against the very purposes and intents of God, as well as denigrate His work and design. We must line ourself up with His will, His way, His work, and His words about our life. Our worth and value is always based on what Father has already spoken over us and it is never based on what others say or think about us or even upon what they may do or have done to us.

CHAPTER FIVE

ANGELS AND DEMONS

Some people, even believers seem to be very confused about spirit beings, so we will start there.

There is a popular misconception and a deception which causes not some, but many people including some Christians to believe that when their loved ones pass on they become angels and even become their own personal guardian angel. Nothing could be farther from the truth. It sounds comforting to think that someone we dearly loved who has passed on is now looking down on us from heaven and protecting us. But Scripture clearly teaches us that angels are created beings just as we humans are created beings, but angels are of a different order and a different flesh. Angels are superhuman, if you will. Remember David asked God why He was mindful of us on this earth, when we were created so much lower than the angels. Even Jesus was made a little lower than the angels in order to suffer death in our place, Scripture tells us so. (See Psalm 8:5, Hebrews 2:7 and Hebrews 2:9).

I Corinthians 15:38-40; But God gives it a body as he has chosen, and to each kind of seed its own body. For not all flesh is the same, but there is one kind for humans, another for animals, another for birds, and another for fish. There are heavenly bodies and earthly bodies, but the glory of the heavenly is of one kind, and the glory of the earthly is of another.

This Scripture is speaking specifically of the bodies of angels as differing from the bodies of humans, animals, fish or any of the beasts of the earth. No person can ever become an angel anymore than he can become an alligator or a fish or a bird. They are created of a different flesh and they are different beings. Scripture clearly tells us so.

We will talk about two kinds of angels. God's heavenly angel servants and fallen angels also called demons.

HEAVENLY SERVANTS:

All of the angels were created by God for His own purposes and have already been created. In other words, God does not create new ones as He goes along. He did not even create new angels to take the place of those angels who rebelled against Him. So we see that there is no way that a person who dies on this earth goes to heaven and becomes an angel. Angels were created and in existence long before we were. We may not understand all their purposes but Scripture tells us that they were created to worship God and openly declare

63

His holiness and beauty. (See Revelation 4:8-9 and Revelation 5:11-14). Angels were also created to be God's messengers, to do His bidding and to minister to us, the heirs of salvation. There are many Scriptures that tell us of the ministry of angels to men, but here are two very interesting ones to look up. (See Genesis 19:9-22 and I Kings 19:5-8). In fact the word angel means messenger. We also know from the book of Daniel that angels war in the heavenlies and they war in our behalf on the earth.

Hebrews 1:14; Are they not all ministering spirits, sent forth to minister for them who shall be heirs of salvation?

Angels have appeared to many different people throughout the pages of the Bible and still appear to many today. Angels do have bodies even though they are immortal beings. Angels can also be invisible to the naked eye. They have feelings and possess great intellectual and physical powers far superior to human beings. This is indicated by Scriptures that reveal they have power over the elements such as winds, storms and fire. They can also manifest in physical bodies and speak to men. Remember Jacob wrestled with an angel and Jacob prevailed. However, Jacob limped because the angel touched his hip socket and it remained out of joint the rest of his life. (See Genesis 32:25). So when angels manifest in this manner we are able to physically touch them and they are able to physically touch us.

Angels are messengers of God who communicate and activate the will of God and execute the judgment of God. They carry out God's orders in the heavens and in the earth. They are at His command and disposal at all times, eager to do His bidding. God has put angels in charge over us as far as our safekeeping and protection, so it is true that we do have a guardian angel. Angels activate or initiate God's ministry to us as He directs. (See Hebrews 1:14). Matthew 13:39-42 tells us that at the end of time the angels will be sent to reap the harvest of souls. In Luke 16:22 we see that angels carried the body of Lazarus into Abraham's bosom when his time of suffering on this earth ended.

There are many stories in the Bible of angels appearing and disappearing, ascending and descending, worshipping God, strengthening men, warning people, leading God's people out of danger, loosing prisoners, stirring the waters, bringing messages, making announcements, giving direction, carrying out the judgments of God, fighting for His people, standing in the glory of God and worshipping, and ministering to Christ. But at no time were angels ever human or will any human ever become an angel. (See II Chronicles 32:21, Psalm 78:49, Isaiah 37:16, and Acts 12:23 as examples).

Colossians 1:16; For by him were all things created, that are in heaven, and that are in earth, visible and invisible, whether they be thrones, or dominions, or principalities, or powers: all things were created by him, and for him.

There are different orders of the angelic hosts of heaven and different ranks such as archangels, seraphim, cherubim, and various powers and authorities. The angelic hosts were with Christ and ministered to Him during His agony in the garden. They were at the tomb when He rose from the dead and they were in attendance when He ascended into heaven. They will reap the earth at the end of the world, and they will be with Him when He returns to the earth again at His second coming. All angels are powerful beings.

DEMONIC BEINGS:

Demons are those who followed Satan in rebellion against God. They are also superhuman beings who were created by God. At one time, before they rebelled against God and followed Lucifer, all demons were part of the angelic hosts who served God in heaven. All demons are fallen angels meaning they fell from their previous state and service to God. There are different ranks or orders of demonic beings just as there are different ranks or orders of heavenly angels. Some teach that demons are different from unclean spirits. However, the words used to describe demons are the same words used to describe unclean spirits, ghosts, apparitions and any other form of demonic being. In other words, they are all the same thing. These are the angels that revolted against God, who willfully and purposefully took a position to make themselves enemies of God. They possess power just as the angelic hosts of heaven do. They have rank and order and various administrations of influence and power just as their heavenly angelic counterparts. However, they no longer have the degree of power they once had before the fall because Jesus Christ became a Victor over the devil and all the hosts of hell when He conquered death and hell and rose from the dead. So now their power is more limited in scope through the power and authority that is in Christ and given to us by Him.

The Greek word Daemon which is the same as our word, demon, means a spirit; in particular a demon or devil. (See Matthew 8:16 and Matthew 10:1). They are condemned to their present state and locked into it. They cannot be redeemed.

Job 4:18-19; Even in his servants he puts no trust, and his angels he charges with error.

We see here that the fallen angels who instigated a mutiny against God were His servants before that great rebellion in heaven when Satan declared that he would take over God's position as the Supreme Ruler of the Universe.

Jude 1:6; And the angels who did not stay within their own position of authority, but left their proper dwelling, he has kept in eternal chains under gloomy darkness until the judgment of the great day.

The devil and his demons always recognize Jesus Christ. They recognize His power and authority. They recognize all supernatural power and that includes the power Jesus gave to you and I. If you are walking faithfully with God they will also recognize you. These are the powers and principalities against which we are commanded to wrestle in faithful battle. God said we do not wrestle against flesh and blood but we wrestle against powers and principalities of the highest order.

Ephesians 6:12; For we do not wrestle against flesh and blood, but against the rulers, against the authorities, against the cosmic powers over this present darkness, against the spiritual forces of evil in the heavenly places.

The King James Bible refers to these authorities as principalities. The Greek word for principality is arche. Translated this word means a leader or a chief of various clans and orders; someone who is a magistrate, a power or a principle ruler. "Powers" in Greek is the same word we know as exousia. That is the word we see in the Bible which speaks of authority. This means the devil, Satan, and his demonic hosts are those who have authority, ability, competency and mastery in the spirit realm. It means one who is a potentate or monarch, someone who is a ruler with delegated influence, jurisdiction, authority, strength and power.

In Matthew 21:23-27, we see the chief priests and elders coming to Jesus and demanding that He should explain to them who had given Him the authority to speak and teach in the manner in which He did. "Who gave You the authority to teach like this?" they demanded. "Where did You get this authority?"

They recognized the exousia with which He spoke and it scared and infuriated them because they considered Him to be a no-body, certainly not a learned man like themselves. They considered Him to be one who was most certainly untrained and unschooled in the things of the priesthood. "So who gave You the authority to speak this way?"

Real authority is something that can be sensed even before it is seen or heard. Authority is not in the tone of one's voice, mannerisms, speech patterns, dress, or any outward demonstration or expression of a person. It is much more an inward power and ability that is resident within someone. When someone has authority we sense it even before we hear them speak or see how they act. There is a leadership quality that comes with authority which presents itself as a strong influence. Power can be discerned in the spirit realm before there is any manifestation in outward mannerisms. The devil and his cohorts discern the spiritual authority of the one who is walking in it. They will recognize the authority of someone who is walking with God and who understands their authority in Christ. They will recognize someone who has head knowledge of this power and authority but does not apprehend and walk in it. They also recognize someone who is walking with the powers of darkness and who has obtained a certain degree of power and authority from that kingdom as well.

There are many demons, although we do not know the exact numbers. But we do know that one third of heaven followed Lucifer in rebellion against God. Lucifer is their leader; he is also called the devil. All demons are under the direct leadership of Lucifer and do as he commands. All of these fallen angels are powerful deceiving spirits and we must be very careful to know and understand what kind of angel we are having communion with. Is this a messenger of God or is it a messenger of Satan? When we come into agreement with the powers of darkness in the form of an angelic visitation we open ourselves up to the operation and manifestation of those spirits in our life. This is a component of generational sin as well. In other words, most generational sin is attended by the operation of demonic spirits.

THE PRINCE OF THE POWER OF THE AIR:

There is one devil and one of his many names is Satan. His followers are called demons. He is a created being who has tremendous power and authority, but he is subject to the power and authority of Jesus Christ and God the Father. There are so many names in Scripture for the devil, some of which are as follows; the prince of this world, the deceiver, a liar, the father of lies, the adversary, the dragon, the old serpent, the prince of the power of the air, the god of this world, the one who has the power of death, the thief, the enemy, the accuser of the brethren, adversary, Abaddon, Apollyon, Lucifer, and the angel of the bottomless pit.

He has many other names in Scripture but this will give you a general idea of his attributes and nature. Scripture describes him as divisive, rebellious, deceitful, proud and boastful. He was very powerful when God created him but has given himself completely over to evil and rebellion against God.

The devil and all demons are therefore at enmity with God. They are locked into their estate because of their decision to rebel against God. They are set on the destruction and overthrow of God's kingdom and all that belongs to Him which includes you and me.

Just as God has heavenly angels who are His ambassadors and ministers and He commands them to carry out His instructions, Satan also uses his demons to carry out his instructions in the very same way. Just as God's heavenly angels are sent by God to minister and protect us, Satan's demons are sent on assignments against us. These assignments are meant to bring destruction, complete wreckage and death into our life. Some of these assignments include poverty, infirmity, sickness, disease, and every kind of physical, mental and emotional torment and affliction upon man.

The devil and his hosts cannot be everywhere at once. They are not omnipresent which means they cannot be in more than one place at a time. Nor are they omniscient which means they do not possess all knowledge. They are limited in knowledge. We must remember that in spite of the fact that they have great power, they are only created beings. We do know they are able to travel through space and manifest themselves in the earth.

Satan looks for ways to get at us so he can bring ruin to us. Scripture tells us that he goes about like a roaring lion looking purposefully for anyone he can attack. If he can attack us he will try to weaken us by causing us to lose heart, distrust God, and turn back from God. His main purpose is to strike against the heart of God by destroying God's people. That is exactly why we must close every open door in the spirit realm so he does not have an opening. He will arrange attacks anyway because that is his nature as a thief, but there is no point giving him an open invitation by standing and holding the door open for him while he comes in.

I Peter 5:8-9; Be sober, be vigilant; because your adversary the devil, as a roaring lion, walketh about, seeking whom he may devour: Whom resist steadfast in the faith, knowing that the same afflictions are accomplished in your brethren that are in the world.

James 4:7; Submit yourselves therefore to God. Resist the devil, and he will flee from you.

We are instructed that we must stand in faith and resist Satan and his demons. We are also told that if we submit to the will of God and resist Satan's attempts to bring his plans to fruition in our life that he will flee from us. So a lot of what happens really depends on us and our response to the attack. We are the ones who decide if we will allow the devil to continue his blatant assault against us or if we will call it to a halt. We then are the ones who determine if he can operate in our life or not by our willingness to stand and do battle with the weapons God has given us for our warfare, and by our heart attitudes. What are these attitudes? We must put our complete trust in God, believe in His Word, put on our armour, take up our weapons and enter into the fray knowing that Jesus Christ has already secured the victory for us on Calvary.

I want to say here that if we have given our life to God through salvation in Jesus Christ, there is no way a demon or many demons or even Satan himself can come in and overtake a believer at will. There must be a sin factor, unconfessed sin that we have hidden in our heart. That is the foothold for a demon or the devil to begin to harass or oppress or vex us. God has placed a hedge about us and assigned angels to guard us. However, we break down the hedge of protection by sin, especially ongoing sin. Scripture clearly points out that sin separates us from God.

CHAPTER SIX

ANGELS ANGELS EVERYWHERE

I am truly amazed that so many people are caught up in the worshipping of angels. We are told in the Word that angels worship God but we are told never to worship angels. And yet, everywhere I go I run into people who do not think it strange to worship angels. Actually the only angels who would willingly receive the worship of men would be fallen angels. That itself should be a frightening eye opener.

I had an opportunity to minister to a women's group a couple of years ago and God put it on my heart to speak to them about the worshipping of angels. For a month I waited on God thinking I must not be hearing Him and soon He would speak to me and tell me what I was really supposed to speak about. But the month came and went and I got no other message. So I made my notes and off I went to the meeting. When I arrived, much to my surprise many of the women were elderly. There was a mix of young and old, but most were elderly. I walked into the room and looking around, my heart sank. These women looked like everybody's grandmother. I thought, "Surely I did not hear from God. This cannot be the message I am supposed to give to these women."

However, since I seemed to get nothing else from the Lord during worship, I just had to go with it. I stood up to speak in fear and trembling. When I moved to the podium the Spirit of God came on me with such power, much stronger than I had ever felt. I had no hang-ups, no nervousness, no fear and no concerns. God filled my mouth and I just gave the message loud and clear with great straightforwardness and freedom. It was a very strong message. When I was finished with my message I said a prayer to close the meeting and walked back to my seat. The organizers of the meetings gathered in a corner and put their heads together. I could see the puzzled looks and some words going back and forth. I thought, "I bet I'll never be invited here again!"

Then one of the leaders came to me and asked if I would join them in praying for whoever might need healing or had any other need. Of course I told them I did expect to do so, and thanked them for asking.

One by one the women lined up and I was completely amazed by their stories. One after another their stories were so much the same as the woman before them. One at a time they told me their stories. I was flabbergasted! Each and every one of them started by telling me they did not worship angels BUT ...! One said, "I don't worship angels, but I do talk with my angel every night before I go to bed and tell her (HER) what I want her to do for me the next day."

I asked this woman, "Why would you be asking an angel to do something for you, why wouldn't you be praying and asking the Father in Jesus' name?"

"Oh no, my angel and I have a wonderful relationship and **SHE** does things for me all the time when I ask. I don't have to pray a long time about it."

Another said, "I don't worship angels, but I do know my angel's name and we have long discussions all the time. Her name is …."

Then she rattled off some long foreign sounding name and told me that she commands her angel to run errands for her. It gave me chills. I tried to convince her she needed to repent and renounce this alliance but she insisted it was wonderful and godly even though she admitted that she bowed down to the angel when she prayed to it.

One told me she prayed to her angel every night and asked the angel to tell God what she wanted. You cannot believe the things these women told me about their angels, which were really spirit guides. How do I know this? The answer is simple; God does not send angels to us to do our bidding but to do His bidding. He does not send angels to entertain us when we are lonely or to sit and have long conversations about whatever is happening in our daily life. When God sends an angel to us it is with intense purpose and meaning. What these lovely older ladies were practicing was spiritism. They were taught and deceived into thinking it was all right to be in communication with angelic beings in a friendly, relational manner, even wrestling with them and tickling each other.

Oh, I was climbing out of my shoes and could barely believe my ears as one after another stood in line, waited their turn politely and then told me all the things they did with angels. There were many more stories. If my hair were not stark white already it surely would have been after that. In each instance I instructed these lovely, gentle, refined looking women that they were not to pray to or worship or call forth these angels ever again. I did tell them that indeed these were NOT angels coming to them, but they were demons in the form or appearance of heavenly angelic beings. They were dark spirit beings appearing as angels of light. Unfortunately many of the women did not want to repent but insisted it was all okay. They clearly desired and enjoyed their communication with these "angels." One woman even told me she hugged her angel every night before bed and another told me that her angel sat on the edge of her bed every night and prayed over her until she fell asleep.

YUK!!!!!!!

Many of these women indicated they also prayed to saints and their dear departed loved ones, so I believe it was such a small leap to begin to pray and summon angelic beings which were demonic spirit guides. No one seemed to see anything wrong with it. They all found it very comforting and no doubt thought that I was ill informed and ignorant.

Well, now much to my surprise, I knew I had indeed received and given the right message. Generally when I am preaching or teaching I do not feel the anointing. I used to feel it very strongly when I first began to minister, but that was over thirty years ago and now it is rare that I feel it in that way. I know the Holy Spirit is moving and ministering to people because I see them crying or they begin to repent, often out loud. But as for me to be feeling the anointing in a strong way, it just does not really happen to me that way anymore. I have to stand by faith. But that day I felt the anointing so strong. It was the most powerful anointing with so much freedom that I have ever experienced while preaching or teaching. It surely was God's word for the day. I do hope they received it. Perhaps after they went to their own homes they were convinced. Maybe they mulled it over in their head, perhaps even pulled out the Bible and looked up the Biblical references I gave.

I guess people have a real need in this day and age to have their own angel in tight communication with them on a daily basis. But why would anyone desire communication with an angel when they can have communication with their heavenly Father or with His Son?

IF IT IS NOT REAL WE WILL JUST MAKE IT UP:

One time during the dead of winter here in Wisconsin, I wanted to take some classes at a local college. I was very bored and I enjoy school, so I set out for the nearest college. It was an impressive citadel of learning. I loved the magnificent marble halls and the grandness of it all. Finally I made my way into the admissions office and asked for a catalogue of the classes and degrees offered. Much to my chagrin I found that many of the classes were on angels and spirit guides. They offered many classes with titles such as; "Meeting your Angel, Meeting your Spirit Guide, Conversations with Your Angel, Spirit Travel, Extra Sensory Perception, and Finding the god within you." They placed a capital G on god in their class catalogue. There were so many more titles of classes along these lines. I really found it hard to believe. To think that they actually gave credit for this kind of nonsense amazed me. I attended and graduated from several Christian colleges and there were not any fluff classes, and certainly nothing that would be considered mysticism, new age or the occult. I left immediately. I do not even want to be in such a place, much less take any classes there. It is not only idolatry, it is actually teaching witchcraft. It is leading people astray in mass. It is like taking someone by the hand and leading them right to the edge of hell itself where these devilish beings are waiting with open arms to welcome them into a new world of communication with spirit beings.

DO YOU BELIEVE IN ANGELS?

Do I believe in angels? Oh, you bet I do! At one time there were four little girls, now all grown to be lovely Spirit filled women of God, who would invite me over to their slumber parties and ask me to tell the stories of angels and miracles. At the time they ranged in age from perhaps seven to fourteen years old. It was so much fun to sit around on the floor and tell the stories of Gods powerful intervention in my life.

Before I received salvation I saw demons all the time in the form of apparitions, ghosts, or spirits. Whatever you might like to call them it is all the same. I was certain that most people saw these apparitions on a regular basis just as I did. So naturally when I received salvation I just assumed that everyone who got saved also saw angels. It was a very long time, a matter of about ten years before I realized this was not the case. I believed everyone saw these things and that everyone heard the voice of God even audibly after their salvation experience.

I have had angelic experiences of both kinds, both before salvation as well as after. I have seen both, real angels sent from God and the other ones from the demonic side as well. An angel actually transported me all the way to the United States from Africa.

After I was first saved, every night in the middle of the night a voice would wake me up calling my name. I would sit up in bed and say, "Yes, Lord, what do You want?"

The angel would tell me to worship God or go to my knees and pray for a specific person. I would pray until I felt a release and then go back to sleep. The angel NEVER sat and chit-chatted with me or touched me in any way. It was holy and the focus was always on GOD, never on me, never on him. Night after night this angelic being came into my room to wake me. I would be instructed to pray or sing to the Lord or just worship Him. Sometimes there would be very specific instruction for intercession regarding a particular person or situation. This angel always gave me instruction as to what God wanted from me that night.

One night the voice woke me and told me to get out of bed immediately. I sensed a real urgency in the voice. I jumped out of bed and turned on the light. I did not see the angel but I saw a huge hairy and horrible looking spider as large as my fist crawling up the bedspread and almost reaching the top of the blanket where I would have been exposed to it. The next night the angelic voice woke me and told me to get out of bed and open the drapes. It was pitch dark but I got out of bed quickly, turned on the bedroom light and opened the drapes. There on the window was a whole bunch of these spiders, maybe six or seven of them. I quickly left my apartment, got into my car and drove to a friend's house to sleep. The next day my apartment was fumigated. Obviously a mother spider had gotten in there from the woods right by my place and she had hatched her eggs.

But never at any time was I ever instructed to fraternize or socialize with the angel who would call me awake in the night. It was never about me. It was never about him. I never asked his name and he never told me. I suppose I could have asked because there are many instances in the Bible when people asked the name of the angel, but we had no casual conversations. There was never any bowing down to the angel or praying to him and no sending him to run errands for me. It was all strictly business. It was all about God and His Son, Jesus Christ.

Those who allow themselves to be involved with spirit beings (demonic in origin) have literally opened a door to hell! They certainly must have no idea what they are doing. They are absolutely deceived by their "angelic" host and they are entertaining demons unaware. But what will the end of it be? Certainly God's judgment awaits such foolishness, and a curse comes down upon the head of the one who is involved in such blatant idolatry, not to mention the attendant spirits (demons) who minister to the person and who will continue on through the family line wreaking havoc as they go, bringing destruction and damnation.

So if you know or even suspect that there was or is someone in your own family line that was or is currently involved in these activities; first of all begin to pray for them. Secondly, ask God to prepare you to speak to them if possible and give you the right words to speak. Ask God to prepare their heart to receive the truth so they can be set free and delivered and so that the generational sin and attendant spirits will be cut off. Also pray for yourself and your family to cut off any affect it could have had on your own family.

We must guard our hearts against any kind of idolatry or witchcraft because both of these things open the doors of darkness and usher in attending spirits (demons). These demons visit us in order to deceive us and are visited on through our generations.

How can we know if we are meeting a real angel that is actually sent from God or a demonic being posing as an angel of light? The Bible tells us that we are to test the angels who appear to us.

I John 4:1-3a; Beloved, do not believe every spirit, but test the spirits to see whether they are from God, for many false prophets have gone out into the world. By this you know the Spirit of God: every spirit that confesses that Jesus Christ has come in the flesh is from God, and every spirit that does not confess Jesus is not from God....

This is a good Scripture to keep under your belt. Don't just go around believing everything you hear or even for that matter, everything you see. Certainly we are not to believe and receive whatever others say without checking it out ourself in the Word of God. Study the Word, get it in your spirit and bury it in your heart. You must know the Word and you must ask God for discernment in order to be able to discriminate between what is holy and what is not. Do not be led about by every wind of doctrine!

One more story about angels. Right after I was saved God showed me there was a call on my life. I was so excited to think that He would use me. One day as I was walking home from work God spoke to me and said, "I have a gift for you today. It's in your mailbox."

Wow, a gift from God. I wonder what it could be! I rushed to my mailbox and scattered the mail over my kitchen table. There were

Sins Of The Fathers

the usual announcements, maybe a bill or two, and advertisements. There was a flyer from some group I had never heard of. I was about to toss it when I heard the Lord say, "This is the gift I have for you."

I pulled it open and read it. I heard Him tell me that I was to go to the conference it was announcing. I looked at the clock and noted I had about one and a half hours to get there and it was at least two hours away. Nonetheless, I immediately hopped into my car and headed off to the conference. It was in a town I had never been in and as I drove a real excitement filled my soul. I couldn't help but wonder why I was to go to this conference with these people I had never ever heard of. When I arrived worship had already begun so I found a place to sit, looked around to check things out, and closed my eyes to enter into worship. The worship was so wonderful and some time during worship I was caught up in the spirit. I have no idea how long I was like that, but during this time God opened up the heart of the worship leader for me to see. I could see music coming out of his heart. It was pure worship, out of a heart filled with love and mercy. The most beautiful music, sounds and incredible colors were actually flowing out of him, and something that looked like liquid gold flowed smoothly out of his heart. God said, "I want you to go back with him and this group and be a part of them."

What? Go back where? I don't know these people, who are they? I couldn't believe He was telling me to do this. Just then I came out of the Spirit and jumped to my feet. I think I made a racket when I jumped to my feet and everyone had turned around to stare at me.

The worship leader was kind of taken back and stopped worship. He looked at me (I was the only one standing at that point) and said, "Are you okay?"

I told him I was. Then he said, "What happened? Why are you standing?"

I said, "God just told me that I am to go back with you and this group to wherever it is you go. Like thunder, He told me to stand up!"

He laughed so hard. I did not think it was particularly funny, but then he said, "God just spoke to me and told me that some of you in the audience would be going back with us and I was to ask you to stand."

He called the elders and the president of the organization to lay hands on me and claim me for their organization. They did. They gathered around me and prayed like crazy. I had perfect peace but I still had absolutely no idea where in the world I was going or why I was going there. I did not even know what this organization was about. I had never heard of the place, but I found out it was somewhere in Missouri. I went home that evening and prayed and the next day I gave notice at work. I told my neighbors I was leaving and sold almost everything I owned. I felt like I was to do that. Within approximately thirty days I was on my way to Missouri with a map in one hand and a jug of water beside me, my car packed to the ceiling with clothes and books.

However, within the time between the call and my actual leaving; I had a visitation. One evening I was lying on my back on the living room floor worshipping God. All of a sudden the room filled up with light. Startled I looked around and saw a huge angel standing in my living room. The room was bathed in a blush of golden light. The most pleasant music filled the room. There was so much love in the room I could almost reach out and take it by the handful. The presence of the angel was so strong it filled the whole room and I felt like it filled my whole being. The angel spoke and told me that God was going to take me home to Him. I was going to die. I thought that was strange since God had just told me I was to go to Missouri and join this particular group, but I thought, "Well, I guess God knows what He is doing. I wonder why He wants me to die there in Missouri."

I was not afraid at all. I just thought it was odd. I kept thinking that perhaps God just changed His mind. But why did He want me in Missouri?

I arrived at what turned out to be a seminary. I had actually no idea it was a seminary and was shocked to find out that is what I was to be a part of. I found a place to stay, met some people and signed up. It was pretty lonely not being from Missouri and not really knowing anyone there, but school was fantastic and I loved it. There was such an anointing for healing on the grounds that I would step on the grounds of the school and begin to weep. Not only me, but this happened to many others as well. This was a place of a real outpouring of the Spirit of God, a true introduction to signs and wonders. It was a place of wonderful healings and great miracles.

I remember as I would drive back and forth from school to my little apartment I would wonder how I was going to die. The angel had told me I would die before my thirty-eighth birthday. This was October, so it wasn't that far off. I did not tell anyone about this visitation for several reasons. I had not been saved that long and I still believed that everyone who was saved had these kinds of experiences of seeing and having visitations of angels, so I did not think it was all that unusual. Secondly, I felt that it was kind of a sacred trust between me and God. Something very special that He was requiring of me and I was more than happy to let Him take me home if that is what He wanted to do, although it still puzzled me why He sent me to Missouri to die.

When I did think about it I would wonder if I was going to die in a car accident, or die in my sleep or by what means? But there was no fear. I had perfect peace about it.

One Sunday afternoon there was a church picnic on the grounds. A couple who had about twelve children they had adopted from various countries was at the picnic. The mother stood up on top of the picnic table to get everyone's attention and make an announcement. She asked if there was anyone who would be willing to come to her home and care for one of her children while she and her husband traveled to another state to minister. My arm shot up in the air. I tried to bring it down, but it would not come down! About the last thing on earth I wanted to do was to babysit anyone. In fact, I had plans that weekend to return to Wisconsin to visit friends. However, my arm was stuck up in the air like it had a steel rod inside of it. She noticed me, thanked me publicly and that was that. When she thanked me my arm shot back down like it had just been released from something. It felt like the iron rod that held it just melted away. Because everyone was applauding and thanking me, I was much too embarrassed to say it was all a mistake. The weekend came and went without a hitch. The child was no problem. Afterward she and her husband returned home, thanked me and as I was about to leave I asked if I could borrow some books from their library. I had pulled about ten or twelve books off the library shelf and laid them out on their massive dining table. She looked very surprised so I tried to reassure her, "I promise I will take good care of them. I take very good care of my books and I will return them quickly."

She responded, "Are you sure you want all these books?"

"Yes, if I can."

"Well okay," she said as she began to pile them one on top of the other into a box.

When I got home I laid all the books out on my bed and wondered which one I should read first. It was then that I noticed for the first time that all the books I chose were books on deliverance. I thought that was not only very strange but I was surprised that all the books were on the same subject. As I was choosing them off the bookshelves I thought I was picking books on all different subjects.

I said, "Okay Lord, You must want someone to receive deliverance, but who?"

I prayed for hours and then the Lord spoke to me and said, "You are the one."

I was shocked. Me? I had already received deliverance when I got saved. I was delivered from all kinds of strongholds and demonic spirits. What in the world would I need deliverance from now? I could not think of anything in my life that would cause me to need deliverance. The Lord spoke to me and told me that the first thing I was to do was to call the woman that I had borrowed the books from. First thing the next morning I did that and told her that God had showed me I needed deliverance. She told me to come right over. It is interesting that I had no idea she and her husband were deliverance ministers. (How appropriate, God! You do everything so well!)

When I arrived at her house she asked me what I needed deliverance for and I told her I did not know, in fact I had absolutely no idea. She asked me a few questions and within just a matter of several minutes she had the devil by the tail. The Holy Spirit led her to ask me certain questions and one of them was; "Have you made any agreements with anyone, entered into any covenants with anyone or taken any vows?"

I did not want to tell her because as I said before I felt I had entered into a holy agreement with God and believed He was going to take me home before my thirty-eighth birthday. Finally I told her and she was really upset and frightened. She kept telling me

89

I had to renounce that agreement, insisting that it was not of God. Immediately I felt anger against her and began to resist her. I refused to allow her to pray with me about this. I felt like she was trying to break an agreement that God required of me. After all, He sent an angel to me with this message. Thank God she kept at me and would not quit. Finally she asked me this, "Will you let me pray for you and ask God to break off of you anything that is not from Him? Anything that is not specifically in His will for you? Will you allow Him to break off of you anything that hinders His plans and purposes for your life?"

I actually had to think about it because I did not want her getting in the way of anything God was calling me to do. Finally I said it would be okay to pray that but only that and nothing more. She agreed. Then she prayed. Immediately there was a powerful manifestation of demonic power and that was that. It was all over. I was so surprised because I did not expect anything to happen. I thought she was way off base and did not understand what God wanted from me. But in truth, I was the one who had no understanding and was deceived.

It is so easy to be deceived and that is why God instructed us to test the spirits to see whether or not they are of God. When God tells us that His own people die because of a lack of knowledge, it is a warning to us that we must take the time to get to know Him and to know His ways. It is not enough to have a surface relationship with Him, but we must really bury His Word inside of our heart and soul.

If God had not rescued me by putting me in a situation where I had to babysit the whole weekend, I would not have met the woman and her husband. Of course I would not have asked to borrow the books, and I would never have known I needed deliverance. In His great mercy to me, God orchestrated the whole thing in my behalf because I was ignorant of His ways.

All His promises are yea and amen. Everything He speaks He will bring to pass. He will not tell you one thing and then quickly change His mind and tell you to do something else. He is not double minded. His word does not return void. What He says He will do. My ignorance in this matter held me a breath away from death and I have absolutely no doubt that I would have died because I had unknowingly entered into an agreement with a demon who posed as an angel of light. It was an absolute miracle that I was rescued from this ungodly visitation and the resultant covenant I entered into by my agreement. There is also no doubt that although I had received various deliverances since salvation that the spirit of death that dogged me all my life was still there. This was some of his work and I needed to be set free of this assignment against me.

FIND THAT HOUSE:

I have also had experiences where angels lead me or directed me to places I had no way of finding on my own. For example, at one time a young woman kept on calling me for help. She lived in another state. Finally I agreed to drive to her state and help her out

Sins Of The Fathers

with clothing and money and whatever else I could do. I arrived in her state in the middle of the night only to find out that there was no place to stay. All the hotels and motels in two adjoining towns had been booked for weeks because there was some special performance in town. I had no idea what to do, so I gathered all my luggage and found an all night restaurant. I found a large corner booth and piled in the booth with all my suitcases stacked around me. Then I began to drink coffee and pray. I had it in mind to try to stay awake until morning but could not. Finally I did not know what to do and I just could not stay awake any longer. So I got out of my seat and walked up to the counter. I had it in my mind to ask the hostess if perhaps she knew of some place I might be able to stay. Just then a large group of people walked to the front of the restaurant to pay their bill. I explained my dilemma to the cashier and the group overheard me speaking so they asked me what was going on. I told them I could not find a hotel or motel anywhere and asked if they knew of any place that might have a room available. It turns out that they were just returning from a Holy Ghost conference in a nearby state and said they would be honored to have me stay at one of their houses. They escorted me home with them and showed me to a beautifully decorated room with a huge welcoming bed. In spite of all the coffee I had consumed over those long hours trying to stay awake, I immediately fell into a deep restful sleep. The next morning when I awoke they made breakfast and told me I was welcome to stay as long as I needed. I explained that I was looking for a young woman who was in trouble but that she had given me a non existent address. I told them that if they would be kind enough to drive me and my luggage through the town; up and down each and every block so that I could look at the houses that God would surely point out which one was the right house. They were very surprised and laughed at me. They tried to tell me that was just silly, but I knew God would show me. Otherwise He would have cautioned me not to come this far at all. I knew God would show me the right house.

I would not be tempted to change my mind even though they insisted it was foolish. I had not traveled all this way for nothing! So, off we went with me in the back seat of their vehicle with all the suitcases piled next to me on the seat and at my feet.

We began at one end of town and went for several miles. I simply looked at each house we passed waiting for God to show me. I knew He would send an angel to direct my path. The driver and his wife still tried to convince me this was really silly and I should just come home with them and have lunch. But within a very short time I said, "Stop! This is it!"

"How do you know?"

"I just know!"

The angel had pointed out the very house to me. I got out of the car, pulled all my suitcases out and knocked on the front door. You can imagine the surprise when the girl opened the door knowing she had purposely given me the wrong address. I figured out later that she wanted help, but she did not really want me to come to her door.

A check in her mailbox would have been sufficient. But God knew what she needed.

THE MAN WITH A GUN:

Before salvation I worked for an attorney as a Para-legal. I loved the work. I found it stimulating and exciting and challenging. It was not unusual for me to work late in the office alone. One evening I was at my desk finishing up some things when a man walked in through the front door. He demanded to know where my boss was. I tried to explain to him that my boss had already left for the day and offered to make an appointment for the very next day for him to be seen. It was obvious he was very angry although at this point I still did not know what it was about. He began shouting at me in a foreign language and pulled a gun from his pocket. He was pointing the gun at me and then waving it in the air, all the while shouting and cursing me. He was extremely threatening.

My desk was located at the far end of the office but right next to a door that led into two long hallways. Out the door and to the right was a long hallway that led to the bathrooms. Out the door and to the left was another long hallway that led down the stairs to other offices and to the underground parking. I remember looking over my shoulder at the open door behind me and wondering if I could make it out of my chair and through the door before I got shot in the back. If I made it through the door and into a hallway, which way would I go, to the right or to the left?

Just then another man walked through the front door into the office. He came straight toward me. I had absolutely no idea who he was or why he was there. I had never seen him before in my whole life. He walked right up to me and stood really close to me, right alongside me directly facing the man with the gun. I was still glued to my chair. I looked up at him and wondered, "Doesn't he see the gun?"

He took me by the elbow and very calmly said, "Come on honey. You know everyone is waiting for us and we can't be late."

He politely smiled at the man with the gun and said, "I am sorry, but everyone is expecting us."

He pulled me up out my chair by his firm hold on my elbow and walked me to the front door of the office. My legs had long ago turned to water and I couldn't speak. He told me he would take me to my car in underground parking. I still did not know if he was a good guy or a bad guy. Perhaps he was a part of this whole thing and he would kill me. When we got to the basement he asked me which car was mine and I pointed it out to him. He got me into the front seat and told me to lock the doors and not to open them for anyone. He told me to sit there until I gained control of myself because my whole body was shaking so hard; then to drive out as soon as I could and go straight home. He said he was going back to the office.

To this day I have no idea who that man was or where he came from. I never saw him again, I never heard from him again. My boss did not believe there ever was a man who rescued me. I found out later from my boss that the man with the gun was arrested and locked up and shortly after that he was deported. The man who saved my life was never to be seen or heard from again. Angel?

SO MUCH FOR VOLUNTEER WORK:

I had another similar incident when I was first saved. I volunteered to work at a local Veteran's hospital. I went through the training sessions and came on board doing little things that were needed. Write a letter, visit a veteran, etc.

In this particular hospital there was a mental ward. I asked my supervisor if I could have permission to go into this ward and pray for the patients. On several occasions when there was nothing else they wanted me to do I was allowed to go in. It was dark in there, only enough light to see the foot of each bed. I could not see anyone or anything else. I felt my way along the footboards of several of the beds and would simply pray from one bed to the next.

One evening after leaving the hospital as I was walking toward the parking lot, I suddenly felt very afraid. I looked behind me and saw two very tall men following me. Or at least they were walking behind me, but I felt like they were following me. I picked up the pace a bit and looked back again to see that they also picked up the pace. I began to pray.

Several nurses had been raped on the grounds in recent months coming or going to their vehicles, so an armed guard was supposed to be stationed at the door. He would walk us to our car. But this night he was not at his station. I looked back to see if perhaps he had returned to his station thinking I would turn back and ask for his help. But when I looked back he still was not there. I did not know if I should keep on walking fast or go back to the hospital. I kept walking.

Within a minute or so the two men had caught up to me and flanked me one on each side. They looked so tall and they looked scary to me. One asked me where I was going. I don't know if I responded or not. Wondering if I could make it to the car or even if I turned back, would I make it back to the hospital safely, I prayed harder, taking authority over any spirits that might be operating against me.

One man put his hand on my shoulder and asked me how much money I had in my purse. At this point I simply lost it. I began yelling and shaking my fist at him. I was shouting at him that I was broke and did this work as a volunteer. The pitch of my voice alone should have scared him half to death. I was shouting that all I had was two dollars and if he thought for one minute I was giving it to him, he was just plain crazy. He probably thought I was crazy! The second man just stood there slack jawed looking at me.

As I continued yelling at him I reached up and grabbed his jacket collar. I began to shake him. I had really lost it! I don't know if I was responding in fear or what! Finally, I remember saying in a very accusing and loud voice, "I have two dollars. I will give you one if you really need it, but you are not going to go across the street and

Sins Of The Fathers

buy a drink with it. It is my last two dollars and I am not sharing it with you for a drink. I worked too hard for it."

He slipped his arm through mine and said, "Come on. Don't you know it is not safe out here? You should not be out here alone. We will walk you to your car."

I did not know if I should be screaming, trying to run in my stupid heels, or what. I was so frightened. The two men, still one on each side of me walked me to my car. One told me to give him my car keys and with great fear and trembling I did. He opened my car door, put in me and punched down the lock on the door. Then he knocked on the window and motioned for me to roll down the window so he could talk to me. I was so scared, but I rolled it down just a crack. He said, "You go straight home, it is very dangerous out here."

Boy, you're telling me! I quit my volunteer position at the hospital the next day by phone and never went back. But I had to wonder what exactly happened that night?

STREET GANGS:

For a time right after my salvation I did street ministry in an inner city. I handed out Bibles to anyone who wanted one and shared the gospel with anyone who would listen. Very often I came upon gangs of both girls and young men. They would often be on the streets or in the playgrounds playing basketball. In the beginning I would see them walking toward me and would automatically put my head down and step into the gutter so they could pass by on the sidewalk. God would tell me over and over not to fear them. He kept telling me that He was making my forehead like brass. I would hear Him say; "Walk right up into the midst of them and tell them your name. Then ask if anyone of them would want a Bible."

Results were varied. Usually they were astonished at first that I would even dare approach them. Sometimes the results were funny. Anyway, more than once I was told by these gangs that I was attended by huge angels.

I don't think the two men at the Veteran's hospital were angels because they asked me for money, but I have to wonder if they saw my angels and decided to be nice to me. I don't know!

There are so many stories like this that I can tell. Angels are real and we should expect God to send angels to our aid in situations when we are in need of help and especially when we are in dangerous situations. God said His angels are to minister to the needs of the saints. That's us!

In the last few years it has become so popular to talk about angels everywhere. But we must be very careful to know what angel it is that is ministering to us. Is it an angel sent from God or is it a fallen angel? So many people are deceived because they want to see angels, they want to hear angels speak to them, and they want the manifestation of angels in their meetings or in their homes. Some people want a personal relationship with an angel but that is not what God created angels for. We must be very cautious to discern the origin of

Sins Of The Fathers

the angel(s) that manifest to us. It is not a game! We must not allow ourselves to be seduced into the worshipping of angels or being led astray by fallen angels who appear as an angel of light.

CHAPTER SEVEN

CHASTISEMENT OR A CURSE?

God tells us that He chastens every son and if you have not been chastened, then you are not His son.

Deuteronomy 8:5; Know then in your heart that, as a man disciplines his son, the Lord your God disciplines you.

Hebrews 12:6-8; "For the Lord disciplines the one he loves, and chastises every son whom he receives." It is for discipline that you have to endure. God is treating you as sons. For what son is there whom his father does not discipline? If you are left without discipline, in which all have participated, then you are illegitimate children and not sons.

God says the same thing in the Old Testament and in the New Testament so I guess that means He did not change His mind about it. If you were not chastened (disciplined) as a child, then I am certain it was difficult for you as an adult to be able to fit into the real world. The word chasten in the Hebrew and Greek means to be educated, trained up, corrected, instructed, punished, reformed, reproved and taught.

As a child without firm instruction as to how things are done correctly or how to act, the child quickly goes astray and tries to find his or her own way. So we see that chastening is actually a good thing and it is very necessary for the growth and education of the child. God gave children parents for a reason knowing that they would need correction and direction and would be unable to provide it for themselves. It is a gross injustice to the child and a tremendous neglect of duty as a parent not to discipline and teach our children what is right and godly. This teaching will make their lives so much easier as time goes on. Our Father in heaven feels strongly about this and undertakes to teach, discipline and correct us as is necessary.

However, when you are in the midst of a trial it can be very perplexing. We are mystified about the whole thing. I think that the first thing we do is go before God and ask Him, "What is going on here? Why is this happening to me?"

It is often confusion that we feel first. We do not understand what is going on. If you are a sincere and dedicated believer, then you have surrendered your life to Christ as much as you know how at this time. You read His Word, you believe His Word, and you believe His promises, yet, here you are in the midst of some trial that has totally come out of left field and caught you completely off guard. You are left sitting alone wondering what is going on.

Scripture is very clear when it talks about sowing to the flesh. It tells us that if we sow to the flesh we will also reap from the flesh. Sow means to plant, to scatter seed, to purposely plant seed and to sow knowingly. So it is clear that sowing to the flesh is speaking about someone who is in rebellion against God and refusing to turn from their sin. They are rejecting God by their continual choosing of sin. They want what they want and they want it right now. They are not going to give in or surrender to God's will for their life. Those who purposefully sow to the flesh will reap from the flesh and those who purposely sow to the Spirit will reap from the Spirit.

Galatians 6:7-8; Do not be deceived: God is not mocked, for whatever one sows, that will he also reap. For the one who sows to his own flesh will from the flesh reap corruption, but one who sows to the Spirit will from the Spirit reap eternal life.

TIME AND CHANCE HAPPEN TO ALL MEN:

Ecclesiastes 9:11-12; Again I saw that under the sun the race is not to the swift, nor the battle to the strong, nor bread to the wise, nor riches to the intelligent, nor favor to those with knowledge, but time and chance happen to them all. For man does not know his time. Like fish that are taken in an evil net, and like birds that are caught in a snare, so the children of man are snared at an evil time, when it suddenly falls upon them.

This is one of my favorite Scriptures. I think it explains so much. The root meaning in Hebrew of the word "chance" here means to impose upon one by means of force. To impose upon someone something that is not their will. For example, it could be an accident or some abuse or violence; whether emotional, mental, physical or even financial. No one chooses a car accident or some other kind of accident that causes injury of any kind. Certainly no one would ever choose any form of violence toward themself or anyone they love, and they would not choose financial calamity. So this verse tells us that suddenly and without any warning, some circumstance may come crashing in to interrupt your life or my life. The Hebrew word gives the meaning that it is something that comes between the time and circumstances you were just in and the time and circumstances that you will soon be in. However, in the meantime, there is this time in between, and this is what it is talking about. This time in between sneaks up on you and slaps you right in the face when you are not expecting it. This verse explains to us that both time and chance are a part of life on this earth. Things happen and it is that simple! We somehow have to deal with it.

Not everything on this earth is going to be perfect in your life or in mine. In fact, if I am correct, not much of anything will ever be perfect in this life on earth. We are the ones who have to change and adapt. We have to adjust to our circumstances as they come to us. We are the ones who have to reach for God's grace and take a hold of His strength in order to make it through the trials and troubles that

Sins Of The Fathers

come our way on this journey that we make from here to eternity. Hopefully through these trials and troubles we are strengthened. It will be so if we set our heart to trust and obey Him that we will be strengthened. He will help us to grow in maturity and wisdom through the things that come to us in this life, however unpleasant or painful at times. It is clear; the one thing that we can count on is that if we are being chastened or tested by God, it will only last for a time and a season. It is not something that will endure. Over and over the Bible says, "And it came to pass."

I like that! I like it because it gives me hope that there will be an end. It encourages me about what I cannot yet see and what I still do not understand. "It came to pass." The end may not yet be in sight, but I will lift up my head and hope in my God. The end may come yet today, and if not today then perhaps tomorrow morning or tomorrow evening. Even though the end is not in sight yet, I know that I can anchor my soul to Him because He has promised me that He will not give me more than I can bear. His mercies are new every morning. Therefore, I have hope in Him that this too shall pass.

Malachi 3:3; And he shall sit as a refiner and purifier of silver: and he shall purify the sons of Levi, and purge them as gold and silver, that they may offer unto the Lord an offering in righteousness.

Zechariah 13:9; And I will bring the third part through the fire, and will refine them as silver is refined, and will try them as gold is tried: they shall call on my name, and I will hear them: I will say, It is my people: and they shall say, The Lord is my God.

Whatever the case or even the cause, there will be an end to it because it came in order to pass. That is what chastening or a trial does. It comes to pass. It is not forever. It is simply for a time and a season. The refiner of fire sits over the fire and controls the intensity of the heat. The purpose is to cleanse and purify His sons and daughters. Whether it is purifying, chastening, or testing; God does allow His people to walk through fire so that we can see what is inside of us. He already knows but we are the ones who need to see what is in our own heart.

Jeremiah 17:9; The heart is deceitful above all things, and desperately sick; who can understand it? "I the Lord search the heart and test the mind, to give every man according to his ways, according to the fruit of his deeds."

Instead of the word "sick," some other versions use the word wicked or incurable. Most of the time, as believers, we walk around so pretentious, talk so grandiose and make our self seem so big and puffed up as though we really are something special all by ourself. But a time comes when God desires for us to see our meager self as we really are so that we may learn to lean into Him with all our heart and soul. So He allows testing to come to make a display of all that is buried within our heart and soul. But even this is only for a time and a season. It comes to us with purpose. It comes to show us who and what we really are apart from Him and it comes to pass!

Remember when the children were lost in the wilderness and trying to find their way into the Promised Land? God allowed them to be tested to show them what they were made of. When we begin to see ourself the way God sees us, there is repentance on the way! (See Deuteronomy 8:2).

In the midst of the testing and trial we are stripped down to our naked self. We begin to see what we are really made of, and we begin to see what God sees. Our nakedness is not hidden from His eyes. Some teach that when God looks at us He only sees Jesus. They say He does not see us as we really are, in our unfinished state. But I disagree. God is not blind. And I don't believe He has poor vision. I believe He sees us just exactly as we are! But He also sees what He has furnished and provided for us when we were purchased by His own sacrifice. We are hidden in Him. He regards us as holy and complete because positionally we are seated with Christ in heavenly places. We used to be profane but His shed blood has made us holy. He is well satisfied with the sacrifice which was offered in our behalf and He has fully accepted that sacrifice.

This means we are each in the process of a personal sanctification. Each one of us are in various stages of that process which is why we must be patient to walk in grace and love with one another.

This process of sanctification lasts our whole lifetime. It is not completed until the moment we look full into His face. Until that time there is a daily outworking of our sanctification. However we appear at this moment, He knows and we should always remember; we are not displaying the finished product. The moment we draw our last breath on this earth we shall be like Him, completely transformed into His image.

In the meantime, when we walk through fire, after our covering has been stripped away from us, (the covering we made out of old fig leafs and odds and ends in order to cover our own nakedness); after that covering has been stripped away from us the only things that are burned away in the fire are the tight bonds that held us captive. In the midst of the fiery trial we look around and see that there is one walking in the midst of the fire with us. His name is "Son of God." His name is "Jesus, Wonderful Counselor, Prince of Peace, Mighty God and Deliverer." He is the One Who is mighty to save.

The Word tells us that our heavenly Father chastens every son He takes to Himself. The word son is used in the universal sense meaning son or daughter. He warns and encourages us not to be surprised when sudden trials come upon us as though some strange thing happened to us.

I Peter 4:12; Beloved, think it not strange concerning the fiery trial which is to try you, as though some strange thing happened unto you.

I remember the Holy Spirit giving me this verse so very often. It seemed like every single time I prayed and almost every time I opened up my Bible, I got the same thing. Every church service I attended the sermon was on this verse. If I attended a conference or got a personal word of prophesy, it was this word. I was amazed that everywhere I went it seemed no one could talk of anything else. Or was it just that the Holy Spirit was ministering this to me in order to prepare me? Yet, in spite of all that, I was very surprised when fiery trials came my way. They come so suddenly with no warning. An unexpected onslaught!

Often Christians are taught that nothing bad can ever happen to them. That gospel is an incomplete gospel and it leaves them ill prepared and ignorant of God's ways. We are assured that trials will come our way. But on the other hand, we say we believe that God loves us. We say we believe that He will not do anything to harm us, yet so very often we blame and accuse Him for everything that happens in life. God does allow trials and tribulations into our life at times. In the midst of all this we must also remember that not everything that happens is from God. We must understand that everything that happens to us is not even from the devil! Remember, time and chance? Time and chance happen to all men. The rain falls on the just and the unjust alike. Also, some things are just simply our own fault because we have a sinful nature. Sin always brings death to us in one form or another because we reap what we sow. When we come to Christ most of us are naturally still very strong willed. Very often we are not willing to turn completely away from our sin. We often want to pick and choose what we will walk away from. We have our pet sins. We rationalize our sin and we tell ourself that God loves us and He understands our need and desires. We try to compromise with God, make deals with Him, coax Him and convince Him. We bargain with God. When He said, "Come, let us reason together," this is not what He had in mind.

However, in the end it is a matter of surrender and this is a work of sanctification. We may think we surrendered all to Him the day we knelt down and said the prayer to accept Him as Lord. But as we go down the road we find there is always more to surrender, as He reveals our true nature to us and puts His finger on us revealing the depths of our being.

So we have several things working in our life; time and chance are working in our life and we have sowing and reaping at work in our life. We know it is fact that whatever we sow we will also reap. If we sow to the Spirit we will reap of the Spirit. If we sow to the flesh we will reap of the flesh and sin always brings a measure of death to us. We also have testing and trials that come upon all believers and the chastening hand of the Lord can be at work as well. But there is another factor that is very often hidden to our view and that is generational sin and generational curses which are quietly at work to bring complete devastation into our lives and the lives of our loved ones. We become so used to the outworking of generational sin and curses that we assume it is the natural order of things without taking into full account that Jesus suffered tremendously to free us from the same.

I know of a town which was — but is no longer in existence. In the past it was a lovely area filled with small but adequate houses, tree lined streets and friendly neighborhoods. Now it has been completely bulldozed under. Even the soil has been hauled away because of contamination. The contamination in the soil caused horrendous sickness and blood diseases. Whole families contracted cancer in one form or another. Every home, every nail, every roof shingle, every fence post, every flower box and every garden was destroyed. None of it is left, not even a trace. Was this contamination in the soil the fault of the people who lived in that town? Were all those people such great sinners that they should suffer such things? No of course not. Very unfortunately it was a "time and chance thing."

Take a minute and read Luke 13:1-5. We see there were some people in the crowd listening to Jesus and they apparently questioned Him about the tower of Siloam which fell and killed eighteen people. Jesus warned them to be very careful not to judge those eighteen who died in this tragic accident. He warned the people not to jump to conclusions when they see others suffering great trials and think that it is because they are great sinners. Jesus then cautioned them to be aware that this circumstance should serve as a warning to them personally that death can come suddenly and without warning so they should repent of their own sins. We must try to remember that at any moment we can be called to stand before Hm.

Sins Of The Fathers

What about asbestos in old buildings, schools, factories and offices where people worked for years without knowing the dangers? What about lead in pipes or paint, chemicals in factories, and mercury or killer mold? These are causes of many diseases including cancer and other wasting diseases. So if a believer works for twenty years in a place where there is such a problem and contracts a lung disease, is it God who put the disease on him or did he get the disease because of his working conditions for twenty years?

Yes, perhaps all this could have been prevented if we had the knowledge of the end result from being in contact with asbestos or second hand smoke or whatever contaminated the soil in that town. But at the time no one knew. Certainly the men who died when the tower of Siloam came crashing down on them had no warning when they got out of bed that morning that it would be their last day on this earth.

At one time I owned a small shop where I sold herbs and vitamins. Many of my customers were believers and many were people who had tried doctors and various medicines for devastating diseases but found no cure. Looking for relief and help they turned to natural medicine, herbs and nutritional supplements. One of these was a man who worked in a nuclear laboratory. At work he was over exposed to radiation and had gotten radiation sickness. He was desperately ill. This man and his wife were believers. Every day as he left his employment he had to be scanned to be sure the radiation levels were okay and he was not in danger. One day he was scanned and it was not okay. Did this man sin in some way that caused God to put this illness on him or was he in the wrong place at the wrong time? Would God put radiation sickness of one of His own children that He has sworn by His own Word to protect? Would that be the action of a loving Father who promised to save and protect His children? Remember time and chance?

Some years ago I made a trip to Africa. I arrived in the early evening and went directly to a hotel. It was much too dangerous to travel at night. First thing in the morning I went to the hotel exchange to trade my American money for African currency. As I stood there at the exchange window I was robbed of all my money. Right there in broad daylight, right in front of my eyes, I was robbed. A man walked up beside me, put a large briefcase on top of the counter where the money had just been counted out and scooped it into his briefcase. He stood right next to me and did this. We were elbow to elbow. I was stunned and I was helpless! As a woman alone in a dangerous foreign country, with a native of that country standing next to me and robbing me in broad daylight, I felt very much the victim.

Being in the streets doing evangelism and ministering in the villages I was exposed to hordes of mosquitoes. Although I took all the required Malaria pills beginning weeks before I left and faithfully took all the required shots and pills for various diseases both before I left the United States and continued taking whatever was required while I was in Africa, I still got Malaria and Typhoid. There are many strains of Malaria that are resistant to the medications. So with

Sins Of The Fathers

many mosquito bites every night I came down with a viral form of malaria that attacks the brain. I suffered horribly.

Without any money for food or medicine because of being robbed, I picked whatever I could; mostly fruit, off the trees or off the ground to eat. Within a short time I could eat nothing at all because of the illness. I became dehydrated and could not even take a sip of water. I could not go to a doctor or the hospital because my money was gone. There were raging fevers; delirium, violent vomiting, and soon I did not have the strength to stand up by my own strength. Then I began to bleed from every orifice in my body. Too weak to go on I begged God to let me die in Africa. Over and over I begged God to just take me home because I was too sick to live. But He had other plans.

Was God punishing me? Did He put Malaria and Typhoid on me? No! I drank unclean water at the house of someone I worked with. They gave me tap water instead of bottled water. They thought it wouldn't hurt me.

God is the One Who told me to go to Africa. Within one week of the time He told me to go, He supplied every cent for the trip. But could He not have protected me? Oh yes, He most certainly could have. And I have to tell you that after I got safely home and was physically revived enough that I became somewhat functional again, I began to have circular conversations with God. Every morning and evening for quite a long time I sat on my back porch swing and told Him over and over again, "God, You could have kept me safe so none of this would have happened! You are the One Who told me to go there! Why didn't You protect me?"

To be honest I felt betrayed. I kept telling Him over and over how I had surrendered everything I knew, how I had been obedient as much as I knew, and on and on. I reminded Him of all the times when I let go of things He required of me. I listed all those things that I thought should have been a safety net for me in my relationship with Him; a safety net that should keep me from all harm.

I sat on my back porch swing and continued in my vain conversations and endless questions with Him which lasted for many long months. But in the end He never did give me an answer. Finally I just had to stop asking! It came to the point that I had to set my mind and my will to get past the circumstances and choose to believe that He is good, that He loves me and that His Word is truth. The fact that I was still alive, although desperately ill with many kinds of secondary viruses and infections, just had to be enough for me. I had to choose to trust Him in spite of circumstances. I had to make a deliberate decision to rely on Him once again and squarely keep my confidence placed in Him. I just had to lock my hand into His firm grip like a small child and go on with Him. Once you have walked with Him there is no other place to go.

I once heard someone say that God puts duties in front of us, they are ours to fulfill. God gives us opportunities, they are ours to accomplish. But the events of our life that we cannot foretell or control, they belong to God and we must put them in His hands.

There are just some things in life that we cannot explain or control and in order to navigate through them we must put ourself and our circumstances in His hands and trust Him to take us through them to the other side.

Many years ago I moved to a Western state and lived there for several years. When I first moved there I could not help but notice how many people I saw in the streets that were lame or crippled. It was very noticeable to me. I found it striking because everywhere I went I saw so many who were crippled. When I questioned this I was told it was because of the underground testing at the nuclear testing grounds.

However, looking back at that situation many years later I made a mental note that this state was also the home of a major cult. Was this then the result of a curse or was it from natural causes?

In the end, what we really want to know is this; what is the difference between a curse and chastisement? We can safely say that chastisement is for a time and a season. It is carefully guarded and watched over by God Who sits as the Refiner of the Fire. He controls the fire and the intensity of the heat. But a curse goes on through family lines for generations unless it is cut off.

HOW IS A CURSE DIFFERENT FROM CHASTISEMENT?

- Chastisement is for a time and a season.
- This time of chastening will definitely come to an end.
- We hopefully learn and grow after being under chastisement.

- Chastisement brings one into a holy fear of God which is a good thing and should keep us from future sin.
- A curse goes on from generation to generation until it is revoked.
- A curse brings only suffering.
- The one under a curse suffers destruction and devastation with no lessons learned from it, only a lot of questions.

I remember so many years whenever anyone had a problem of any kind someone would say, "What does God want you to learn from this?"

I came to the place where I thought that if I heard that one more time I would scream. But in reality, God does want us to learn from everything that happens to us, from every chastening, and every experience whether good or bad. We are meant to learn and grow. It is not always a conscious thing. Sometimes we simply pack it under our belt, store it in a file somewhere in our memory bank and go on. But before it is totally lost in the cobwebs up there, we have the opportunity to mull it over and see what God would want to teach us about the circumstances and people involved in our daily life at any given moment. We should always be learning and growing. We should be able to learn from every single person we meet whether they know God or not. There is always something we can learn. Perhaps we may not always be able to learn from their intellect, but we can learn from their circumstances, their gifting, their lifestyle, their heritage and even from their bondage.

If you believe God has His hand on you in chastisement, you need to repent of any known sin in your life. In particular you must repent of any specific sin that could have brought you under His rod. Repentance may not always bring an immediate release. Sometimes God allows us to stay in the place of chastisement so that we really and truly learn whatever it is He is trying to teach us. But again, you can rest assured that chastisement will not last forever. It will only be for a time and a season and then He will release you and draw you out again into a large place, a place of freedom and restoration.

Proverbs 13:24; Whoever spares the rod hates his son, but he who loves him is diligent to discipline him.

The rod of correction is just that. It is a rod and it smarts when it touches us. Micah 6:9 tells us to listen to the rod, because the rod will speak to us. The rod will speak to us by helping us to hear what the Lord is saying to us in correction. The rod will caution us and it will speak to us of the fear of the Lord. Remember that the devil is a liar and a thief. He comes with only one purpose and that is to kill, steal and destroy. Believers are subject to satanic attacks and if they do not learn to claim the promises and resist Satan they may become physically, mentally, emotionally and financially afflicted just like other men. (Read James 4:7; I Peter 5:7-9; Ephesians.4:27 and 6:11).

CHAPTER EIGHT
THE CURSE CAUSELESS

Proverbs 26:2; As the bird by wandering, as the swallow by flying, so the curse causeless shall not come.

Exactly what does that mean? Do you ever puzzle over certain Scriptures? It means very simply that a bird flying over your head does you no harm. It simply flies in the air above your head. Just so, a curse put on you when you are undeserving cannot do you any harm. It is powerless and has absolutely no effect.

Then why do many curses seem to be so effective, especially in things like witchcraft or voodoo? They become effective because of fear. Fear opens the door in the spirit realm which allows a curse to take on power and become effectual. Another way the curse becomes effective in your life is if you have unrepented sin. Please notice I did not say unconfessed sin. I said unrepented sin. There is a great deal of difference between the two. A believer might confess a particular sin with lip service simply because he or she knows it is a sin. All the while this one knows in their heart that they are not willing to give up this sin yet. That is simply a confession of lip service, it is not sincere repentance. If we truly repent of our sin it means that we genuinely desire to be free of that particular sin and to turn our back on it forever. It means we want nothing more to do with it. In fact one of the words for repentance means to turn away from sin. The enemy of your soul can open the door for the curse to come by bringing fear on you through guilt and condemnation, especially if there is guilt because of unconfessed sin.

Faith in God is always your defense. So you must put on your armor, honestly repent of any known sin and stand in the power and authority in the name of Jesus Christ and in the power and authority He gives you in His Word. The Word tells us that if we resist the devil he will flee from us. We must ask God to search our heart and show us anything that is in any way displeasing to Him, anything that is a hook inside of us that the devil can use to bring destruction into our lives. Remember when Judas, the High Priest, and the people came to get Jesus in the garden? Jesus said, "Satan has nothing in Me."

John 14:30; I will no longer talk much with you, for the ruler of this world is coming. He has no claim on me, but I do as the Father has commanded me, so that the world may know that I love the Father.

There was no sin hidden in Jesus' heart that Satan could use as a hook to be able to lead Jesus where he wanted Him to go. There was no sin, no taint, and no darkness buried within His heart and soul. Therefore, it is clear that Jesus laid down His life. The devil did not take it from Him. Jesus yielded to the plan of His heavenly Father by giving His life as a ransom for you and me.

We must learn from this and not allow Satan to have a foothold in our life in any manner. David cried out to God to create a clean heart in him. Faith in God is always our defense. Holiness is a rewarding conformation to the will and the heart of God. Some people shudder at the word holiness and think it sounds religious. It is not religious. Holiness is a work of sanctification by the Holy Spirit deep within us. This work is accomplished in us over time but only by our surrender and never against our will. So we would do well to come before His throne and ask Him to search us and show us any wicked way that is still hidden in the depths of our mind, our heart, in our will or our emotions.

Psalm 51:10; Create in me a clean heart, O God; and renew a right spirit within me.

One time many years ago I had a friend who was a minister. He was married with several children and had been a minister for many years. I had ventured into his church one Sunday after many months of deliberation.

This is how it all came about. I was not yet saved and I am certain that was no doubt very evident to any believer who met me. Apart from my knowledge, a man that I worked with and his wife took me on as their special prayer project. Although I did not know it at the time, it was the beginning of a tremendous war for my soul. Many times since my salvation I have thanked God for their faithfulness and tenacity because I know that I was quite the mission field. I am so very grateful for their deliberate care for me in prayer and intercession. They labored over my soul for a very long time and finally many years after they began to intercede for me, I received Christ. Very often I think about this and I am amazed that God was so patient with me. I find it amazing. His long suffering with me and grace toward me is beyond my comprehension.

Anyway, they kept on inviting me to their church in the little town where we lived in Arizona. I resisted for so many months. I had no desire and just could not even force myself to go. There were so many demons entrenched in my life. A demonic battle seethed with terrible ferocity inside of me although as time went on a small part of me actually began to want to go to with them to their church and check it out. But still the major part of me was disgusted by the mere thought of it. The darkness intensified within me fighting every thought of joining them in church or any other place for that matter. A part of me was drawn to them and a part of me felt such discomfort around them that I could not stand to be near them. When I looked at them I actually saw light but had no understanding of what I was seeing. It bothered me and at times I had to turn away.

II Corinthians 2:15-16; For we are the aroma of Christ to God among those who are being saved and among those who are per-

ishing, to one a fragrance from death to death, to the other a fragrance from life to life.

My new found friends started by inviting me to lunch at their house. They would say things like, "We are going to put on a roast Sunday afternoon and sit around and talk and enjoy the sunshine. We would love to have you over so you can meet the children. Will you come?"

A couple of times I said I would join them, but when the time came I would back out. On several occasions I promised I would meet them at church and then go with them to their house for Sunday lunch. I actually got dressed and made it as far as the front door, but when I stepped outside my door I became terrified that I would not be accepted by the good people in church. So I turned around, went back into the house, changed clothes and found something else to do. Finally one day I decided I was actually going to do this. There was this small part of me that really wanted to go with them and the desire had been growing. So I decided that the next Sunday, no matter what, I would meet them and check it all out. I made it as far as the church parking lot but I could not get out of my car. I sat in my big red convertible in the church parking lot and cried. Finally, embarrassed as people walked by and frustrated that I was so afraid, I just turned around and went back home again. After months of their faithful prayer for me (they did tell me they were praying for me), I made it all the way to the church and actually got out of the car. I went inside and found a seat. My friends were so excited to see me there, but I did not sit with them. I sat in the last pew in the last row in the back of the church right next to the door just in case I had to make a quick getaway.

I have no idea what the pastor was talking about that day. I don't even know if I heard a single word he said, but on that day I experienced something I had never felt before in my whole life. At the end of the service as everyone filed past me and out the door, a little old lady came right up to me. She cupped my face in her hands and held me so gently. She told me that Jesus loved me so much that He gave His life for me. Hot tears boiled over and streamed down my cheeks. I had never felt anything like that before in my whole life. I did not know it at the time but it was the love of God the Father and the love of Jesus Christ that I was feeling that Sunday morning in that little country church. It made me cry so hard although I had no idea why I was crying. God was definitely knocking on the door of my heart. Although many years passed on from that day before I accepted Christ as Savior, I never forgot the feelings I experienced that Sunday morning. It was a true manifestation of God's presence and His love.

After the service that Sunday morning my friends introduced me to the minister. We shook hands and then we all went to my friend's house for lunch. The minister began to call on me once in a while when he was in my neighborhood and he would talk to me about Jesus. On one occasion he asked me to go along with him downtown to visit a witch's shop. He said he wanted to witness to her and that

Sins Of The Fathers

he regularly visited her shop to talk to her about Jesus. I did not want to go because of previous experiences with witchcraft. In fact, I wanted nothing at all to do with it because it still really scared me. But for some reason I consented and went along.

In her shop there were many shelves lined with jars and bottles filled with various herbs and parts of this and bits of that. All of the jars were labeled, some with very familiar sounding names and some with very odd names. There were many different kinds of candles some of which were also labeled with names of spells that could be cast, and an assortment of every sort of thing one might use in practicing witchcraft or the occult. The shop seemed very dark and threatening to me. I did not like the feeling at all. It dredged up things from the past that I was still running away from. But my new found friend had convinced me that it was okay because he was a pastor and it would be perfectly safe. Consequently, against my better judgment, I went along with him.

He boldly walked into the shop and greeted the tall pretty woman standing behind the counter by name. I was surprised at his boldness because I was cowering behind him following closely in his shadow, hoping not to be noticed at all. He walked right up to the counter where she stood holding a small mortar and pestle in her hands in which she was mixing something. He smiled and said hello to her and asked how she was doing. They exchanged pleasantries and then he began to share with her about Jesus Christ. She did not interrupt and in fact she made no comments at all; nothing positive and nothing negative. She seemed to be intently listening to every word. She actually seemed very polite. She looked full into his face as he talked to her. When he was finished speaking she looked down at the mixture in the mortar, sprinkled something into it and then proceeded to tell him that he was going to be unfaithful to his wife; that he would have an affair, and as a result he would lose his pastorate.

She put a curse on him. She spoke it all very calmly with a slight smile on her face. He simply laughed at her and said it would never happen. I was afraid and wanted nothing more than to get out of there. I wondered why I ever let him talk me into going there with him.

Not many months passed before I was told that he came before his congregation and confessed sin. He stepped down from his pastorate because he said he had an affair. I was not there but I was shocked to hear of this and immediately I remembered the curse that was spoken over him. The curse did indeed come on him. However, it was so many years later before I ever understood the meaning of all this.

The curse she put on him by the spoken word found a place to rest because the devil saw something inside this man's heart that was an open door, something that had not been dealt with before God. The devil always knows what it will take to bring us down. The witch was simply speaking the information that the devil was feeding her. She was acting as a medium for the powers of darkness. The devil saw the open door of sin in his heart and walked right in. Had this pastor gone before God right then that very night when he got home from the witch's shop and dealt with the source of this matter which was buried in his own heart; if he had thoroughly repented of the lust the devil saw inside of his heart; and then resisted temptation, that evil could not have overcome him. When we resist the devil he will flee from us. If we do not resist him we open a door in the spirit realm by allowing temptation to continue inside of us and by somehow thinking we can manage the situation in our own strength and power. When we do this we will most certainly fall. The devil saw a hook inside of this man and took strong hold of it.

God said that the curse cannot come upon us without a cause. The cause the Bible speaks of here would be something that is hidden in the depths of our heart and soul. Some sin tendency we have not dealt with. We must be unmerciful when we deal with our sin. We must keep very short accounts with our sin. We cannot linger or dally in temptation or sin, but we must immediately and sincerely repent. It is so very important for us to live holy lives before God. He requires it of us. However; it is only in His power that we are enabled to do so. Sometimes we think we are so strong in our own power, but the Word tells us that it is NOT by our own power or might, it is not by our wisdom and cunning, or even by our gifting that we stand. It is only by the blood of Jesus Christ and in His power alone that we can stand. We cannot trust in our own strength and power, but we must have our hope and trust firmly anchored in Him and His finished work in our behalf.

How very sad that this man fell. As I said, I was not yet saved and so I did not fully understand or appreciate the ramifications of his circumstances and how much it affected his church. I am sure that many in his church were caused to stumble by his actions. I cannot even begin to imagine the heartache it caused his wife and children. I do hope that he and his family found God's merciful healing touch and restoration for the pain and shame that he and his family endured. He was removed from ministry at once and I have no idea whatever happened to him after that. I never saw or heard of him again and never had occasion to frequent that church again because shortly after that I moved out of state.

I am however very certain the witch knew she had accomplished her goal. And once again I was afraid.

Do you remember when God told the children of Israel that when the time came for them to enter the Promised Land, they would have to fight for their land and drive out those who had possession of it? This was the land God was giving to the children as their inheritance. He warned them that if they did not drive out the inhabitants, they would be grieved and harassed by them all the days of their life. It would be a recurrent problem and a continual vexation to them. God warned them not to make any concessions with them but to regard them as enemies and destroy them completely.

Numbers 33:53, 55-56; "And you shall take possession of the land and settle in it, for I have given the land to you to possess it. But if you do not drive out the inhabitants of the land from

before you, then those of them whom you let remain shall be as barbs in your eyes and thorns in your sides, and they shall trouble you in the land where you dwell. And I will do to you as I thought to do to them."

There is a parallel here. That is exactly what God is speaking to us regarding our old sin nature. God has a land for us to inherit after we are saved. Our land is the plan of God for each one of us individually. But we cannot possess our land in peace and safety if we do not drive out the prior inhabitants of our land. The prior inhabitants are the sin and bondages that have ruled over us in the past. We must not allow these things to remain in our life. We must deal with each one of them ruthlessly. There can be no compromise.

CHAPTER NINE

IS IT A STRONGHOLD OR A CURSE?

In the Bible one of the words in Hebrew for "heart" is leb or lebab. This word is used to indicate feelings, the will of man and his intellect. It means his inner being and is indicative of his personal life. In Greek (origin Latin), the word for heart is kardia or cor. It means the heart and mind which are made up of our thoughts, feelings (emotions) and our will. The Bible often uses the words, heart, mind and soul interchangeably. The King James Bible also uses the word "reins" which in Hebrew is kilyah and is pronounced as kil-yaw'. It literally means the kidney or the mind, the inner being, and the heart and soul of man.

In Old Testament times people believed that the inner being of man, the reigns, was in the kidney area. So in referring to our inner man which includes our mind, will and emotions, I may use these words interchangeably.

Everything we do is created and released from within us. Our sin, our life, our works and actions all come out from what is within us. These things are buried in the depth of our being, in our heart and soul (mind, will and emotions). All our actions are motivated and set into action by the thoughts that are resident within our own heart and mind. Our character and personality is the product of our heart (our inner man). All our thoughts and actions proceed from our heart and inner man. This is what defines us as to who we are in personality and character. I will use the term "heart and soul" repeatedly because they are inextricably linked. One cannot be separated from the other. Whatever abides in our heart will work itself out in our soul through our emotions and actions. We can speak, but our actions will always speak louder than our words. That is why Scripture warns us that we are to guard our heart carefully because we will live out what is buried in our heart.

Proverbs 4:23; Keep thy heart with all diligence; for out of it are the issues of life.

So we see that the heart and soul is the center of all our human activity. Every thought and action comes out of our own heart or inner being. Our thoughts, our temptations take root in our heart and they are birthed in our soul and find release in our emotions, words and actions. We are controlled and motivated out of our heart and inner being. If our ungodly thoughts (temptations) are not dealt with, then the temptation will continue to come and will continue to grow in strength. If these temptations are not cut off they will be empowered within us. Each temptation becomes stronger than the last time and begins to penetrate deeper into our heart and soul. This is a major assault against us so it must be dealt with. Scripture tells us to flee from temptation. If this admonition is not heeded the temptation will quickly become a stronghold in our life. A stronghold is a defended area of thought and action in an individual's life. This area is safeguarded by the devil and his cohorts. By continual giving in to temptation the enemy of our soul is able to build a stronghold or a fortress, a safe place that he may inhabit. This is a safe place from which he can take dominion and set up his rule over that area of the person's heart and mind. The Word says to resist the devil and he will run from us. It tells us we can combat him with the power of the Word and God has given us specific weapons for our warfare.

WHAT IS A STRONGHOLD?

A stronghold begins as a thought or temptation and quickly becomes a thought pattern, which then quickly becomes a behavior pattern that is established in a person's life because it is not resisted. It is first launched in an individual's heart and mind in the form of thoughts. This in its very simplest form is a temptation to sin. If this person being tempted should choose this sin and continue in the practice of this same sin, the devil is able to create a stronghold in their mind, through their thought life and in their emotions as well. Why do I include emotions? Sin is generally pleasurable at least for a time, therefore it would involve the emotions, passions and pleasure centers. A stronghold is a fortified place from which the demon attacks the thought life and emotions of a believer. He does this by placing thoughts into the mind, desires into the emotions, and a constant barrage and harassment of the individual, filling them with a desire for a particular sin.

HEART AND CONSCIENCE:

Our heart is the source of our conscience. If we continue to allow temptation without taking our thoughts captive, of course we will act out the temptation, which is sin. When we continue in this way, our heart (soul) becomes hardened by our continued sin and we are no longer bothered by our sin. The Bible says our conscience becomes seared. This means that our heart becomes so hardened to this particular sin that our conscience no longer concerns us with it. We have made our heart insensitive to the Holy Spirit and we can come to the place where we no longer hear His voice at all.

God said He would not strive with man forever. That is a very dangerous place to be because there can come a time when God actually releases us to the desires of our own heart even if those desires will bring destruction to us. In other words, as believers we can strive with God and continue to insist on having our own way, ignoring the power of the Holy Spirit at work within our soul, until God releases us to have the thing we continue to pursue against the guidance and direction of the Holy Spirit. But this will always bring leanness to our soul, a lack and spiritual deficiency because we insist on having our own way. At this point we have departed from God. There are many examples of those in the Bible who hardened their heart against God, against His prophets, and against His people. Pharaoh is an example of a man who hardened his own heart against the will of God and met a bitter end.

Out of our own heart we will draw forth whatever is within us. That is why, when we come to a salvation experience, God will begin a work deep within our soul to bring about a complete change of heart within us. When we are truly saved we will have heart surgery performed by the Holy Spirit and we will become a new man who no longer desires to operate out of a cold, hard heart. As we continue to yield to God and allow the work of the Holy Spirit in our life, our heart will be changed.

Ezekiel 36:26; A new heart also will I give you, and a new spirit will I put within you: and I will take away the stony heart out of your flesh, and I will give you an heart of flesh.

Scripture tells us in James 3:10, that we can have a mixture of good and evil in our heart at the same time. God is looking for a change of heart. He wants us to come to Him with a pure heart. We are to concentrate on those things that are good, lovely and of a good report. We are to deal with our sin and we are to fill our mind and heart with the Word and with good and positive things so that our heart and mind are renewed and changed. This change will surely bear fruit upward out of our mouth and through our actions. We are to draw living water out of the wells of salvation.

Isaiah 12:3; Therefore with joy shall ye draw water out of the wells of salvation.

Our heart and soul (our inner being), is what determines who we are and what we are like. If we have love in our heart it will manifest in many different forms. If we have hated in our heart it will manifest in many different ways. If we have envy and jealousy hidden in our heart, that also will become clear by the way we behave and the things we speak and do. As we draw near to God the Father through Jesus Christ, the Holy Spirit begins to do His work in our heart and soul to change us. Sometimes it takes a while for those changes to become evident, but eventually everything that is changed inside the heart will begin to manifest outwardly in every way. The changes inside will begin to manifest in an outward display of our words, actions, dress, attitudes and even in our mannerisms, because we live out of a heart which is now lined up with the heart of God and filled with His desires for us.

WHAT YOU ARE INSIDE WILL BE DISPLAYED ON THE OUTSIDE:

I remember thinking about this many years ago when I ministered in certain areas of the city which were high crime areas. There was a lot of alcohol, drug addiction, crime, prostitution and uncleanness of every sort. So very often the houses of those I ministered to were so unkempt. Some were just plain filthy. They were more than messy or dirty, and very often there was a feeling of deep oppression in the house which made it really uncomfortable to be there. It was not just physical dirt and filth; it was a sensing of a spiritual filth. You knew when you entered in some of the houses that there were serious spiritual problems. You could actually feel it. But as these people individually gave their life over to Christ, one of the first things that changed was their outer person and their home. Why? Because the outer person, meaning their own individual style, dress, home life and even the actual home itself, was an outward manifestation of their inner life. They soon began to clean up their clothing, change their style, and clean up their houses. All the disorder, disarray and clutter were soon moved out to make way for cleanliness. This was absolutely an expression of a change of thinking, or one could say, "A change of heart." The bondage was broken and therefore their thought life was changed. In this area of their life it was a renewing of their mind which became outwardly visible in a very personal way.

To this day, there are houses I go into that are physically clean, yet I am so uncomfortable while I am there. I generally cannot stay very long, I have to leave. When this happens I understand that I am uncomfortable because there are strongholds build up in the people who live there and I can feel the oppression over the house and in the house itself.

Very often at funerals we hear someone say that the person who passed had a good heart. Because this person displays some act of kindness or goodness at one time or another or perhaps because they have a good sense of humor and seem to be a "good Joe," they are remembered as being one who had a good heart. Let us examine a few hearts and see what we find.

Genesis 4:1-8; Now Adam knew Eve his wife, and she conceived and bore Cain, saying, "I have gotten a man with the help of the Lord." And again, she bore his brother Abel. Now Abel was a keeper of the sheep, and Cain a worker of the ground. In the course of time Cain brought to the Lord an offering of the fruit of the ground, and Abel also brought of the firstborn of his flock and of their fat portions. And the Lord had regard for Abel and his offering, but for Cain and his offering he had no regard. So Cain was very angry, and his face fell. The Lord said to Cain, "Why are you angry, and why has your face fallen? If you do well, will you not be accepted? And if you do not do well, sin is crouching at the door. Its desire is for you, but you must rule over it." Cain spoke to Abel his brother. And when they were in the field, Cain rose up against his brother Abel and killed him.

Cain was Adam and Eve's first son. He was born to them after they were driven out of the Garden of Eden. As he grew he took to farming. A brother was born next and he was named Abel. Abel grew up to be a shepherd.

A day came when the two brothers offered sacrifices before the Lord. Cain made a grain offering to the Lord and Abel offered the best of his flock and the fat of the lamb to the Lord. God accepted Abel's offering but not Cain's. Cain became furious with his brother over this. He felt sighted by God and jealous of his brother. God tried to deal with Cain and calm him down. God told him that if he would do what was right he and his offering would be accepted. The word in Hebrew, Charah, which expresses Cain's anger means to burn with anger, to be furious, to blaze with jealousy, and to be incensed. God was telling Cain that he needed to get a grip on his emotions because they were completely out of line. He needed to deal with those things that were buried in his heart. No doubt he had been jealous of his younger brother for a very long time, perhaps even since his birth. This was not just a sudden outburst that came out of nowhere. It had been buried in his heart for some time and was fueled by his thoughts which caused great anger, resentment and jealousy to grow in power until it exploded into pure rage.

Cain and Abel were both of an age where they were able to choose for themselves how they would worship God. Cain was obviously a religious man who was very strong willed. His heart was not right with God but he still tried to maintain the outward works. Cain understood what kind of sacrifice God required for a sin offering, yet he came with what would have been a tithe offering. Blood was required for sin atonement, but Cain brought an offering of what was grown out of the ground, an offering of what was already cursed

Sins Of The Fathers

by the fall. So there was no acknowledgement of sin on Cain's part. He was not coming with a repentant heart to honor God and receive forgiveness of his sins. He gave no acknowledgement whatsoever of personal guilt of sin. Cain came before God in pride ignoring what God had ordained for the sacrifice of sin. However, Abel came in humility before God as a sinner, bringing a fit sacrifice for his sins. So we see that Cain's heart was hard and unrepentant. His offering was a display of self will, self interest and self righteousness. We know that Cain murdered Abel in a fit of rage. When God questioned him as to his actions he denied any care for his brother hardening his heart even further. Let's see what happened to his succeeding generations.

Cain was cast out and made to wander as a vagabond in the earth. He built the first city called Nod. He had many children and became the first Mayor of his own city. He had a son named Enoch and built another city which he named after this son. Many of his children were talented and brought forth many fine inventions and musical instruments such as the harp and organ. Another son became one who learned to forge brass and varied metals. He became a skilled engraver and artiste and taught others in such fine artistic endeavors.

However, in spite of all the talents and gifting, there was soon another murderer in the family line. His name was Lamech (See Genesis 4:22-23). This was now the second murder on record in human history and the murderer was a direct descendant of Cain. Lamech was also the first polygamist.

139

Sins Of The Fathers

Soon the children of Cain became immoral, degenerate and depraved. Eventually they were all destroyed by the great flood.

Whatever is in our heart is what we will live out and speak out and it will come down upon the heads of our children and their children whether it is good or evil.

It is very easy to see what is in people's hearts as you see what is on television, in the movies, and listen to the way people talk in grocery stores, restaurants, malls, in places of entertainment and in everyday encounters. It is easy to see what is in a person's heart because they live it out right before your eyes. What God requires is a pure heart.

CHAPTER TEN

MY CHILDHOOD

My own childhood was tumultuous at best. My father and mother surely loved each other but both had explosive tempers. They married and divorced each other three times. I guess that speaks of both the love and passion and the volatile moods of both of them. I do not think that one was necessarily more to blame than the other, I cannot really say. I only know that my mother left or was forced out of the marriage when I was three months old and I never saw her again until just before she died.

After my mother left I lived on a farm with my grandparents. I always felt loved by them and especially by my grandpa. He was a special man. Long and tall with sparkling blue eyes and a beard. I could crawl up into his lap at any time. He would wrap his long arms around me and sing a Russian lullaby to me while he rocked me in his arms. Even when I was sixteen years old I could still climb into his lap. That would put a smile on his face. He would wrap those long arms around me, hold me close, rock me and sing to me. I felt so safe with him and I felt loved by him. My grandmother was great! She was spicy, a real spitfire. I had so much fun with her and loved to make her laugh. She also had a hot temper and would chase me around the barnyard with a broom yelling at me, if I did something wrong, but she was never able to catch me. We would both end up laughing until the tears rolled down our cheeks and we would fall down laughing and hanging onto our sides. Then, still laughing, she would say something to me in a language I did not understand. I would howl with laughter and try to repeat it. Then we would both scurry into the house to do whatever was to be done.

I do not know exactly when my grandparents took me in, but I have been told that I lived in foster homes for a while; once with a blind man and his wife, and once with an explorer and his wife. Actually I found out later in my early adult years that this man was a very famous explorer and I was able to read some articles about his work. Then I lived with this relative or that one for a time. Finally, at age three I was in court, headed for an orphanage. Of course I don't remember any of this, but that is, I believe, when my grandparents took me in to live with them.

I do remember different times when my mother would come to visit and try to see me. I would be out playing in the yard or in the barn or the tool-shed and my Uncle, one of my father's brothers who also lived on the farm with my grandparents, would grab me roughly by the arm. In one hand he held tightly to a shotgun with me struggling to be free in the other. This always caused great fear in me. I remember I was not much taller than his boots and my feet dangled off the ground as he hauled me into the house. He would push me forcefully under the bed and say, "No matter what happens do not come out. You just stay there."

Then he would stomp out of the room totting his shotgun. I remember one time when this occurred I asked him what was happening. He told me that my mother had come to visit me and he was going to shoot her. I did not know her because she left when I was three months old. However, I couldn't help but wonder what it would be like to be shot with a shotgun. Would it hurt? Finally, after some time passed he would come to get me. I could hear him enter the room and then his big angry voice telling me that I could come out now. I never knew what happened. All sorts of thoughts went through my mind; "Did he kill her? Did she die? Is she laying out in the road or the driveway? If you are shot do you bleed?"

It seems there was always a rivalry and jealousy between this oldest brother (the one totting the shotgun), and his other two brothers. Growing up I heard stories of the jealousy and fighting between them. At one point this particular uncle tore down his other brother's house with his own hands and then burned the timber while the brother was at work. There seemed to be a general atmosphere of animosity and hostility bubbling below the surface at all times. My gun totting uncle seemed to have control and rule over the family and no one seemed to buck him. Thinking back over these things as an adult I came to believe that he was probably a bully and bullied the whole family. He certainly was abusive. If he decided that he was angry at someone, then the whole family was commanded not to speak to that person or have anything to do with them. Years would go by when no one in the family would speak to this one or that one for some slight or imagined infraction. When I became born-again and was baptized in the Holy Spirit I made the head of that list. My uncle did not speak to me for over 25 years. Although I tried to speak to him more than once, he would completely ignore me as though I did not exist, refusing even to look at me. If I walked down the street in the tiny town where he lived where the main street was only three blocks long, he would cross the street when he saw me coming. He told the family that my name was never to be mentioned in his presence, as far as he was concerned I did not exist. To him I was never born. So we can see here a strong family history of unforgiveness, condemnation and rejection toward others, even bitter hatred.

I MET MY DAD:

When I was about three and one half years old this uncle insisted that my dad come to get me and take me to live with him. He said it was too much for my grandparents to care for me. I'm sure that was true because looking back I can see that my grandparents were really very busy and worked so very hard. They spent their days, milking cows, sowing crops, cultivating, picking potatoes, planting, pruning, weeding, haying, shoveling manure, cleaning the barn and all the things that go with tending a farm. I remember my grand-mother making her own lye soap out in the yard in the summer time in a huge vat. I recall her standing and ironing seemingly endless piles of clothes with a hot iron laid atop the old wood stove to heat it up. I played at her feet while she washed laundry by hand with washtubs of water that had been pumped by hand from the well and then heated on the old wood stove. There were endless pies and hot breads and countless meals and dishes. When I think about it I have no idea how she did it all and then managed to pitch in and help with the haying and canning and everything else. I am sure it was much too great a burden for both of them to see to a small child. So my dad came to get me.

My introduction to him was chilling. I really did not know who he was but my grandparents always welcomed everyone who came to their door. So one day at noon time, a big tall man walked in and stood in the doorway; at least he seemed big and tall to me. I did not ever remember seeing him before, so I listened intently to what my grandmother and grandfather said to him. I remember how he stood in the doorway of the kitchen, one hip swayed away from the door frame, one knee bent forward and holding onto the woodwork above the door with one hand. He looked like a giant to me!

My grandma was scurrying around moving plates and adding chairs to make room for him to come and join us at the noon table. It must have taken her completely by surprise when he showed up because she did not seem to know he was coming. Anyway, she invited him to sit down and eat and I quickly echoed her invitation. "Yes, come on Ed, sit down and eat with us."

By this time I had walked over more closely so I could investigate him. I extended my hand up to him along with the invitation to join us at lunch, not knowing he was my dad. My invitation was quickly met with a hard slap across the face and I was told to call him "Dad." That was the beginning of our relationship.

I guess I was taken to live with my dad then, in a two room cottage down the road, along with his new wife. I really do not remember much about it. I still spent almost all of my time with my grandma and grandpa on the farm up the hill just as it was before he came. I guess he was at work.

My father, now saddled with a child he did not want, was abusive and held great resentment against me because he had to care for this child that weighed him down and apparently held him back in some way.

It was not very long before I began to understand who I was, or at least who he said I was. Even though a spirit of rejection had entered early on, even in the womb, now that spirit was gaining strength and power over me on a daily basis because of the reinforcements I was receiving by constant curses spoken to me and against me.

My dad would always tell me; "You are worthless, no good. You will never amount to anything. You do not have a chance in life, because it is in your blood. You are a tramp just like your mother and you can't even help it because it is in your blood. You have bad blood and you are a bad seed. It's not really your fault but there is no help for you. You will never be worth anything. It would be better if you were never born."

I had seen a picture one day in my coloring book and asked my gramma about it. It was a picture of a man walking down the railroad tracks with a kerchief tied to the end of a stick which was slung over his shoulder. My gramma explained to me that in this kerchief the tramp apparently held all his worldly possessions. My gramma told me the man was a tramp. So I began to wonder why my dad would say that I was a tramp. I could not understand it because I saw no correlation with this colorful man in the picture book and myself. I didn't even own a kerchief and a stick although I could have gotten a stick easy enough from all the trees in the yard or in the pasture land. Also, I knew there were railroad tracks out in the woods beyond the pasture, but I was always forbidden by my grandparents to wander out there. In fact, they told me that sometimes tramps built camps there and it was dangerous. I was never to leave the yard without their permission.

The mind of a child that young is very graphic, yet I still had no understanding of the meaning of his words toward me. But soon enough I learned by his oft repeated litany, that my mother ran off when I was three months old with another man and it was my fault. Apparently that is what made me a tramp. Whether or not it was a fact and she really did run off with another man, I have no idea.

My grandma must have told me about Jesus at a very early age. She must have told me that He lived in heaven and heaven was up in the clouds. Or at least, that was my childish understanding. So, I remember that even as young as I was, I used to go out into the pasture and lay on my back to look at the clouds. I wondered how far up the clouds really were. Looking up at the clouds I asked, "God, do You really live up there? Can You see me? Do You know I'm here? If I had a tall enough ladder, could I climb up there and see You? Would You love me?"

Right about that time I remember asking may grandma what those blue lines were on my arms, my hands and wrists. She told me those blue lines were my veins and inside of my veins was all my blood. So I would lie on my back in the pasture on the green grass, scanning the clouds, thinking maybe I could see God if He would just poke His head out even if only for a minute. I really wanted to see Him and see what He looked like. I felt that it was very important for me to discuss this with Him but I could not seem to get Him to poke His head out and talk to me. Finally, I would just talk to Him anyway, hoping somehow He would hear me or know I was there. That hill in the pasture where I could lay down and scan the clouds seemed to be the only place I knew where He might be found. I didn't know if He could hear me or see me, but I had to give it a try. I would lie on my back in the green grass, hold up my arms and hands and show Him my veins. I would always be very careful to explain to Him what they were and why I had them. I would tell

Him about the blood that flowed through my veins for the purpose of keeping my body alive. But I would diligently explain to Him that it was VERY BAD BLOOD and it made me a bad girl, a girl that no one could love. Lying there in the bright sunshine on the green hills of the pasture I still felt perhaps there was some hope for me if He could just clean all the blood out of my veins. Either clean it up or take it out completely, I really didn't care which. I just knew that the blood in my veins made me bad and made my daddy not love me or want me. But if God could remove the blood or change it, then maybe my daddy would love me and I wouldn't be a bad girl anymore. Children are always so eager to please their parents, even when those parents are abusive.

It is very interesting to note that when I became a young woman about the age of sixteen or so, I was diagnosed with a blood disease which consumes the whole body. I find this to be no accident but believe that it was a direct result of the demons that were at work in my life bringing destruction in my body. The door that was opened for them to gain entrance to my blood was by the actual word curses spoken over me again and again, by repeatedly telling me that I had bad blood. I do also want to say that after salvation, God healed my blood. He cleansed my blood by His blood.

THE DEVIL PURSUES THE ANOINTING AND THE GIFTING:

I believe the devil tries to invade and destroy the life of every single child one way or another. If he can lure them into teenage sex

149

and uncleanness, get them involved in alcohol, drugs, or gangs; if he can defile their flesh and defile their mind, it brings him the greatest satisfaction. His desire is to get a foothold in the lives of children and bring destruction while they are still very young, then it is far more difficult for them to recover from the devastation. However, no matter how hard he fights, God is always greater. God is always able to bring restoration if there is forgiveness and repentance.

The devil begins his work as soon as possible so he can continue to build on it throughout the person's whole lifetime. If he can get involved in the person's life early on, while they are still a small child, it is easier to bring that child quickly into bondage. We must open our eyes to the destruction of our children and our loved ones. We must stand in the gap for them to cut off the generational sin and curses so that they do not have to labor under them. We want our children to be found free in Christ and to be able to live out their life in the fullness of what Christ has purchased for each one of them. The father is to be the gatekeeper for the whole family as the head of the home. That is why it is necessary for the father to take his rightful place in the family. The father and mother are to be a strong support system for each other and for their children. Together the parents are the gatekeepers for the children and the home bringing protection through teaching and by being examples of godliness and wisdom. Through prayer and spiritual warfare they are to keep the enemy at bay. As parents in this age we fail miserably and allow our children to enter adulthood unsaved and thus unprepared for life.

My own life as a child and teenager became so very difficult emotionally. I heard on a daily basis how I had ruined my dad's life on the day I was born. He told me often how neither he or anyone else ever wanted me to be born, that it would have been better if I had died in the womb. It was a constant litany of hateful things repeated time and time again until it was burned into every fiber of my being, especially my brain. I thoroughly believed every word.

I did not know any Christians although I was sent to a parochial school where the instructors were less than loving. I was forced to face the class on my knees and pray out loud every Monday morning. For a very long time I had no idea why I was required to do this, but then one day I was told that I had to do penance for my parents because they were divorced. I was told that I had to atone for their sins. The shame I felt was awful. I was made to kneel in front of the teacher's desk facing the other children. All the kids laughed and made fun of me while I prayed the rosary out loud. I became convinced that not even God could love me otherwise those who said they belonged to Him would not be so cruel.

So once again, shame and condemnation were my lot in life. The devil finds every person, every tool he can possibly use to reinforce the work he has already begun in a person's life. He works daily to establish it through any person or vehicle that will lend itself to him.

No one had to convince me I was worthless, I already believed it. As far as praying every Monday morning on my knees in front of the class was concerned, I already did believe that the third and final divorce of my parents was my fault because my dad told me so over and over. And I did believe that my mother actually left because she did not want me. I did not know anything I could do to change my life. I felt hopeless and desperate wanting only to die. That seemed to be the only solution. Thinking back I find it odd that I did not ever think about running away, but I suppose that was because I was so strongly convinced that no one wanted me and there was no place I could go.

When it was time for me to go to middle school my parents sent me to a secular school. I loved it. Outside of school fear dogged me all the time. I was afraid of the dark even as a teenager. I was afraid to let people see me. I became very fearful of all adults because of the power they were able to wield over my soul, (mind, will, emotions). I was terrified of being unpleasing in any way because it would bring a barrage of criticism and hateful condemning words. I was even afraid to get sick because then I was told I was causing a problem and wasting their money.

So I learned at a very early age to walk quietly on eggs at all times. I had many mantras; "Do not offend anyone. Do whatever you are told. Never talk back. Agree with whatever others say or do. Never register your own opinion. Blend in quietly. Do not make any noise. Be seen but never heard. No one wants you so do not give them an excuse to put you out. Work hard. Do not cause any problems."

I was silenced as a child, never allowed to sing or speak in the house unless I was directly spoken to. I find this very interesting

Sins Of The Fathers

because much later on in my life, I learned that God called me as a minister of the gospel and a teacher in the Body, which means I must be able to speak. As a small child I used to love to sing and dance and perhaps I was a chatterbox, I don't know. But immediately the enemy went to work in order to quickly extinguish the call on my life by trying to put a muzzle over my mouth to stifle me. It was when I got saved that I immediately understood there was a call on my life. Fear was a major enemy and it was very difficult at first. I remember the first couple of times I stood up to speak in front of a church I actually almost fainted with fear. I had to began to war against this assignment. Even as a believer, it was many years before I felt comfortable speaking even to my friends much less to a crowd.

It is interesting that this silencing was an assignment by the devil to cut me off from ministry. Even as an adult I have noted certain people who have tried to come against me to silence me, but I no longer allow it. I have even been told that I cannot minister because I am a woman. I just say, "Oh, you need to take that up with God because He is the One Who called me, equipped me and anointed me. So you can be the one to tell Him that He must have made a terrible mistake!"

A terrible stronghold of fear of man had been built in my life, but when God delivered me, He gave to me a spirit of holy boldness and enabled me to feely speak His Word with power and authority. That is what the devil was after all those years when I was a child.

He was trying to create a mentality and personality of silence in me. He succeeded for many years, until God got a hold of me!

By the time I was eleven years old I had become very withdrawn and introverted. I felt as though school was the only safe harbor for me. I loved school and I was an excellent student although at home I was told all the time that I was really stupid. At home I was made fun of constantly and called names which meant "stupid" or "idiot." I was shocked when one day after school I was called into the principal's office and was given a letter from the principal of the school addressed to my parents. Of course I was terrified that I had done something wrong. I considered throwing it away and not giving it to them but I did not know if the principal had requested a response or not. If he had asked for a response to his letter and I threw it away, it would not have gone well for me. I had never been called into the principal's office in my whole life, had never been in trouble of any kind, and had never been given a letter to take home to my parents before. My parents read the letter while I held my breath. The letter simply stated was a request from the principal that I should be transferred to advanced classes because my IQ was in the genius range. My dad tore the letter up in pieces and threw it away as he cussed me. That was the end of that.

School was the one place I could speak, although by now I had become so withdrawn that I rarely ever spoke unless someone first spoke to me. I did not believe that anyone would want to hear anything I might have to say. But all in all, school was my safe place. I loved to go there and dreaded coming home again. I had no friends because I was too afraid to reach out to anyone and I was not allowed to have anyone in the house anyway, so I did not really know anyone.

On a regular basis it was burned into my soul that my being alive was an intrusion into the lives of those around me and I had become a major hardship to them. I felt so guilty for being alive.

I was still being transferred back and forth from aunts and uncles and then back home again. Each year when school ended I had to sit down and write letters to the relatives in order to find a place to live for the summer until school started again. So with great fear and trembling, I would sit down and write first one relative and then another. I would ask them one by one if there was anyone who would take me for the summer until school started again. I made many promises. If they would take me I promised to clean their house, keep their children, do the cooking and whatever else was necessary. This was not humiliating for me as much as it was worrisome. What if no one would let me come to live with them? I was always afraid the relatives would say "No!" Then what would I do? Where could I go if no one on earth wanted me? Who would help me? How would I live?"

To add to my dilemma, I found stress and fear of man to be my constant companions. I had become a very nervous child. By the time I was eleven years old my long beautiful black hair began to fall out by the handfuls.

Sins Of The Fathers

My father reiterated to me almost daily from the time I was about three and one half years old that the day I reached eighteen years old I had to leave his house and was not welcome to return. He would rant and rave about it. So the night I graduated from high school at age seventeen; I knew my time was up. That evening after the ceremony I went home and packed a small suitcase. When I woke up the next morning I said goodbye to my dad. I walked out of the house knowing I was not welcome to come back again. I began walking to the bus stop which was about one mile away. There I would catch a local bus which would take me to the train station. Then I would head for the only place I could think to go, that was the town where I had lived in foster homes or with relatives. After I started out the door my dad came behind me and told me he would walk to the bus stop with me. He said, "Hey kid, I'll carry the suitcase."

When the bus arrived he handed me my suitcase. He reached out to shake my hand and said, "Good luck kid!"

That was that. I am sure he was very happy and greatly relieved to be free of me at last.

It was many long miserable years after all these things before I actually got saved and I only got saved because of God's great mercy and grace to me. But once I was saved it was not long before God began to address the issues that had held me captive all those many years until I was well into adulthood. He helped me understand that a spirit of rejection had entered into my life even in the womb. That spirit drove my father to bitter hatred toward me, even as a little girl.

156

Even before kindergarten he regularly and constantly displayed his bitter rejection of me. The spirit of rejection had dug in and taken deep root in my life and was to be played out over and over again as I moved from age to age and circumstance to circumstance.

Before salvation, not having an understanding of spiritual things, I had no way to explain my life except that apparently everything that was said about me must be true. I absolutely believed that for some unknown reason or another, I really was no good and nothing good would ever come of my life; no one could love me and no one wanted me because I was a bad seed. I believed what he always said, that I was born that way. I believed that God, if there really was a God, had really messed up and made a serious mistake when He made me. I also believed that if there was a God, He must also hate me. Since no one else could love me, certainly He wouldn't be able to love me either. I grew up without hope, with no future, nothing to look back on and nothing to look forward to.

CHAPTER ELEVEN

GENERATION TO GENERATION

It is interesting to note that my father felt so rejected by my birth-mother and passed that rejection onto me through his constant denunciation of me. His unforgiveness toward my birth mother and his deep feelings of rejection from her opened a door to bitterness in his life.

My birth-mother was for whatever reason, also rejected by her whole family. She had nine or ten brothers and sisters and none of them had anything to do with her. She was considered the black sheep of the family. I suppose she loved my dad when she married him and no doubt he loved her as well. I think that was obvious by the fact that they married each other three times and then divorced each other three times. They would not have gone back with each other over and over if they did not truly love each other. However, when a spirit of rejection is at work in a heart and mind there are wounds that just keep on bleeding. If they have not been bound up healing cannot come. As long as the wounds are there, the enemy has a place to plant his foot. As long as he has ground, he will work it from every angle.

I have found that one who suffers from rejection will very often be rejected by all the family members, not just one. I found that this is especially true in cases where there is alcoholism and abuse. A home where alcoholism reigns supreme is never a safe place. No one knows what will set an alcoholic off so everyone learns to walk on eggs. Everyone quickly gives in to this person because it is easier to give in than to suffer their wrath. Very often the whole family will jump on the bandwagon and all stick together with the abuser. It always feels like there is safety in numbers. Human nature looks for the safest place when bombs are exploding all around. It is the easiest and simplest solution and people do it all the time. They just duck their head and agree with whoever is the most volatile because it takes great courage to come up against the one who is wielding the axe.

In my case, my dad was a very difficult man because he was unable to forgive my birth-mother for leaving him. He was so infuriated and carried such rage inside of him all the time that no one ever wanted to come up against him or get in the line of fire. It was much easier to side with him and try very quickly to get out of his way, than to be caught in his wrath. I do not know why my birth–mother was rejected by her family, but a spirit of rejection will most often draw another spirit of rejection, then they play off of each other. So it went from my mother and my father to me and then on to my children. I do not know if that is where it all began, or if it began with the generations that went before. I have no idea what the parents of my birth-mother's lives were like in Ireland, or their parents for that matter, (my great grandparents). But I do know it all had to start somewhere and it continues on until it is cut off by the shed blood of Jesus Christ.

We also see in this story the tremendous power of the spoken word. There is such power in our words. We can bless or we can curse. In this case word curses were enacted and became effective. As believers we are called to take responsibility for our words. We are called to bless and not curse.

I recall hearing or reading at one time that cursing, gossiping or backbiting is like taking a feather pillow to the top of a tall building. Once on top of the building, holding the pillow out over the city and cutting it open with a knife, the feathers scatter into the wind. The wind picks up the tiny feathers and scatters them to other buildings and onto the streets below for blocks in every direction. Soon they are carried over the whole city. Once they are scattered they can never be gathered up again. Our words are like that. We must be very careful what we speak over and about one another.

Ecclesiastes 12:11; The words of the wise are as goads, and as nails fastened by the masters of assemblies, which are given from one shepherd.

Sins Of The Fathers

This is a wonderful Scripture. It tells us that our words, the words of the wise, can be as goads or nails which are fastened in place. A goad is like a huge nail or spike that is driven into a place to secure whatever hangs on it. God's Word is like a goad for us to hang onto. It is like the footholds in the wall of a climbing gym. They are anchored in place and cannot be moved. God's Word is like that and our words can be like that as well. So we must be very careful what words we choose and what words we speak over each other. Words can carry and affect blessing or words can be derogatory bringing pain and cursing. Words can release God's power over another or unleash the demons of hell. Words can build up and words can tear down. Words can create and words can desecrate.

There is so much more that could be told, but it no longer matters. Why? Because I forgave. I had to forgive. It was required of me. But even more so, God brought me to the place where I really desired to forgive anyone and everyone that I thought had sinned against me. I wanted all the anger, rage, resentment, unforgiveness, bitterness and utter hopelessness out of my own life. I did not want to carry on the family history and further it. I wanted to forgive because Jesus promised me that if I would choose to forgive, He would forgive me of all my sins and I had so very much I needed Him to forgive me for. I wanted and needed to forgive because I saw that my own sins were the same as my dad's sins and my mom's sins, and ever so much more. Each generation does more than the one before. Also, I wanted to see my father and step-mother saved and living in the peace of God. I wanted my birth-mother to be saved if she was still alive somewhere, although I had no knowledge of her name or where she might live if indeed she was still alive. I desperately wanted to know that each of them felt secure in His love and His forgiveness and I wanted them to know the peace of God in their own life and have hope of the resurrection. I wanted and desperately needed to live in His freedom, in His presence, and in His love. I wanted to live out the plans and purposes He had for my life, even though it took so very long for me to get saved and I had wasted so much of my life. I also chose to forgive because I wanted God to restore the lives of those I pillaged along the way by my own sin, most particularly my husband and my own children.

ONE SPIRIT OPENS THE DOOR FOR ANOTHER:

When one spirit is at work in a life, sooner or later it will open the door for other spirits to enter in as well. As an example, in relationships, a person with a spirit of rejection often draws another person with a spirit of rejection. Or a person with a spirit of rejection will draw or be drawn by someone with a spirit of lust. These spirits play off one another and feed off of one another.

FEAR AND PRIDE ARE STRONG BEDFELLOWS:

Rejection opens the door for a spirit of fear to enter in. Fear opens the door for many other spirits to operate in a person's life. When there is rejection and fear the pendulum can swing either way.

Rejection and fear can operate and result in fear of man because of the shame and dishonor received causing someone to become a man pleaser and a doormat. By man pleaser I mean someone who will keep peace at any price and I use the word "man pleaser" in the universal sense meaning man or woman. Or rejection and fear coupled can take on the form of rebellion. In either case pride is an end result. A perfectionist behavior and attitude is often associated with the man pleasing spirit. The one who is a perfectionist is afraid of being rejected again and so poses a front of absolute perfection. They become controlling in their quest for perfection. Everything must be in perfect order at all times. This opens the door for a Jezebel spirit, a controlling spirit to begin to operate. The perfectionist raises the bar so high over their own head in order to protect themselves from further humiliation and rejection. This person will also raise the bar over your head expecting you to measure up to their standards as well. It is a false standard and you will always fail because God never meant for man to be the sole fulfillment of another human being. This is His role in the universe. Also, by your failure to measure up the person holding the bar is satisfied that they are somehow better and able to breathe easier now.

This kind of perfectionist behavior comes out of a spirit of fear. This spirit of fear will operate or be discernable in the characteristic traits of fear of man, fear of failure, fear of not measuring up or not being good enough and of course, fear of rejection. In this scenario there would be several spirits in operation. First there is rejection.

Rejection always causes fear. When fear enters in the door is opened to pride.

It is not long before one spirit opens the door to another and life becomes very complicated and painful. That is why once we receive deliverance from any stronghold or generational sin, we must be certain to fill our inner house, our heart, with the Holy Spirit. We must garnish our house with the Word of God and a sincere life of holiness before God.

Luke 11:24-26; "When the unclean spirit has gone out of a person, it passes through waterless places seeking rest, and finding none it says, 'I will return to my house from which I came.' And when it comes, it finds the house swept and put in order. Then it goes and brings seven other spirits more evil than itself, and they enter and dwell there. And the last state of that person is worse than the first."

REJECTION AND SUICIDE:

Not long into my adolescence I began to think about suicide. Rejection ruled over me with an iron fist. It was never ending and it was buried deep inside of me. The very first time I considered jumping from a building I was only sixteen years old but I could not work up the courage to do it. After that the thoughts of suicide came and went from time to time until finally they became an all consuming desire. I spent hours on end and day after day contemplating

Sins Of The Fathers

how I might end my life. I suffered horribly every day knowing no one loved me and I was really unworthy to live. Now, as an adult with small children, I was desperate to end my own pain but I did not want my children to have to live the rest of their life with the pain of an unfit mother who committed suicide.

Now it is interesting at this point to note that all these things I believed were just lies. They were illusions. None of it was truth. My children certainly loved me. My grandparents had truly loved me. Some aunts and uncles I lived with while I was young also loved me. And now God had blessed me with a good husband who truly loved me with all his heart. But I was the one who was unable to perceive love or receive or give love. I did not understand love and could not identify it in my life because my life was filled with the pain of rejection. The lies of the devil began in my earliest childhood and had now I clothed myself in them as my full identity. I believed all the lies! I accepted them and never even questioned them anymore. I just allowed the lies to rule my whole life, all my emotions, my thought life and personality. Eventually I divorced my good and kind husband. I did so blindly without ever recognizing that God had richly blessed me in an effort to bring healing and deliverance into my life even though I still was an unbeliever. Then, on a downward spiral I abandoned my own children.

As I said earlier, one spirit opens the door for another to begin to operate. I began taking prescription pills; tranquilizers, because I could no longer function through the days and nights. I washed them down with liquor time and time again. I wanted to blot out reality. I would be out for days on end but would always wake up again, disgusted with myself and hurting so bad, knowing I was such a pitiful creature I could not even kill myself. My life was literally hanging by a thread. Somewhere along the way other spirits entered in and gained control of other areas of my life; guilt, false guilt, condemnation, and now another. The spirit of rejection which ruled over me for so long drew a spirit of lust and perversion. Rejection always seeks love to heal its wound. Rejection had already opened the door for a spirit of suicide. Then another door opened in the spirit realm and a spirit of infirmity entered in. I didn't want to live and so my heart and mind were ripe ground for the devil to come in and place sickness and disease on me.

Looking in the mirror one day I saw for the very first time that I was a very pretty young woman. I was very shocked when I got a good look at myself. It may sound strange to say, but until then I did not really spend a lot of time looking in mirrors since I felt so unworthy of being loved or even being noticed. But that day, after taking a good long look at myself, I decided (based solely on my looks), that surely there must be someone, at least one person, who would love me. I would have done anything just to feel loved. It did not even matter who that person might be. Because of that attitude I got into some pretty awful messes and ended up in very dangerous situations more than once. I used my looks and body in a desperate search for that all illusive love, although in the end, after salvation,

God showed me that I had absolutely no understanding at all of what love really was. He taught me that the love I so desperately sought had to come from Him. That was the only kind of love that could heal my broken heart and fill me up as a person. I had to learn about love from my Savior.

A verse in Scripture tells us that there is a woman who tears down her house with her own hands. I was certainly that woman. Although I functioned on a high level in my job, kept my house clean and organized, and outwardly kept things together, inside I was destroying my self and my children whom I loved with all my heart. And even though I loved them I had no idea how to show that love or give the proper attention and nurturing they now so desperately needed from me.

I believe it all began in the womb when my parents who were both filled with their own hurt and wounds decided that the last thing on earth they both wanted was a baby. I was told on several occasions that my mother tried to abort me but failed. Abortion was illegal in those years and so she tried to do it herself. I certainly do not condone abortion in any form because God is the One Who gives all life and no man or woman has the right to take that life or decide whether or not an individual has the right to live. Only God can give or take life. However, for anyone who has had an abortion, I do absolutely believe that God can and will forgive any sin if we sincerely repent and turn to Him with all our heart. He is not a respecter of persons.

No doubt it was at this time when they were both so upset about the pregnancy that a spirit of rejection found entrance in the womb. Now as an adult, so many other spirits were operating in my life that I was a woman possessed and driven by many demons.

It always amazes me that God was so merciful to me, such a sinner. I am still astounded (so very many years later), that He would ever have bothered with me when no one else would. To understand that His grace and love extended even to me has carried me for all these years. To know that He lifted me up and revealed Himself to me, that He poured out His love and healing to me, that He cleansed me of all my sin; such grace and mercy is beyond description. Always, even to this day, it brings tears to my eyes and causes my heart to be filled with love and intense gratitude to Him. It is sad to know that I could have known such love and healing all along if I had only known Him many years before.

RUNNING ON EMPTY:

Many years later I saw and understood that when we are running on empty we turn to others and expect them to fill us up. We look all around trying to find someone we hope will be able to fill our emptiness. We somehow believe it is the obligation of our husband or wife or children or parents or friends to fill up our lack, to make us feel secure and comfortable. But in truth, that job belongs to God. He is the One we should be running to.

One evening I was sitting in my kitchen after classes I attended. There were three glasses of water sitting on the table in front of me. Two of the glasses were half full of water while the third glass was filled right up to the very top. I knew if I tried to move that full glass I would have to be careful because it would overflow. God spoke to me and said; "This is why marriages fail."

I found that very interesting since I had not been asking Him about marriage nor was I seeking marriage. In fact, I was not asking Him anything at all. I was just sitting down to take a deep breath after class trying to relax for a moment. But I often find that is when God speaks so clearly to me, when I am just simply resting quietly and not doing anything in particular. Anyway, He continued to speak and gave me great revelation regarding the subject of failing marriages. He said; "When two people marry they come together just as these two glasses of water that are each half full. Each one then expects the other to pour off out of his or her store and give to the one who is only half full in order to satisfy their need. They selfishly cry out, "Meet my need and satisfy me."

Since they are both only half full there is really very little to give. Then the one who is demanding satisfaction feels cheated because their desires, their needs or wants were not completely satisfied by their mate. But they have no understanding at all. If they would come to Me first and spend time with Me, they would receive from me in abundance. Then they would be like the glass that is completely full and running over. They would be able to go to the other

Sins Of The Fathers

and pour off out of their abundance, each one to the other. Their love would grow and they would both be satisfied. I never meant for any human being to be able to completely satisfy another human being. I want My children to come to Me and turn to Me for their needs and then turn back to their fellow man and satisfy them out of the great riches I give."

I have never forgotten that. First we must receive from Him before we have anything to give to any one else. That is the reason Scripture says, "Freely you have received, now freely give."

CHAPTER TWELVE

DEATH TO LIFE

The spirit of death was a strong influence on my life for many years and began to take control of me at age sixteen. It was a generational spirit but I did not understand any of these things at the time. This spirit continued to manifest in different ways. I was no longer just thinking about committing suicide, now I began to take terrible chances in my behavior. The spirit began to manifest through me in ways that were reckless, rash and out of control. I was rebellious and wild lacking self control. It was years later that I learned my grandfather whom I loved so much also had been suicidal and that my dad was suicidal for many years before his death.

Death began to manifest all around me. On one occasion a reporter came to visit a girlfriend of mine who was staying at my apartment for a time. I had never met him before. He began telling us that he was going to testify before the grand jury in a very short time. I had no idea what this was all about and he did not say, but I recall being concerned for him. I even asked him if he was afraid that someone would come after him. He told me I was paranoid and watched too much television. After he left our apartment he was murdered.

One of my uncles murdered his wife and then killed himself because he thought she was cheating on him.

Now the manifestations were no longer just in my thoughts or even my actions, but now others were also being involved. I was being surrounded by similar spirits operating in other people. One spirit draws another and they seem to work in cooperation with each other and feed off of each other's energy.

I was now found getting mixed up with some very unsavory characters. I found it exciting, not realizing to what depths I had sunk. On one occasion I was thrown from an automobile in the middle of the night traveling through the desert at high speed. I could have been killed.

There are many stories I could relate regarding this issue but suffice it to say I needed deliverance from a spirit by the hand of God. As I said earlier, these spirits do not just decide to go away on their own. We must be set free of the bondage that was established in our life. The bondage was created and established with our help. I say "with our help" because these bondages were fashioned by our agreement with the powers of darkness through our own thought processes, actions and behavior patterns.

I guess because I was shifted around so much as a small child and teenager, I developed a habit pattern of running off to live in another place or another state whenever things became unbearable for me. It was as though a change of scenery would make a difference, but I always had to face myself again once I got wherever I was going. There was no escape. I could not seem to get away from me and the thoughts that tormented me. Once again I was deeply suicidal and could no longer handle my life. I went to a new city. All I could see about my whole life was one long string of failures and disappointments. Loneliness and isolation can be felt intensely even in the midst of a crowd. I could not find a way to touch anyone's heart or let them touch mine. Life was bitterly disappointing and empty. By now my children were both far from me. I grieved over the loss of my children and I was plagued by it day and night. I often thought of trying to gather them again and try to make us a family but I knew that I was unfit as a mother. When I thought about my children I always thought I had gone too far, done too much, been too pathetic, and I never thought they would ever want to be with someone like me. I guess now that I was looking back on all of my past, this was probably the beginning of recognizing my unrelenting sin, although I did not yet understand that part of it.

I rented a room under an assumed name and told the landlord that no matter what happened he was not to disturb me under any circumstances. I had made up my mind I had to kill myself and I did not want to be rescued. This time it had to work for me.

I went into the room, bolted the door, and pulled the shades and the drapes closed. The next thing I remember is that I was pacing the floor and shaking my fist at the ceiling. My heart was broken that after all I had been through. No matter what I tried, nothing worked and nothing in my life made sense. It was so disappointing to me that my life was so empty and useless. That is not what I desired. I had tried so hard to change it but no matter what I did, I was unable to bring any change. I was a complete failure in every way.

I paced the floor and began to sob. All the while I shook my fist at the ceiling calling on God to show Himself to me. When I think of this today (and I do think of this often), I am ashamed of my arrogance and ignorance and amazed that God would have even heard me or bothered with me. But I called out to God to show Himself to me and prove that He was real. I asked Him to name Himself because I really did not know who He was. I told Him that I heard His name was Confucius or Buddha. "Someone else told me it was Allah. Somewhere I had heard your name was Jehovah. Others say you are Jesus. But how can I know if any of this is true? If Jesus ever really lived, He is dead now, He was crucified! So how can anyone say you are Jesus? How can I ever know which one you really are or if you are even real?"

I challenged Him. "Someone along the way told me that you are a loving God. If that is true, why would you ever allow starvation and wars and all the varied tragedies of life?"

There was no response. I challenged Him further demanding to know if He knew who I was and all that I had gone through. Did He know my children? Did He know their names and ages? I raged at Him demanding to know where He was when my children went through horrible things and I was helpless to fix any of it. Stillness was the only response. The rage inside of me spilled out in bitter anguish. The next thing I remember is that I was howling in grief. I fell to my knees and begged if He was real that He would reveal Himself to me in some way. I remember telling Him that if He could only prove to me that He was real, I might not have to kill myself. Perhaps that would give me a reason to live. If only He could prove to me that He was real and if He could let me know if He loved me. I told Him that if He loved me, that would be reason enough for me. If He could just show me who He was and that He loved me, it would be enough for me to go on. This went on for some time as my heart was being ripped out of my chest with pain long since buried.

Finally, I remember saying, "God, whoever you are, if you will just reveal yourself to me and show me that you love me, I will give you my whole life. I will do anything for you. I will go wherever you tell me to go and I will do whatever you tell me to do. I will say whatever you tell me to say and I will belong to you all the days of my life."

Suddenly I saw a vision. I saw Jesus Christ hanging on a cross up on a hill. It was like I was standing back on another hill very close by, close enough to see Him very clearly. He was covered with blood. His whole body and His face were horridly bloodied, and the sight was most shocking to see. I had never seen anything like that. He was not yet dead but He was suffering tremendously. He was in sheer agony. In that moment, when I saw Him there, I understood for the very first time in my whole life that Jesus Christ was my Savior and I knew then that it was my sin that nailed Him to that cross.

All of my life I had never understood or realized that I was a sinner. I always thought I just had a bad life or people did bad things to me. I was never aware or conscious of my part. But now I saw that I was the one who was condemned and He was the One Who paid the price for me. Suddenly before my eyes I saw a path opened up to me. I looked at the path. It was a winding path behind me, extending from this moment in time back through my past, through my whole life back to my earliest beginnings. I saw it clearly. It was a path of sheer destruction and devastation. It was the path of a life of desperate and deplorable sin. As I watched Him hanging there dying in my place, I was overwhelmed with shame for who I was and who I had been.

In this vision I heard the voice of God speak to me for the first time. It was like a thundering in my soul. He told me many things that night. One of them was that I needed to forgive my parents, both father and mother and my step-mother as well. He told me that if I would choose to forgive them he would fill my heart with a great love for them. That did not make any sense to me and for a bit I argued with Him about it. Then in the vision I saw my dad and step-mother holding hands and walking toward the cross together. It was like I was standing behind them and watching them from a short distance away. I saw them walk up to the cross and stand there, still holding hands, and still looking up at Him. I heard Father God say,

"What more have you done than this?" (speaking of Jesus' death on the cross). "What more have you done than this, that you could possibly hold their sins against them?"

It was in that instant I had the realization that Jesus died not only for me, but He also died for them. And yes, they were sinners. But they were sinners for whom He died. He purchased salvation for them as well as for me and I had no right to hold their sins against them.

I simply said, "Okay Lord, I forgive them."

I was thirty-six years old now and for the very first time in my whole life I felt like I had a reason to live. I actually experienced the most tremendous joy and happiness I had ever felt. I had a new care-free feeling I had never known before in my whole life. I no longer needed drugs or pills or alcohol or any of the worldly pursuits I had previously given myself to. Jesus really was my answer.

I do not know how long all this went on throughout the night, but I know when I first bolted the door to kill myself it was early evening. When I opened the drapes and unbolted the door it was morning. It was a blustery winter day in Wisconsin. I put on my jacket and went for a walk. There were no sidewalks and I had to walk alongside the highway. I was elated even more than words can describe. As I walked along the highway I was sure that every single car which passed me must have known that I belonged to God. I felt like I glowed in the dark. I was certain everyone could see it!

At that time I still did not know anything about God, or healing, or deliverance, or about anything in the Bible, but I knew one thing.

I knew all my sin was nailed to the cross I saw in the vision and Jesus took it all on Himself. I knew I was free!

When I saw my father and step-mother the next time, which was not long after my salvation experience, my heart was overflowing with love for them. I knew this was nothing short of a miracle and something only God could have done for me. He took a heart that was cemented in bitterness and unforgiveness and He gave me a heart of flesh. He gave me an understanding and a compassion for them so that I was able to see them in a new way.

For the first time in my life I understood that my dad could not love me. He was unable to love me. He did not have it in him. His life was so embittered by his own heartache that it crowded out anything good he ever could have felt for me. His whole life was colored by unforgiveness toward my birth-mother and entrenched in terrible pain. Understanding his pain now made it easier for me to bear mine because although I had changed, he did not.

It still took a long time after that for my heart to be completely healed. It was a long process over many years. It was like people say; pretty much like peeling the layers of an onion, one layer at a time. God does not open us up and remove everything at once. It would be too painful for us. He is very merciful, so He does His work a little at a time. There were instances when what He opened up to me was so horribly painful that I did not want God to remove any more layers of pain. It just hurt too much. I did not think I could live through it. But surgery is always painful and all the infection of our life and rottenness must be removed so our life can be free and unrestricted.

We can only be filled to the degree we have been emptied of all those things that have consumed us and devalued us as His children. We must be emptied out so that He can fill us up.

Psalm 30:5; For his anger is but for a moment, and his favor is for a lifetime. Weeping may tarry for the night, but joy comes with the morning.

CHAPTER THIRTEEN

THE SPIRIT OF DEATH

In this book, when I refer to an unclean spirit I am not simply speaking of sexually unclean spirits. I am speaking of any type of demonic spirit. In other words, any spirit that is in rebellion against God. These spirits may be called by many different names which include devil, demon, fallen angels, powers of darkness, unclean spirits, or powers and principalities.

Also, I want to make it perfectly clear that a person who is saved cannot be possessed. However, any spirit can harass, intimidate, afflict, torment, and influence the person's thought life, personality, character and actions if it is allowed to do so.

We can have one or more spirits operating in our life, or through us, or against us, or however you might like to phrase it. By this I mean that a demonic spirit, or perhaps more than one, can influence our life, our thoughts and actions. The demon or demons bring a compelling pressure which is exerted over us in the spirit realm. The aim of course is to control our thoughts, personality and character drawing us to sin and establishing us in deep bondage. This demonic power is able to manipulate, deceive and persuade its host. Yet, the person under this demonic influence more often than not, is completely unaware of the operation of demonic powers in their life unless they are purposefully involved in some form of witchcraft in which they have set their heart to contact and enlist the help of the demonic realm. Often within our family members or ourself, this influence is hidden from us. We are blinded to it. When we do see the manifestations in our own personality or the personality of other family members, we simply think, "Oh that is just how they are! Our whole family is like that!"

It is so very interesting to note that any one spirit can take on so many different manifestations. After God began to show me some of the patterns of iniquity in my generational line, I began to understand that the spirits operating in and through me and other family members can change the manifestations even though it is often the same spirit operating in or through the person. Even as a spirit goes down through the generations from one member of the family to another, the manifestations of that spirit may differ in various family members.

For example, I was told constantly that it would have been better if I had died rather than to be born. This opened the door for a spirit of death to enter into my life because I was a child totally submitted to my dad.

At the age of sixteen the same spirit began to manifest in my life in a suicidal manner and continued to manifest in that way in my life until my salvation.

Remember, God said, "My people die for lack of knowledge."

A lack of knowledge in this case means having a lack of the knowledge of God and an understanding of His ways. After salvation I thought that everything that was in conflict with God's will or God's ways within my life was broken off of me when I got saved. I had such joy after salvation that it never occurred to me that any spirit could still be operating in or through me (in my mind, will or emotions), or influencing my attitudes or behavior in any way. It never occurred to me that this was even a remote possibility.

Hebrews 3:10; Wherefore I was grieved with that generation, and said, They do always err in their heart; and they have not known my ways.

THREE TYPES OF DEATH:

I want to tell you about a spirit of death. This is an actual spirit that comes to take us. That does sound rather creepy, doesn't it? But we are going to take a look at this spirit. Death is not just a physical condition of the body. Nor is death simply the ultimate and probable end of illness or disease. Death is a spirit.

There are three types of death. The first is spiritual death which is what one experiences if they live in sin and refuse to accept Christ as their Savior and repent of their sins. Another type of death is the death of the body. This is of course the act of breathing out our final breath of life on this earth. This is something each one of us must face unless we are taken in the rapture of the church first. Scripture tells us that death is the last enemy that shall be destroyed. And since life is a gift from God, death is our last enemy to be overcome as well. We must resist death and embrace life. The last and final type of death of course is referred to in the Bible as the second death, which is total and complete separation from God for all eternity, being cast into hell.

Let us take a look at the following Scriptures which tell us a little about the spirit of death.

Exodus 12:23; For the Lord will pass through to smite the Egyptians; and when he seeth the blood upon the lintel, and on the two side posts, the Lord will pass over the door, and will not suffer the destroyer to come in unto your houses to smite you.

I Corinthians 10:10; Neither mumur ye, as some of them also murmured, and were destroyed of the destroyer.

In both of these Scriptures the spirit of death is called the destroyer. However in the following Scripture the same spirit is called "him" who had the power of death, the devil.

Hebrews 2:14; Forasmuch then as the children are partakers of flesh and blood, he also himself likewise took part of the same;

that through death he might destroy him that had the power of death, that is, the devil.

The spirit of death is referred to here as "him." This means he is an actual being, a created being. He is referred to by several names as we have seen and in II Samuel 24:16 he is called "the destroying angel." So we now also know he is angelic in being. Other references to his nature and character are revealed to us in the following Scriptures.

Job 18:14; He is torn from the tent in which he trusted and is brought to the king of terrors.

In the book of Job this spirit is referred to as "the king of terrors."

Revelation 6:8; And I looked, and behold, a pale horse! And its rider's name was Death, and Hades followed him. And they were given authority over a fourth of the earth, to kill with sword and with famine and with pestilence and by wild beasts of the earth.

The spirit of death can be an influence on a person's life through generational sin or curses without the person ever realizing this. An example would certainly be the Kennedy Family. There is a litany of early death of the Kennedy men and women alike throughout their history.

A spirit of death can manifest in various ways such as severe depression leading someone to consider suicide, or manifest in murder. Both of these are manifestations of the spirit of death. One is passive and one is aggressive. Suicide is an inward act of murder and homicide is an outward aggressive act of murder. Suicide is murder of one self, while homicide is committed against another human being. But both are the same spirit manifesting in different ways.

A spirit of death can torment someone for years with various sicknesses and diseases, often driving them to the brink of death. It can also manifest in an intense desire for death, with the person not necessarily wanting to commit suicide, but having an intense desire to simply die and thereby find some peace from the constant torment they find in life.

In our Western civilization we have the mindset for the most part that when anyone dies it was just God's will for that person. How sad that we believe God takes people before their time. We lack an understanding of God's will for us on this earth. God can certainly take anyone at any time according to His plan and design. However, in most cases, He has stated in His Word that there is a plan set in place for our life and He wants us to live out the fullness of our life.

We tend to forget that the devil is a deceiver. He comes with one purpose which is to kill us, steal from us and try to destroy us in any way he can. He is looking for any open door. This is why healing and understanding healing as a part of the atonement is so very important for us as believers.

When it was time for my father to die, the doctors had been saying for several years already that there was no hope for him. However, God put it in my heart to contend for his life. It was like a mandate from God. It came to my mind continually to contend for his life until he saw the salvation of God. I continued to cry out to God day and night for his soul. He still did not know Jesus Christ as His Savior. Every single day I took authority over the spirit of death and bound it commanding that my dad could not be taken until he had an opportunity to hear the gospel message with a right mind, a sound mind of understanding and clarity. I prayed for him to have a mind that was not clouded with pain or blinded with bitterness and unforgiveness. Of course it was all still up to him, he had to make the final decision.

The war was on and God made me steadfast in this battle. I could not bear the thought that my dad might die and not know Jesus Christ as Savior. Day after day I took authority and demanded that he could not be taken by the spirit of death until he had an opportunity to understand with a clear mind that he was going to stand before the God Who had created him, the God Who had loved him all of his life. I prayed for a clear revelation of God, along with true repentance; and a deep and sincere sorrow for his sins. I prayed that he would humble himself and put his hope and trust in God. I prayed for him to look at eternal life in glory with the Lord of Glory as a reality for himself. I also prayed relentlessly that the spirits of unforgiveness, bitterness and hated, that had operated in his life would be completely cut off. I prayed that all family-line curses and attending spirits would forever be cut off and that they could go no further down the family line. I prayed that they would not be able to continue through my life or the lives of my descendants. I asked God to search me and know me and show me if there was any wicked way in me, anything I needed to repent of, any doors I needed to close. I contended in battle for my dad, myself and my family.

Revelation 1:17-18; When I saw him, I fell at his feet as though dead. But he laid his right hand on me, saying, "Fear not, I am the first and the last, and the living one. I died, and behold I am alive forevermore, and I have the keys of Death and Hades."

Jesus now holds the keys to death and hell. And God the Father attends us in those moments with goodness and gentleness. He is not willing to lose even one soul and He will go to the greatest extent to save a soul. I know this personally.

One night about two o'clock in the morning, I rolled over in bed and heard Him say; "All the shields of the earth belong to Me. All tribes and tongues, they are Mine. Every man, every woman, every child; they were created by Me and for Me. They are released and go to live their lives on the earth and then when it is time I call them to come back and stand before Me. It is then that they must give an account of their life before Me."

I understood God was speaking to me about my dad whom I had been praying for. Just then the most incredible thing happened. After

God finished speaking these words to me, the love of God poured all over me. It was like the waves of the sea washing over me, a strong, weighty love rolling from the tip of my toes up to the crown of my head. I felt the love of God so profoundly like nothing I have ever known before. I knew God was showing me how much He loved my dad. I knew in that moment that God would go to the greatest lengths to save a soul. He is not willing that any should perish. Not even one. I had such great peace and hope knowing that God was contending in this battle with me. I was not begging or pleading or fighting alone, but God was in the midst of the battle fighting for one he created to be in fellowship with Him. We were co-laborers in the battle.

My father died after several months of intensive warfare, but he accepted the Lord before he died. In fact, he died crying out to God, calling on His name. He died on his knees with his head bowed and his hands folded in prayer.

I know my dad is safely in heaven and all his sins are washed away. Now he can constantly behold the face of the One Who so freely surrendered His life so that he could have eternal life with Him. Jesus is the Victor. He took the keys to death and hell! His mercy is a river ever flowing to us, His children.

God said that He has no desire for us to die prematurely. He is the One Who numbered our days and they are counted out before Him. He desires for us to see the fulfillment of our days. But how many are cut off before their time? Death must come to us at God's appointed time, not when the powers of darkness decide they want to take us out.

Psalm 116:15; Precious in the sight of the Lord is the death of his saints.

I knew an elderly man who had been a pastor. He was a godly man. Although he was quite old, he still stood tall and straight and read his Bible every single day. His eyesight had gotten pretty bad with age but otherwise he was still healthy. He lived with his daughter and son–in-law in a large house and had lived a good, reasonably happy and long life, more than most people could say about their own life.

One day he got up out of bed, cleaned up and dressed and sat down to breakfast. After breakfast he did what he did every other morning. He went into the front room and took his Bible. There he stretched out on the couch where he read and then sang to the Lord. After he had spent some time with the Lord he called his daughter into the room and said, "Gather all the family together to meet with me in the morning. The Lord is going to take me home tomorrow after my quiet time. I want to have time with them to say goodbye to each one and to pray a blessing over them."

His daughter did not doubt what he had told her because this man had raised his children to know the Lord and to hear His voice. So she called each one and told them what time to be there at the house the next morning. The chairs were all fixed in a half circle

Sins Of The Fathers

around the couch. He had laid out hymn books on each chair before anyone arrived. Then he laid himself out on the couch as he usually did and read his Bible and sang to the Lord. The children and grand-children began to arrive. They also knew that "grampa" heard from God all the time and so they were prepared to say goodbye to him.

Everyone found a chair and seated themselves. He spoke then and told them that he was going to go home but wanted to pray over each one and bless them individually. They came to him one at a time and talked with him for a moment. Then each one separately knelt down beside him by the couch as he laid his hands on their head. He kissed each one and told them how much he loved them. Then he prayed a blessing over each one. After he had prayed for the very last one, he lay back on the couch, folded his hands in his lap, closed his eyes and gave up his spirit to God. He drew his last breath on this earth.

What a sweet and precious way to meet the Lord of Glory.

One day a friend of mine called me up and asked me if I would go to a local hospital to pray for someone who was dying. I did not know this particular woman and was not at all sure that she or her family would even allow me to come into the room, but I decided I would go anyway. She welcomed me into her room when I told her I had received a telephone call from our mutual friend asking me to visit. After we talked for a few minutes I began to share the salva-tion message with her. I asked her if she wanted to pray a prayer of repentance for her sins and to ask Jesus to be her Lord and Savior.

She did, so we prayed together that day. Little did I know but her husband who was sitting very quietly in the corner of the room the whole time told me many years later that he also prayed that day; the same prayer as she prayed.

She died a few days later in the same hospital bed. She died laughing and shouting with joy that Jesus Himself had come into the room to take her home. What a glorious way to enter eternity. It was about twenty five years later that I met her husband. I had no memory of him whatsoever. When I was called to the hospital to pray with this woman, both she and her husband were total strangers to me. So it was odd that he remembered me all those many years later when I ran into him at a summer gathering. He thanked me for leading her to the Lord and that is when he told me he also prayed the prayer that day. By his demeanor it was easy to see he was a believer. He was a gracious, sweet, tender hearted man full of the love of God.

Believers should die without fear. I had a friend who was a tremendous prayer warrior. She was one of my best friends for so many years. As she lay dying she was still so full of joy. She talked and laughed just as she always had and she praised the Lord with every dying breath. She knew she belonged to Him and she would never be separated from Him now.

Only God knows the exact number of days. We do not. That is why we must live godly lives and live with a view to eternity. I think very often about people who go through their whole lives gathering up and storing up things. They name their properties after themselves and they live luxurious lives. But I do wonder if they ever ponder their own death. Do they think about it? Do they prepare themselves spiritually? Or do they just somehow think they will deal with it when it comes? I don't know. But within a split second we can be in eternity standing before Him. That should be a very frightening thought to anyone who is not spiritually ready. I have heard people say things like, "I will repent just before I die. That will be time enough."

How silly. We do not know the moment of our death and we have no idea how we will die. Many people do not have the time to repent. Death can be instant. But even more so, there must be a genuine repentance. And another thing, the longer we put off surrender the more hardened our hearts become. Someone who keeps refusing salvation may end up like Pharaoh, with the heaviness and hardness of his own heart weighing him down on the bottom of the sea of death.

About two years ago I had a stroke. I was living alone at the time so there was no one who could see me or listen to me or judge if I was acting strangely. I was in horrible pain on the whole right side of my body and dragging my body around my front room talking to God. Now when I look back over this whole incident it is laughable. I kept on asking God, "God, is this serious? Should I be calling 911?"

If I had not been alone at the time, whoever was with me would have known not only by the pain and paralysis of my whole right side, but also by my conversation with God that I was in serious trouble. The stroke was already affecting my brain. I could not think clearly and I could not reason. I simply continued to call on God and ask Him what I should do. Finally I called several people and asked them to pray for me. Because my brain was already being greatly affected I could not tell them exactly what was happening in my body except to say that I was in really serious pain and felt really funny. The first person I called told me they were extremely busy and did not have time for all this. They were trying to get ready for a celebration. They told me they were just too busy to pray with me. However, in the end they angrily relented and did say a short prayer with me. Then they quickly hung up the phone. I felt reluctant to call anyone else at this point. I did not want to bother anyone, so I dragged myself around my front room for another hour or so asking God what to do and calling on Him for help. Right about this time, I began to go in and out of my body. That is the only way I can explain what was happening to me. I felt like I would float up out of my body and then after a bit I would come back into my body. It was when I would come back into my body that I realized what had taken place. This all may sound very strange unless you have ever had a similar experience.

After floating in and out of my body several times I had the rational that I must call someone for help. I did not remember that

I had already called several people. At this point my brain was not functioning at anything resembling normal and so it never even occurred to me now to call 911. I dialed the telephone number of a friend and asked for prayer. Apparently I had already called her once or twice earlier that morning and asked for prayer, so this time the person called my daughter and told her that it seemed like I might be having a stroke. I do not remember dressing myself or much of anything after that phone conversation with my friend. I don't even know if she prayed for me but I suspect she did because she is a strong prayer warrior. All of this had been going on now for several hours. I continued to have episodes when I left my body and came back again. Then in an instant, in just one split second, I stood before the Lord. I was so amazed that I was there and He was there. We were both standing there together - standing face to face looking at each other. I saw Him and I was so close I could reach out and touch Him. I always imagined what it would be like to stand before Him and now I did. I looked around and was amazed at what I saw. Both of us were suspended in space. My first thought was that there was nothing holding us up. I could see there was absolutely nothing under our feet, but we were completely suspended in space together. My next thought was that I was being held up by the power of His presence. I was so amazed. I remembered the Scripture that He upholds all things by the power of His word.

Colossians 1:16-17; For by him all things were created, in heaven and on earth, visible and invisible, whether thrones or

dominions or rulers or authorities—all things were created through him and for him. And he is before all things, and in him all things hold together.

My next thought was that He was simply standing there looking at me. I searched His face and looked into His eyes and was aware that I saw nothing in His face or His eyes that was frightening to me. I saw no anger or disappointment. When I had looked down at my feet I believe I was barefooted. I got a glimpse of my gown, only a momentary glance. Afterward I could not remember anything about it except that it was white. I hope it was pure white, not spotted or wrinkled. The next thought that went through my mind was that all that I was, all I had ever been, everything I ever said or done was laid bare before Him. Everything within me, every thought that ever went through my mind, both good and evil, every word I had ever spoken, every passion or desire, every heartache; it was all laid bare before His eyes. I was very conscious of that the fact that He could see everything about me. Absolutely nothing was hidden or covered over and I remembered the Scripture that says everything about us is laid bare before the One with whom we have to do.

Hebrews 4:13; And no creature is hidden from his sight, but all are naked and exposed to the eyes of him to whom we must give account.

This is such a sobering Scripture. Think about this for a moment. We take so much for granted. We skim over Scripture without really thinking about it. But a day is coming for each one of us when we will stand before Him and nothing will be hidden, nothing will be covered. We will be seen as we really are. There will be no fig leaves, no excuses, no blaming, and no cover-ups. Just simply laid bare before the One with Whom we have to do; Jesus, our Lord and Savior.

I stood at the bedside of someone who was dying not too long ago. As his family was gathered around his bedside they told him to calmly walk toward the light, to look for the shaft of light and follow it. But when I came to stand before Him on that day, nowhere did I ever see any shaft of light. There was no long tunnel, no music, and no voice calling me to walk toward the light. There was nothing like that. Just bang! In one split second I stood before Him and that was that! It was all over, all done. It was just He and I and there was nothing I could do about it. I could not go back into my body by myself. Only He could send me back.

Much to my surprise I heard myself say to Him, "Lord, if it's my time it's okay. But if it is not my time yet, then send me back because I have really messed some things up and I would like to do it right this time if I can."

I know, I know! It is not by our works of righteousness, I know that! It is not in our power or strength. I know all those things. I am just telling you what happened.

Immediately I was back into my body. The next thing I remember is that my daughter was at my door with a worried look on her face. And the only thing I remember after that was that I was suddenly in a hospital and people were asking me questions. When I arrived at the hospital I was so completely out of it. I babbled and danced and flagged my arms while I sang to the nurses. I am certain they thought I was mentally ill, but I felt so much joy I could hardly contain myself. I laughed and even belly laughed all the while my frustrated daughter was trying to get me checked into the emergency room. She was telling them I had a stroke but I think they were certain I was really crazy because I could not contain the joy I felt.

Yes, I had suffered a stroke which affected my whole right side, my memory, energy, strength and a whole array of other medical maladies. However, I was so giddy with pure delight and happiness for so many months after that because I had stood in the presence of the Lord. I laughed and laughed all the time. I felt such love and joy unspeakable, full of glory! I knew I had tasted a little bit of heaven that day. What a glorious and splendid home awaits each one of us who belong to Him.

One thing I realized afterward was that whatever we are in our life and in our heart, we are so much more of that in His presence because there are no earthly hindrances to confine us or withhold us. If we are evil, then when we stand before Him we will still be evil, and even more so, because absolutely nothing will be hidden, covered over, or buried deep inside of us. Whatever we are in our heart we will be so much more the same the moment we stand before Him. Everything is laid bare in the presence of the One with whom we have to do.

The last enemy we have to overcome is death.

CHAPTER FOURTEEN

SPIRIT TIES

Spirit ties, also called soul ties, are simply a bond that is created linking people together in the spirit realm. This bond can be created between two or more people or with a whole group of people. It can be created through any type of strong emotions or circumstances. This bond can either be a good thing such as a strong bond of godly friendship, or it can be an evil tie which binds one person to another or to a group in a way that is wicked.

For example, anyone who ever fought in a war and shared a foxhole or the inside of a tank with other soldiers soon formed a bond with his or her fellow warriors. This relationship is created out of necessity more often than not because in combat one must be able to fully trust and rely on the fellow soldier he or she is next to. Fighting side by side, soldiers must be able to believe they can trust the one next to them. A bond is created as they rely on one another; as they share their food, their fear, their tears, their pain, their stories and perhaps their prayers.

Often these soldiers were strangers who knew little of each other or perhaps they knew and even disliked each other before they jumped into a foxhole together. Suddenly they had to have confidence in each other for their own safety and protection. They become bound to one another by their shared experience. They are now connected to each other by common thoughts, emotions and conditions. A bond or spirit tie has been created between them. The terrible circumstances they shared together placed cords around them and drew them into a brotherhood of sorts.

Men and women, who were in prison camps during together during the World War II, or any other war for that matter, experienced the same type of bond. They were bound together by their shared experiences of hunger, fear, suffering and pain.

Groups such as biker gangs or street gangs experience the ties of brotherhood. In fact, this is often what draws someone into a gang. They are attracted by the need they have to feel as though they belong somewhere. The same bond can be formed in places such as the local pub where night after night the same people frequent the place and begin to share their thoughts and feelings. Relationships are formed and before long a bond of friendship is forged. This can happen in the workplace or in any place or circumstance where at least two people are drawn into some form of relationship which mentally and/or emotionally binds them together. This is especially true in a sexual relationship. The Bible clearly tells us that when two people have sexual intercourse they become one in the spirit. (See Matthew 19:5-6).

BECOMING ONE FLESH:

Genesis 34:16; Then will we give our daughters unto you, and we will take your daughters to us, and we will dwell with you, and we will become one people.

In the above Scripture in Genesis we see that whole tribes or families can become one family through intermarriage. They become joined together through sexual intercourse to become one flesh. That is why God warned His people not to enter marriage with the inhabitants of the land they were taking over. He wanted His people to be pure, separated to Him and not mixed and intermingled with foreign cultures. When they mixed in intermarriage with these foreign cultures they accepted their culture, their rituals and their foreign gods and soon began to take them as their own.

Therefore, it is of the utmost importance that when we come before God we must take time to examine our heart and repent of every sexual relationship outside of marriage. In every sexual relationship we become one in the spirit with the other person. We take on their spiritual DNA, if you will. I wonder how many people actually realize that they open the door in the spirit realm to whatever their sexual partner has been involved in and they open the door to the spirits that may be operating in that person's life or family line.

Sins Of The Fathers

Not only that, but by being promiscuous, sexual intercourse not only opens the door to the spirits operating in the sexual partner's life, but also to his or her other sexual partners as well, because they also have become one through sexual union. How many people are hopping from bed to bed and defiling themselves without giving any thought to what they are opening themselves up to. It is not simply a matter of diseases but it also of great consequence to consider the spiritual ramifications of being linked spiritually to all kinds of people you do not even know. You not only do not know them, you know nothing of their personal life, habits, sin patterns, bondages or the spirits which are operating in their life. It is a fearful thing to contemplate.

Right after a baby is born there are certain hormones released in the mother's body immediately after the birthing process. As she holds this child to her breast a strong bond is formed. Mother and baby now have a spirit tie that will last a lifetime.

A spirit tie can be formed in any friendship or relationship that is nurtured. It does not matter if one is saved and the other is not saved, or if neither of them are saved. This has nothing to do with salvation. This has to do with a spiritual union or bond that is formed between two or more people because of their shared physical union, emotion, their condition (such as illness), or their circumstances.

Just as a relationship built on love will become a bond, so also, a spirit bond can be created between two people through negative emotions such as unforgiveness, bitterness, hatred, or even through envy and jealousy. That is why Jesus told us that we must forgive before the sun goes down and not hold any resentment or unforgiveness toward another person. Unforgiveness and bitterness binds us to the one we refuse to forgive. It is like having a chain wrapped around us dragging the person we refuse to forgive behind us. Everywhere we go, whether we are all alone or with someone else; even in a crowd, we remain bound in our heart and our spirit to the person we hate. Our heart and mind are controlled by the bond of that relationship and all the emotion that goes with it. It begins to color all our actions and eventually even our relationships with others.

Any spiritual bond which has been created can easily become bondage depending on the life and lifestyle of the one the tie is created with because of the inextricable link of one to another. It can then be passed on to future generations as a habitual pattern of behavior or lifestyle.

WHEN THE DOOR IS FLUNG OPEN:

In ministering to others I have noted that a spirit can remain in place for a very long time and just seem to be dormant or inactive. It seems like it lies low for a time and no one really notices by any particular behavior that it is still there. Because it has been inactive the person tends to believe that he or she is free of it. Then through a series of circumstances or crisis this spirit will raise its ugly head and begin to manifest once again

Sins Of The Fathers

An example is the case of a young woman I knew and grew very close to. I met her when I was first starting out to minister in different churches or women's groups. She was very young when we first met, just in her mid teens actually. She was very intelligent and upbeat. I thought it was odd for her to want to be my friend since she was about fifteen and I was in my early forties. But we did become very close friends and I did grow to love her.

I had a college age fellowship which met in my home and lots of different young people came. We all sat around, talking through the night, solving all the world's problems, sharing what God had done since we last met, playing guitar and worshipping. The presence of the Lord would come and we would pray for one another and just enjoy fellowship with Him and each other. Over time many different personalities ventured into the group; a prostitute, a new ager, and some very hurting young people. My young friend was a part of this group as well.

One day she came to visit me and she seemed kind of down in the dumps. There was something about her person that seemed so different than usual so I asked if I could pray with her. She agreed. I laid my hands on her and immediately I received a word of knowledge that she had sinned sexually. God showed me that she had slept with a man, even a stranger she had just met. I was shocked and really saddened by this information. I told her what God showed me. She broke down and sobbed. When I asked her about it, at first she made excuses but then finally she shamefully admitted it. I prayed and she cried.

I thought that was the end of it. She continued to visit me frequently over the following weeks and it started to become obvious that there was a definite change in her behavior, dress and attitudes. It was very upsetting to see these changes in her personality and mannerisms. This precious young woman who wanted to go into the entire world to preach the gospel was being taken over by manifestations of unclean spirits. Was she still seeing this man? Was she still having sexual relationship with him? I asked her and she denied it, so I did not really know what was going on. She quickly came to the place where she either did not want to receive help or was unable to receive it. She was being hindered in her thinking processes and unable to clearly evaluate her own circumstances and mental state. She was no longer her own person.

I was aware that there was a history of mental illness in her family and currently there were several members of her immediate family who were severely mentally ill and had been for many years. One member of her family was violently mentally ill. So this was definitely a case of generational spirits. However, until now she had personally never displayed any history or symptoms of any kind of mental illness. In fact it was quite the opposite. But now very suddenly all that changed. The next thing I heard was that the police came and took her to the local mental hospital. I do not know the circumstances that led to this action, except that I was told she also had become very violent. Upon visiting her I was shocked to see that she looked so completely different. Her gorgeous bright eyes were dull and the vivacious sparkling personality I had come to know so well was now dull and lifeless. This was a striking young woman who was vivacious, full of life, loving every moment of it, talented, artistic, outgoing and very articulate. Now she looked like a shell of the person I had known. There had been a complete collapse of her personality. She now began to manifest the very same symptoms that were operating in other members of her family.

The next thing I knew she was a long term patient in a local mental hospital. We talked from time to time and every once in a while I would get a glimpse of the beautiful young girl I had known, but then in an instant she would be gone again, buried beneath her new persona. She would be completely changed again like someone else had taken over. It was the same body but a totally different person and personality.

She was confined for a very long time and finally released with a heavy load of medication. I still loved her and longed to see her set free. I thought for certain this was all a temporary situation. But before long she was once again a patient in the mental facility. It was not long before I heard that she had escaped with another patient, this time it was a young man. She did contact me and told me they were lovers. I could not believe the things I was hearing. I was informed that the police were looking for her because she and her boyfriend broke into a gun shop, wrestled the owner to the floor and stole several shotguns. Then they stole a car and headed for places unknown.

This precious young girl, who was barely beginning her life; this one who had such a pleasant fun loving personality, who had glowed with vitality and life, was now a fugitive wanted by the police and was considered armed and dangerous.

She confessed to me that the man she had slept with was a Satanist high priest. Is it no wonder then that the spirits which were operating in her family from past generations had now found an open door into her life? They were powerful spirits that had been entrenched for years in her family line and now they had a new host. As long as she walked with God and lived a holy life she was protected, but when she opened the doors to the powers of darkness they did not hesitate to enter into her life and manifest in and through her as they had in previous and even current generations of her other family members. They had a new home.

She would call me from time to time from various states and beg me to pray with her. Demons would be manifesting to her. She would scream and cry over the telephone telling me that she hiding behind the couch, or under the bed, or in a closet, because she was so terrified. I would pray for her and then not hear from her again for several years. Then without any notice she would call again crying and screaming with terror because demonic spirits were manifesting to her.

Now I know most people would say that she was delusional, suffering from hallucinations or fantasy. Some would no doubt say it was all a figment of her imagination. However, I do not believe that for one minute. She was actually seeing demons manifesting and tormenting her because she had opened up her life to the powers of darkness. I know this is the case because these are the kinds of demonic manifestations I had before I got saved and delivered by Jesus Christ.

I think we can conclude several things from this story. One is that a generational spirit can lay dormant and inactive, waiting quietly on the sidelines, watching, completely out of sight. It remains hidden away until a door in the spirit realm is opened through unrepented sin. Then this particular spirit, whatever it might be, comes to stake a claim in the personhood of the one who has opened the door. By so doing this spirit can continue down the family line taking captives through generational sin and bondage.

An evil spirit will remain in place throughout continuing generations until it is cast out in the name and the authority of Jesus Christ. Of course God can and may deliver anyone from any stronghold or spirit at the time of salvation if He so chooses. However, very often the person has to walk through some circumstances which will reveal and bring recognition of their own sin and their agreement and cooperation with the works of darkness. A time of recognition and repentance is most often a part of deliverance. Deliverance comes through revelation, recognition and repentance. Most often, there must first be a revelation that there is a generational sin problem in operation. Once we have that revelation we are able to recognize the varied manifestations or expressions in the personalities of those in the family line. Finally, there must be a sincere repentance for the sins that opened the doors in the spirit realm in the first place and for our cooperation with those spirits in our own life. Then in the power and authority that is given to us in the name of Jesus, we can break the curse, break the spirit ties or soul ties and declare our freedom in Christ.

HOW ARE SPIRIT TIES FORMED?

Spiritual ties can be formed through:

- Friendships
- Strong healthy emotional bonds such as love or friendship
- Strong negative emotional bonds such as envy and jealousy
- Fear, Resentment, unforgiveness, bitterness or hatred
- Sexual intimacy whether married to the person or not
- Any sexual sin including molestation or rape
- A spirit tie can be created through any type of abuse, whether physical, mental, or emotional; especially long term abuse
- Crisis and trauma
- The bond of gang members
- Close ties through societies, organizations, or even places like the local pub

- Any shared experiences that create emotional ties or makes one dependant upon anther such as war, illness, or disability

- Through any person who has taken or been given control over the life and emotions of another. This can be any one in authority

SPIRITUAL PIRACY:

A door is very often opened to the powers of darkness when one suffers a traumatic experience, a major crisis of some kind. It can be either physical or emotional; or when one suffers great loss. This loss can come in many ways; through rejection and/or abandonment. It can come through the loss of a loved one by death. Even the loss of a lifetime dream or vision for the future can cause such deep suffering that a door can then be opened in the spirit realm. Often it is in the midst of great crisis such as a major accident, molestation by a family member or trusted friend, or rape which violates the whole person that doors are opened to the powers of darkness and spirits enter in. It is at such a time that an armed invasion of the soul can take place. It is spiritual piracy. It is the strongman and he is armed. He comes for only one purpose, to kill, steal and destroy.

When I worked in Hollywood with prostitutes I found that almost every girl or woman I spoke with had been raped or molested. Rarely did I ever meet anyone who was just out on the streets selling their body because they chose that as their profession. Most often with the sexual abuse spirits entered in. The victims were driven either

210

by sexual desire or by hatred and bitterness and wanted to control others by the use of their body. Both of these extremes are definitely sexually unclean spirits in operation.

As believers we must know what is ours before we can claim it. We must have a full understanding of all that Christ purchased for us on Calvary and we must be willing to war for what is rightfully ours.

WHAT CAN I DO TO BREAK SPIRIT TIES?

- We must come before God and repent of any sin on our part that would bind us to another person in the spirit in any ungodly way.
- We must repent in particular of any sexual relationship(s) that we have had with any person or persons we were not married to.
- Our world has become so secular and driven by sex that many people have given themselves over to promiscuity.
- Sexual sin is rampant. It has become so commonplace that even our young children have begun to think that promiscuity is normal.
- For this reason a person may not be able to remember names attached to individuals or even able to remember every incident.
- Or perhaps time has dulled the memory and names and places were forgotten.

Sins Of The Fathers

- But in an effort to be free, we must sincerely confess whatever we can remember and ask God to forgive us of any incidents that we have forgotten.
- Ask God to break all ungodly spirit ties with any sexual partners you were not married to.
- Ask God to break off all ungodly spirit ties if you were ever a victim of molestation or any form or sexual abuse
- Ask God to loose you from any ungodly restraints against your person or personality such as emotional control.
- Ask God to lose the other person(s) from these spirit ties.
- Ask God to forgive the other person(s) and begin to do a deep work in their life as well.
- Ask God to heal your heart
- Ask God to forgive and heal you for your part in any of these sins that tied you to another person with a spirit or soul tie and ask God to forgive and heal them as well.

CHAPTER FIFTEEN

LET'S TALK ABOUT DELIVERANCE

Let me say at this time that deliverance can take place at any time and in any way. Someone may lay hands on you and pray for you or a deliverance can take place privately just between you and God in the solitude of your own home during a quiet time or a prayer session. That is how I received most of the deliverance in my life, although from time to time, God used another person to minister to me.

When I lived in another state I belonged to a very large congregation of several thousand people. On a regular basis we had nights of worship. They were glorious and I always looked forward to them. For hours on end we would simply worship God. One evening I came in early in order to find a good seat because it was always crowded. I found a nice seat in the beginning of the second section of the church. It was toward the front and I could see everything and everyone. As the church filled up I noticed an older black

Sins Of The Fathers

woman enter. I watched her find a seat closer to the front and turned my attention to others who were coming in.

After about an hour and a half of worship there would be a fifteen minute intermission so everyone could run out to the bathroom, get a drink of water or just stretch. People began to make their way out of the sanctuary. Suddenly, I had tunnel vision. All I could see was this one little woman. I heard the Lord say to me, "Go, hold that woman in your arms."

That is all He said to me, nothing more. I had learned long before this that whatever God says is exactly what He means. He did not tell me to talk to her or do anything except to hold her in my arms. So I walked over to her and took her by the hand. I drew her to her feet and placed my arms squarely around her shoulders and pulled her close. The moment I did this I felt like I was locked onto her. I knew I was not to let go. When I first touched her it felt like a magnet was between us holding us together in a very powerful way. I held her like that for a very long time. In fact I held her like that throughout the whole intermission. Soon people were coming back into the sanctuary and finding their seats but I still could not let go of her. The music began and I wondered what she thought. Finally I felt a release and pulled away from her. I did not say a word; I simply walked back to my seat, sat down and entered into worship again. I thought nothing more of it.

The next evening I arrived early and saw the same woman enter the church again. During the intermission the same thing happened.

Sins Of The Fathers

God told me to go to her again and hold her in my arms. I felt a little silly about it since I had held her so long the previous night, but I made my way over to where she was seated. I pulled her to her feet with a smile and clasped my arms around her shoulders again. When I touched her again it was the same as the night before. I could not let her go. I held her again through the whole intermission. Finally the intermission ended and worship began. Then I felt the release. I let her go, smiled at her and walked back to my seat. On the third night the very same thing happened, only this time I was embarrassed. The whole time I was holding her so tightly in my arms I was having a war going on inside of me. All kinds of thoughts were hammering away at my mind. I wondered what she thought and what others might think as well. I wondered if I was really hearing God or not. I wondered what was going on. Finally and none too soon, the intermission ended and I was glad because this night I really felt like I was acting very strange. The worship began but I still could not let her go. I did not know what to think now. Suddenly from deep within me I felt the most terrible pain I have ever felt. It felt like there were meat hooks tearing up my body on the inside. I failed to notice just yet that she was beginning to wail. A deep painful wail began to rise up from somewhere deep inside of her. Very quickly it became a very high pitched wail and now I was certain I would finally be thrown out by the ushers.

This woman wore a scarf around her neck. She took the scarf from around her neck and wiped her tears from her face and then she wiped my face. She did this several times and still I was unable to let go of her. She was crying out from the depth of her being. Surely people noticed, but no one made any attempt to do anything. She cried, groaned and wailed. She wiped her face and she wiped my face with her scarf. Finally she spoke. I still had my arms around her although now I held her loosely. Until now neither of us had spoken even one word to each other. Now she said, "Many years ago my daughter died a very tragic death. I loved her so much. I used to spend a lot of time worshipping the Lord. But since her death I have not been able to worship. But tonight He has delivered me."

She was free! It was all so simple! Just be obedient and go put your arms around her. You don't have to talk, just hold her close. God is so incredible He can do it any way He pleases and we get to be a part of it!

One time I was sitting in church and all of a sudden, most unexpectedly, I fell over onto my side in the pew. An excruciating pain filled my head. The preacher was not even talking about deliverance. I think he was talking about grace. The pain in my head was beyond anything I had ever experienced. It was unbearable. I could neither sit up nor stand up. I laid there in the pew holding my head waiting for the service to end. Finally, when it was over the pastor walked over to me and asked me what was going on. I told him I had no idea. He asked me if I could walk. I could not. I do not recall how he got me to his car, but he drove me home from church and got me into my house. As I walked through the front door I just knew in my spirit that God was going to deliver me. However, I had no idea what He was going to deliver me from. I went up to my bedroom and sprawled across my bed. The pain in my head was intolerable. I wrapped my arms around myself and rocked back and forth on my bed crying out to God. I tried to put on a worship tape when I first entered the room but within seconds I realized I could not bear the sound of any voice. Rocking myself back and forth, moaning in pain, I began calling on God to set me free. "Oh God, You are my Deliverer. Deliver me, My God. Deliver me. You are the only One Who can deliver me, Lord. You are My High Tower, My Shield and My Defense. Hear my cry and deliver me, Lord."

That was all I could say. I kept on repeating the same words over and over. This went on for perhaps twenty minutes or more while the pain inside of my head made me feel like my head would explode. Then, all of a sudden, the pain subsided as suddenly as it had come. I felt as though clean clear water was running through my soul and filling up my body. I knew it was finished. A joy began to fill me up on the inside and I jumped off the bed onto my feet. I began to sing to the Lord and dance around the apartment. I knew I had been delivered although I had no idea what I had been delivered from.

For the next several days I was so full of the joy of the Holy Ghost. I kept on praising God and thanking Him for the blood of Jesus Christ, my Savior, Who had set me free. I also kept asking Him what it was that I had just been delivered from because I still did not know. After about three days of seeking God, He spoke to me. He showed me that I had been delivered from a spirit of condemnation which had been manifesting in my life since I was a small child.

I was free!

Now once you are freed from any spirit that does not mean that the same spirit will not try to gain entrance back into your life again. Remember that Jesus warned the people who came to hear Him by telling them that a spirit, when it is cast out, will try to gain entrance once again into that same life. If that person who has now been delivered and set free, does not fill that void in their life with the Word and the presence of God, then the unclean spirit will come again and bring with him seven other spirits who are more wicked than himself. (See Luke 11:24-26).

After this deliverance God helped me become aware of thought patterns that did not line up with what His Word said concerning me as His child. Any words that were condemning toward me, any negative thoughts about myself, He quickly highlighted in my mind. He helped me recognize this as a temptation that would bring me in concert with the enemy by coming into agreement with the thoughts the devil was placing in my mind. By coming into agreement and accepting these thoughts I would once again give the devil ground to invade my thoughts and thereby, my life. I had to become aware of what was going on in my mind. Any suggestions that did not agree with the Word of God had to be cast down. I had to take authority over my own mind and submit my thoughts to Christ. God reminded me constantly of His word that said I have the mind of Christ. God still reminds me from time to time to check my thoughts, to listen to those tapes playing inside my head and take control over them.

There is no neutrality in Christ. Jesus explained that anyone who was not with Him was against Him. We must align ourself with Him completely and in every way. In so doing we will find comfort and protection. He alone is our safe place, our hiding place. We must dwell in Him as He dwells in us. We are to be found in Him as He is found in us. Day by day we become conformed to His image more and more. It is like looking into a mirror. We become like whatever we behold or keep in our gaze.

How many individuals have been delivered from demonic powers only to be overcome by them once again at a future date? This is because they have not filled their soul with love for the One Who delivered them. They left a vacuum that the powers of darkness desire so desperately to fill. The doors in the spirit realm must not only be closed to the powers of darkness, but the emptiness must be filled with a pure love for God and His Son, and be filled to capacity with the Word of God. The Word washes us and provides a protection to us because God can speak to us through His word. The Holy Spirit can convict us through the Word. The Word is powerful, a tool in the hand of God to divide flesh from spirit. It is a living Word.

Hebrews 4:12; For the word of God is quick, and powerful, and sharper than any twoedged sword, piercing even to the dividing

asunder of soul and spirit, and of the joints and marrow, and is a discerner of the thoughts and intents of the heart.

The powers of darkness desire a human host that they can manipulate and inspire in order to use that person as an influence and force in the lives of others. A human host is like a base of operations for the demonic.

IF YOU THINK YOU NEED DELIVERANCE:

If you think there are generational spirits or any other spirits operating in your personal life or your family line, begin to call out to God to bring deliverance. It is His heart's desire to see you set free. The price has already been paid in full. It was on Calvary's hill that He purchased your freedom. You do not necessarily need to seek out some person to minister deliverance to you. Jesus is your Deliverer. If you just pray and ask Him to set you free, if you sincerely repent of your own sins and especially any sins which have to do with the matter at hand, you will find He is faithful. He would not pay such an awful price to purchase your deliverance and then withhold it from you. God is a faithful God. Set some time aside, separate yourself and seek God as to what He would have you do. If He wants to provide deliverance through another individual, ask Him to show you who it is that should be the one to minister to you. There are a lot of people who pray all kinds of rambling prayers while you sit there in front of them. They will often rush to get a bucket or a garbage bag and insist you vomit, spit, yawn, or make other bodily noises as they pray over you. Unfortunately, very often when it is all over with, you go away just the same as when you came. But now you have an additional problem; you wonder what went wrong! You blame yourself and think that somehow you fell short.

I am not saying that spirits never manifest in this way or that they do not make it difficult when someone is trying to cast them out. Certainly they resist and they can manifest. What I am saying is that it is never a matter of ritual, or of following a certain formula or recitation of certain prayers. It is the anointing that breaks the yoke.

Isaiah 10:27; And it shall come to pass in that day, that his burden shall be taken away from off thy shoulder, and his yoke from off thy neck, and the yoke shall be destroyed because of the anointing.

Certainly at times the spirits do manifest and try to make it difficult to proceed with the deliverance. Sometimes they talk or shriek or throw the person needing deliverance around. And at times people do vomit or whatever. But this is not always the case.

THE CHILDREN'S BREAD:

I do remember one deliverance session at one of the Bible Colleges. It was summer camp and a father came with his deaf mute son. On the second night of the summer camp the evangelist who was ministering called out the young boy and laid hands on him for healing. I am not certain what God spoke to the evangelist or showed him, but the boy went back to his seat unchanged. Later, after the service, the evangelist asked the father of the child if he could pray for him again. I was still hanging around the tent so I began to watch. The father gave his permission for the evangelist to pray again. This time the evangelist took authority over a deaf and dumb spirit and immediately the young boy began to manifest demonic activity. His body became rigid. I don't know if he was levitating or not, but he was in the air and three or four men, deacons I suppose, rushed over and grabbed him. They held onto him by arms and legs and they had a fight on their hands. The evangelist bound the spirit that was tormenting the child and continued to call the spirit out of the boy. The child screamed and carried on terribly and finally fell to the ground in a heap. He seemed unconscious but within just a few seconds he was roused and he began to speak out loud. It was obvious he could now both hear and speak. I for one was astounded at this great miracle.

Incidents like this take place regularly in other countries, especially third world countries because so much voodoo and witchcraft is practiced in many of those countries. Generally, people who live in these places have a clear understanding of the spirit realm and of the working of evil spirits.

I have received deliverances from spirits on more than one occasion and I am so very grateful for it. I recall after the deliverance I just spoke of earlier, when I was set free of a spirit of condemnation. The following Sunday morning I asked the pastor if I could share what God had done for me. He gladly agreed. He gave me the podium and I shared with great excitement how God had set me free. After the service several people came to me and told me that I should never tell anyone such things again because people would think badly of me. I was really shocked. When I first asked the pastor if I could share I was excited because I thought people would be so encouraged to know that deliverance was provided for all of us no matter what our need might be. I thought they would rejoice with me because I received something I really needed even if I did not know it at the time. But that was not so. I guess they felt it was all right for a young boy who was a deaf mute to be delivered from a spirit because he was a total stranger. But surely not someone from the midst of their own congregation!

As I go from place to place I find it strange to see how various believers feel about deliverance. I often find that they somehow consider it dirty or vile. Actually the spirits that are cast out are dirty and vile, but the deliverance itself is an act of God. Jesus poured out His own blood so deliverance would be available to us. We should shout it from the rooftops.

Mark 7:24-30; And from there he arose and went away to the region of Tyre and Sidon. And he entered a house and did not want anyone to know, yet he could not be hidden. But immediately a woman whose little daughter had an unclean spirit heard of him and came and fell down at his feet. Now the woman was a

Gentile, a Syrophoenician by birth. And she begged him to cast the demon out of her daughter. And he said to her, "Let the children be fed first, for it is not right to take the children's bread and throw it to the dogs." But she answered him, "Yes, Lord; yet even the dogs under the table eat the children's crumbs." And he said to her, "For this statement you may go your way; the demon has left your daughter." And she went home and found the child lying in bed and the demon gone.

Jesus said that deliverance from demonic powers is the **CHILDREN'S BREAD**. It is the **CHILDREN'S** bread!

Have we become a nation of believers that always desires to have its best foot put forward? Have we become a nation of proud doers? Do we care more about what others think of us than we do about pursuing God and receiving what He has purchased for us? Have we become a nation of believers who make a pretense of worshipping God while we deny His power? Are we so proud that we cannot humble ourself enough to admit we need what Jesus purchased for us? Instead of being humiliated by deliverance, perhaps we should be humiliated by our arrogance and self righteousness.

CHAPTER SIXTEEN

WHAT ARE SOME OF THE BIBLICAL CURSES?

The Bible lists many different curses throughout its pages. Here are some of the curses pronounced in Scripture for various sin:

DUETERONOMY CHAPTERS 23 THROUGH 30:

- Fear, terror, cowardice
- Worry, your heart failing for fear of what is to come
- God turned against you as though He were your enemy
- Loss of children for one reason or another, either death or rebellion. Watching your own children go into captivity through drugs, alcohol, gambling, or promiscuity
- Waiting for your children to return to you. Scripture says your eyes fail with longing and looking for the return of your children

Sins Of The Fathers

- Your labor spent in vain (putting your money in a purse with holes)
- Inability to succeed no matter what you do. Lack of success in everything you put your hand to. No matter how hard you work you never get ahead. The devourer crouches at your door
- Inability and lack of opportunity to use your gifts and talents
- Constant confusion, mental and emotional illness
- Barrenness
- Depression and despair
- Fear, worry, anxiety and other nervous disorders
- Phobias, fears, heart failure
- Self destruction in many forms including suicide
- Blight on your crops
- Rain withheld
- Burning fever, consumption,
- Fearful and devastating long term wasting sickness
- Malignant consuming diseases
- Accident prone
- Poverty
- Addictions
- Loss of love relationships through divorce, infidelity and betrayal, runaway children
- Multiple marriages and divorces
- Total family breakdown

- There are many curses listed in the Bible for idolatry and witchcraft

AM I GUILTY OF IDOLATRY?

Many believers have committed idolatry in their past and are not even aware of it. Idolatry can be in the form of bowing down physically, mentally, or emotionally to any other god. More basically, it is giving credence or honor to a person or an object made by man such as statues, beads, pictures, candles, pieces of bone, hair, cloth, tarot cards, horoscopes, drugs etc. Idolatry is also honoring any person whether living or dead by placing them in your heart above God. Idolatry is a heart matter. You can bow your heart and mind to any person or object and by so doing, make it the objective of your worship. People are snared when they begin to worship something they consider to be a good thing. An example is given in the book of Numbers when Moses was instructed by God to make an image of a fiery serpent and set it on top of a pole so that those who had sinned could look at it and be healed. This was a miraculous event. The serpent on the pole was lifted up so that all the children of Israel could see it, even in the farthermost regions of the camp. This signifies that when Jesus was lifted up, it was for everyone. Even for those in the most extreme circumstances, even those who were farthest away from Him, even those who had miserably sinned and failed, even for people like me. It was by faith that the healings occurred when they looked at the serpent on the pole just as it is by faith that we are healed. Yet the people made an idol out of the serpent on the brass pole. They worshipped it. They bowed down to it and burned incense to it; which was an act of worship. It was never meant to be worshipped even though it was "a good thing."

Numbers 21:6-9; And the Lord sent fiery serpents among the people, and they bit the people; and much people of Israel died. Therefore the people came to Moses, and said, We have sinned, for we have spoken against the Lord, and against thee; pray unto the Lord, that he take away the serpents from us. And Moses prayed for the people. And the Lord said unto Moses, Make thee a fiery serpent, and set it upon a pole: and it shall come to pass, that every one that is bitten, when he looketh upon it, shall live. And Moses made a serpent of brass, and put it upon a pole, and it came to pass, that if a serpent had bitten any man, when he beheld the serpent of brass, he lived.

II Kings 18:4; He removed the high places, and brake the images, and cut down the groves, and brake in pieces the brasen serpent that Moses had made: for unto those days the children of Israel did burn incense to it: and he called it Nehushtan.

Unfortunately, in our country, we worship so many things. Our children are taught to honor rock stars, movie stars and athletes by mimicking their actions, their behavior and even their dress. This is a hero worship and it is idolatry. Sadly, many and even most children today are not taught to honor the true and living God. They are not even taught to honor their own parents or those in authority. They are being brought up in gross idolatry.

I spoke with a young girl recently who said she was a Christian. I asked her what kind of Bible she read. "I don't have a Bible!" she said.

"You don't?" I asked.

"No! What do I need a Bible for?"

"Well, how can you get to know God and His Word?"

She snapped back at me; "I don't need a Bible to know Him. I just do!"

Okay! I know there are many countries in the world where a Bible is actually inaccessible, but in our own country, they are freely abundant. In our country, of all the places on this earth, we are the ones who **NEED** a Bible. We need to read and understand what it says. Every kind of falderal comes at us bombarding our senses day and night and most of it is meaningless. We no longer seem to have a sense of what is good and what is evil. We have lost the most treasured gift of godly wisdom. We have forced God out of our courtrooms and classrooms and boardrooms. We have become like the people of Nineveh whom God said did not know their left hand from their right and could no longer discern truth from error. They no longer possessed any moral fiber, any idea of what was good or bad, or what was holy or profane. We need to have a good grasp on truth. The only way to find and know truth is through the Word of God and through relationship with Him. But as a nation we have chosen to ignore Him. God decided to destroy the whole city of Nineveh and everyone in it because its people had closed their eyes and ears to God and chosen their own way. However, they had enough sense to hear the Prophet Jonah and repent. God relented and spared them.

God upbraided the great Prophet Jeremiah at one point because he was not discerning. God told him to separate what was holy from the profane. What does the word profane even mean? It is not a word we hear anymore. Profane means to take something that is holy and make it common. That is what has happened in our churches and in our people, because we can no longer discern what truth is. We have begun to accept anything that comes down the pike in the name of glitz and glamour and flamboyance. It seems that we are always looking for something new, some new tidbit, some new word to make us shiver with delight and making idols out of personalities. But the anointing goes so much deeper and the anointing is what we must be searching out.

On several occasions I had the opportunity to hear a woman who had been imprisoned and tortured in another country for her faith. She was small framed and frail looking. She appeared to be much older than her years but her faith was rock solid. She said that she felt sorry for us in the United States because we had so much in the way of books, C.D.'s, conferences, tapes, Christian television programming and so on, but we lacked relationship with Jesus Christ. She said our churches were showy and so were many of our preachers, and yet there was so little bread. She said that everywhere she went, the gospel had already been so watered down, that it was lacking truth and lacking substance. She told me that our people are for the most part on a starvation diet and lukewarm in their faith. They take their faith for granted, and make idols out of the ones who were sent to bring a message of hope and repentance. She said that in her country they had none of these things we had and they were violently abused if they were found to be believers. Yet their faith was strong and true. She told me that the believers in her country prayed for us. She said they feared for us because of our lukewarm half heartedness and because of a lack of reality and substance in our relationship with the Father and His Son.

Idolatry can be building a shrine to a saint or burying a statue in your yard to gain the favor you desire. It can be wearing certain pieces of jewelry or medallions. In certain countries food and drink offerings are set out for the gods daily and various animals are worshipped. Idolatry takes many forms. In America we have been blessed by God. In the past God has put His hand on us and made us very prosperous as a nation, and in return we have become more creative with our personal gods. We rarely bow down to our personal gods anymore, or set them on a shelf to be displayed and admired, or give them a place of honor in our homes. Now we worship our gods in the arena of sports. We worship material goods, name brands, wealth, reputation, position and scholarship. We worship the work of our own hands and we often worship our self and each other.

We can also practice idolatry by placing another person on the throne of our heart. Anyone or anything we put before or above God is practicing idolatry. We can make idols out of a loved one, a mate, or one of our own children. We can make an idol out of a friend, a pastor, a professor or anyone else.

THE CURSE OF BARRENNESS:

I am not going to speak about each of the curses I listed but I want to share about barrenness. Generally speaking, barrenness is a curse. I have had opportunities to pray with young women who were unable to conceive. They asked me if they were under a curse of barrenness. I in turn, asked them if they had an abortion in the past. Some said "yes" and others said "no." If they said yes to that question then I would ask them to pray a sincere prayer of repentance and renounce the works of darkness. At this point I never had a single woman, no matter what age, come to me for this purpose without a clear understanding that abortion is murder. The moment I asked if they had ever had an abortion they could no longer rationalize it in their own mind. The Spirit of the Lord brought understanding and conviction and there was no longer any diminishing of their sin in their own eyes. Each one understood the depth of their sin. After they repented of their sin and renounced the works of darkness I took authority and broke the curse off of them because the Bible clearly indicates a curse for the sin of murder. Abortion is a sin of murder as much as if a screaming child was offered into the burning arms of the god Molech.

Ezekiel 20:26; And I defiled them through their very gifts in their offering up all their firstborn, that I might devastate them. I did it that they might know that I am the Lord.

God says here that because of their idolatry and sensuality he closed their womb. The Hebrew word used here for "desolate" is very interesting. It is "shamem" which is pronounced shaw-mame'. It means to be devastated or stupefied. It also means to be astonished, to come into desolate places and to lie wasted. That is exactly what abortion does to one's soul; it brings one into desolate or waste places mentally and emotionally. An abortion definitely affects one's mind and emotions.

If the one being ministered to responds that they had never had an abortion then I ask if anyone else in their family line ever had an abortion or was barren. Just because abortion was not always legal does not mean that women did not do it. Very often it was the case that they knew of someone else in their family history that either had an abortion or was barren for some unknown reason. So we would come into agreement in prayer and pray a prayer of identificational repentance for the sins of family members or past generations. Then we would pray to break the generational curse of barrenness.

In some cases the woman simply could not conceive even though there had been no abortion and there appeared to be no medical reasons. In these cases all the rest of their family members had no difficulty with conception or bearing healthy children, so there appeared to be no reason for the barrenness. I simply prayed a blessing over their womb and asked God to open it. Every one of the women I prayed for conceived within a period of several months time. One woman had two sets of twins and several other children in the years to come. She joked that maybe I shouldn't have prayed quite so hard.

On the other hand, just like everyone else, Christians are subject to contagious diseases or certain physical maladies because of improper nutrition, hygiene, lack of exercise, improper care of their body, an accident, unhealthy living conditions or unhealthy lifestyle, just as much as sinners are. Also there are hereditary influences in families. However, if it is a curse, it can be broken through the blood of Jesus Christ.

CHAPTER SEVENTEEN
WITCHCRAFT AND THE OCCULT

In Hawaii I saw a priest standing on the edge of a cliff dressed in his very ornate island priestly garb. I asked someone standing nearby what he was doing. I was told he was calling in the sharks. He was calling out to them wherever they were in the midst and the depths of the ocean and calling them to come into the shore. As he called to them they did come in to the shore. I actually saw them coming in. I was told that the little pillars of pebbles along the roadside were offerings to the island gods or the mountain god. Often there were coins placed between the little pebbles or bits of food offerings. I was warned that if you should touch one or remove it or take any part of it, a curse would come on you and your family. I was also told it was not wise to take any sand or stones from the island because a curse would come on you if you did.

When I was in Africa I found there are still many who practice various forms of witchcraft. In the open markets, in rural villages, and in the privacy of their own homes, witchcraft is practiced and often it is mixed with Christianity. There are many curses in the Bible regarding the practice of witchcraft. In the United States we practice witchcraft on a regular basis and in many different ways. It is not relegated to the rural villages of Haiti or Africa.

One day as I was in the open market in Africa, I was going down a long set of stairs out into the streets. A woman walked up behind me put her hand on my shoulder. She slipped her hand momentarily into the inside of my blouse at the shoulder. I thought a strap was showing and she tucked it in. I couldn't think what else it could be that she would be touching me and putting her fingers inside of my blouse at the shoulder. It both startled me and made me nervous to have a complete stranger touching me this way. So I turned, smiled and said, "thank you!" and hurried on.

When I got to the bottom of the stairs a woman I was with turned and asked me what had just happened. I told her I thought the woman who was behind me must have tucked my strap back inside the shoulder of my blouse. The woman was horrified that she had touched me and told me she was a witch and had just put a curse on me. Immediately we both prayed and broke the curse.

I didn't even know this woman who was behind me on the stairs! I cannot imagine why she picked me except that the darkness knows the light! Remember? I said that the enemy recognizes you and he recognizes power and authority if you walk in it.

Several years ago I lived in a rural area in another state. There was a coven that met in the woods behind my house. I could hear them on the full moon chanting and making every kind of noise and sound in their worship. I also heard screams of animals as they were tortured. Usually it would wake me about two in the morning. I would stand at my window and pray in tongues as they continued through the night. One Sunday afternoon after coming home from church I decided to venture into the woods to see what I would find. I had spent a great part of the night before walking or standing by my bedroom window praying in tongues while this unholy worship went on all through the night. For a great portion of the night I could hear a dog screaming in misery. So after Church that morning I ventured toward the woods just a few feet from my back kitchen door. As I got near the edge of the woods I heard God speak to me and say; "Do not go in there!"

I turned around immediately and headed back into my house under the fear of God. He told me absolutely not to go in the woods. There was no way I was going to disobey. It was not uncommon to see witches and warlocks walking down a particular country road in that area, going to their meeting place. They would walk alone sometimes and at other times they would be in groups, each one wearing their long black gowns and sometimes with a man wearing a large pentagram on a chain around his neck.

Some people didn't take it seriously, but I did. Desecrated animals were often found in the pastures and woods and the police did investigate it regularly.

Sins Of The Fathers

I owned a shop in a very small town selling herbs and vitamins. On a regular basis, witches came into my shop wanting to purchase herbs to make potions and such. For this reason I did not order or stock whole herbs.

On one occasion I was confronted by a warlock who came into my store and decided he wanted to change the contents of the bottles in my shop. He walked in at the same time as two other women came through the door. I do not know if they were together or not. The two women separated one to either side of the shop and it came into my mind to watch them for shoplifting. I not only sold herbs and vitamins in the shop but I also had devoted one half of the shop to antiques and very fine and expensive hand made jewelry. So I wanted to be aware of them and what they were up to. The man came forward and stood before me. He was very well dressed and wore a huge medallion on a long chain over his expensive looking white sweater. He extended his arms out in front of him about eye level and began to rub his thumbs and forefingers together while he kind of hummed a single note. I decided right then I was not going to even ask him what he was doing, I hoped he would just go away. But of course, he didn't! Finally after a few minutes, when I could no longer ignore him and pretend he wasn't there, I asked him what he was doing. Still rubbing his thumbs and fingers together and humming the one note, he said he was taking in the essence. The essence of what? The essence of everything in the shop was his reply. That was about enough for me. I went back to my work before me and hoped he would just leave now. Instead he turned and headed toward the long shelves of vitamins and herbs. He stood in front of some of them for quite a while and continued doing the same thing; rubbing his thumbs and forefingers together while emitting this low grade single note sound. Finally, after several minutes I could not take it any longer so I walked over to him and asked if there was anything I could do to help him find what he needed. He told me that he was taking in the essence of everything on the shelves and he was changing the contents. He assured me that my business would immediately escalate and I would be made rich in a very short time. At that point we began what turned out to be a very long and intense spiritual standoff. I told him he absolutely could not change anything in the shop. I forbid him to do so and told him that he needed to leave immediately. That is when he turned and stood nose to nose with me demanding to lay hands on me because there was an illness that was resident in my body. He saw it in the spirit realm. This "seeing" was real but I can tell you that it was not by the power of the Holy Spirit that he had this information. His "seeing" was through a demonic power, of course. He tried to convince me to let him lay hands on me for healing. I have no doubt he possessed the power through demons to heal, at least temporarily, but not without further demonic influence on the person he laid hands on. But that power, that seeing, was definitely not of God. I kept on quoting Scripture to him and demanding that he leave my shop. I could feel the power of the Holy Spirit in me, on me and all over me, feeding me the words to speak to him. I never even would have thought to say the bold things that I said to him apart from the power and boldness of the Holy Spirit. He did not leave easily, but finally he did leave. I was amazed at the altercation that had just taken place and the power of God to stand in the face of such demonic challenge. I immediately called a friend and asked her to come and together we prayed through the whole shop asking God to cleanse it from any demonic power or manifestation.

Whatever happened to the two women who walked in the door with him? I have no idea. In the midst of our confrontation my eyes were glued on him and never left him for a moment. I completely forgot about them. I did check later on to see if any of the expensive jewelry was missing but I really could not tell to be honest. Perhaps they were not with him and got frightened when they witnessed the confrontation. In any case, when I looked around they were gone. I never saw or heard them leave and I never saw any of them again. Perhaps they were practicing witches who were attending him and praying through the whole event. Perhaps they were demonic spirits manifesting in the flesh, as I have seen many times in the past. I just do not know.

On another occasion I looked up from my counter where I was doing some bookkeeping and noticed a slight framed woman wearing a scarf over her head doing voodoo on my shop window. She was muttering, chanting and carrying on. I chased her away and prayed through the shop.

I walked into a gas station one afternoon and went to the counter to pay for my gas. There in front of me stood a warlock dressed in his long garb with a huge pentagram on a large chain around his neck.

It seemed for a while like I was seeing witches and witchcraft everywhere around me. Coincidence? Witchcraft is much more common than you might want to think. I do know several men who were warlocks who are now saved and serving Christ.

So very many people are deceived and drawn into witchcraft because they seek power. Some are looking for excitement or simply looking for something new. Perhaps they tried the church at one time or another. Maybe they heard about the power of God in the Church but they did not see it. Or perhaps they went to a church a couple of times and got hurt or offended. Perhaps they got turned off because of religion. They didn't see relationship, they only saw religion. The Church in the United States of America has grown sleek and lazy. Perhaps they noticed it was full of teaching, full of the operational gifts, and full of itself. It grew to be lukewarm and complacent. The Church sat down in the middle of the race and decided to rest a while because they were content and comfortable. For the last many years it appears they passed out and were down for the count. It has not been asleep as some thought, it was actually comatose. Why? Because they grew fat on religion and overfed with lots of head knowledge but little relationship.

Sins Of The Fathers

Because they have not been busy **DOING** what they have been called to do! They still gave money and lots of it, but how many have sold out for Christ? How many have completely surrendered their life over to God and taken on His will while laying down their own? How many have been willing to pay the price, to count the cost of complete surrender? Complete surrender means giving up your own way, your own thoughts, and surrendering your life in order to do things God's way, by His power and in His timing. That means a real dying to self. It is a humbling process. Death is always humbling! Death to self is the great equalizer.

Recently I had an opportunity to speak with two groups of youth. The first group was in high school, the second group was made up of middle schoolers, kids up to twelve years old. I desperately wanted to warn them of the dangers of mysticism, witchcraft, new age and the occult. It is all around them. A small child cannot watch a cartoon on television without being inundated with witchcraft in every form. It has even crept into our churches and actually is being practiced within our churches and no one is speaking out against it.

Many children have magic in children's church or Sunday school. But children cannot discern good from bad, real from imaginary. So filling their mind with even imaginary magic is setting them up to be deceived. Also, there is so much on television and in the movies that leads the children right into the realm of witchcraft and the occult. So very often they are led into it while being held by the hand of their own parent.

Sins Of The Fathers

I was amazed how many of the kids responded when I asked if they had ever played with a Ouija board, took part in a séance, had their palms read, or had ever taken part in any type of witchcraft ritual. It has become so commonplace to this generation of children that they thought nothing of it until I began to share with them about the open doors for the powers of darkness to enter into their life. Most of the children from both age groups raised their hands, even the very youngest kids. They saw no danger in it at all. Then I asked how many had friends who were involved in actual witchcraft, meaning they openly touted themselves to be a witch or a warlock and practiced casting spells. Many of the kids raised their hands. Some had family members involved. And we wonder why our children are having such a hard time. Who is holding back the scourge? Who is drawing a line? Who is speaking up in the churches?

I got to pray with a lot of youth that evening from both groups. Some were terrified because of poltergeist activity in their own homes. Some were afraid because of things their parents were involved in. Some asked for prayer for their brother or sister and many were afraid for their own soul and wanted to repent and be cleansed. Even several weeks after this meeting, kids were still calling me at my home and asking to make an appointment with me to be able to pray this stuff off of them. I am just amazed and frustrated that no one is talking about this from the pulpits!

If anyone in your past generations was involved in witchcraft or any form of the occult, there will be attending spirits that continue to

243

pass on through the following generations looking for a host or hosts to inhabit in the family line. This must be repented of and broken off. A cleansing must take place.

While in a church in a third world country, I was calling the people to come up for prayer. I raised my arm to motion for people to come forward. When I did this, suddenly a woman went flying through the air at full speed above the heads of those sitting on the benches. I could not believe my eyes. I had never seen anything like this in my whole life. The woman landed near my feet. I was stunned, absolutely unable to move. My feet were nailed to the floor on the spot where I stood. My mouth was wide open and my eyes were huge. I think my arm was still suspended in mid air.

She lay as though she was dead for a moment. Then she began to roll back and forth with such force and power that she couldn't be controlled. The velocity that propelled her was ripping her clothes right off her body. She was being stripped naked by these forces that controlled her body. Several deacons or men from the congregation ran forward and tried to catch her and wrap her clothes around her, but her body moved so fast they could not catch her or even hang onto her. She shrieked and screamed and I think I was still standing there dumbfounded. Finally, after some time about four of five of the men were able to subdue her enough to gather her up, arms and legs flailing, and carry her screaming and spitting to a back part of the church. You could hear her cursing and blaspheming and you could hear them commanding the spirits out. Finally, after quite a

Sins Of The Fathers

long time, they all came walking back into the church. You could see there had been a mighty battle. Her face and hair were all dirty from the struggle, her clothes were in shreds, but she was free, smiling and praising God!

While driving down the roads in Africa I saw more than one witchdoctor barefooted and dressed in his reeds and leaves with beads around his wrists and ankles; shaking bones, waving his arms, pointing his fingers and muttering as I drove by.

What does Scripture have to say about it? Scripture tells us that witchcraft is associated with idolatry and demonic powers. Any time we are involved in any form of witchcraft we have opened ourselves up to the powers of hell. The young girl who followed Paul around was possessed with a spirit of divination. Now it is interesting to note that everything she was saying was true. She was not lying about these men or disparaging them in any way. She was speaking truth about them. Then one might ask, "Okay, what is wrong with it then, if she was speaking truth?"

Acts 16:16; And it came to pass, as we went to prayer, a certain damsel possessed with a spirit of divination met us, which brought her masters much gain by soothsaying.

There were three things wrong; first of all the information was coming from an evil spirit. While she was going through the streets following Paul, her proclamations were meant at first to distract others who would be willing to hear the apostle speak and open up

245

their heart to God. It was meant to draw them away from him. The spirit within her was standing in contest with this apostle and vying for the attention of the people. Second, this prophetic voice from hell was meant to equalize its standing with God and the apostle by showing the people that true words and information can also come from other means, in this case from the powers of darkness. Does that make sense? The powers of darkness often fortify their standing by speaking truth or at least a smattering of truth. This causes people to place their trust in them. The third thing is that anyone with strong discernment can tell the difference between the Spirit of God and unclean spirits. There is peace and purity in the Spirit of God working through men, but there is a completely different feeling when listening to one who is inhabited by an unclean spirit, even if they are speaking truth. If you have strong discernment, everything inside of you goes off; bells and whistles. You cannot ignore it. It is the Holy Spirit warning you that all is not what it appears to be. So anyone in the crowd who was following after Paul could also hear the young woman proclaiming this fact. If they had discernment they would be able to pick up on the difference. If they did not have discernment they would not understand. That is exactly what the unclean spirit was trying to do; to throw them off, to bring confusion, to muddy the waters. To mentally and emotionally put Paul in the same category with this young woman in the mind of anyone who was following after. To put them both in the same category and count them as the same, when clearly Paul was filled with the Holy Ghost and the young woman was filled with the devil.

When spirits, demons, would appear to me before salvation, they would often give me messages that were at least partial truth. Partial truth was the hook that always pulled me in further. In the beginning these appearances or apparitions terrified me, but they also puzzled me. When I was first being drawn in, I did not believe in devils or demons or ghosts or any such thing, but as time went on I began to say to myself; "There has to be something to this, because what they told me is true," or "What they said actually happened now."

As I puzzled over this and contemplated the truth of the message I was given, I would be sucked more and more into darkness. That is how a demon posing as an angel of light often works. This entity will often come speaking partial truth to a person which draws this person further into the works of darkness. Now, not always! Sometimes everything they say is actually a lie! But sometimes in order to draw a person in, they will give partial truth in order to deceive this person and draw them deeper into the works of darkness. It is the hook in their jaw to lead them into bondage.

The word divination in Greek is actually rendered as the spirit of the python. So we clearly see that a spirit or multiple spirits attend such people and it is the spirit or spirits that are operating in and through them, divining or even performing signs and wonders. The person through which these spirits operate becomes a medium or a host for them.

I Samuel 28:7; Then said Saul unto his servants, Seek me a woman that hath a familiar spirit, that I may go to her, and enquire of her. And his servants said to him, Behold, there is a woman that hath a familiar spirit at Endor.

The witch of Endor was a necromancer. A necromancer is either one who believes they are able to communicate with the spirits of the dead or pretends that they are communicating with the spirits of the dead. What they are really doing is communicating with an entity of a familiar spirit. A familiar spirit is a demonic being. So a necromancer or a medium is one who believes or pretends to converse with the dead through a demonic spirit with the end result of obtaining information that will reveal something of the past or to try to influence and affect the future. It is conjuring of spirits and it is divination. A necromancer is a witch, a channeler (one who channels spirits), or may be called a medium, a fortune teller, or a diviner.

All of these activities are strictly forbidden through Scripture.

Leviticus 19:31; "Do not turn to mediums or necromancers; do not seek them out, and so make yourselves unclean by them: I am the Lord your God."

What exactly is a wizard? A wizard is one who conjures spirits, or in other words, someone who believes they can bring up the ghosts of the dear departed as we just talked about. This person is also a necromancer. However, these are not spirits of the dear departed as it appears on popular television shows. They are not ghosts, but they are demonic spirits who have information regarding the departed. Again, this can be a familiar spirit. This is information that the demons acquired of the individual while they were alive on earth.

Leviticus 20:6; "If a person turns to mediums and necromancers, whoring after them, I will set my face against that person and will cut him off from among his people."

All of this type of demonic activity was strictly forbidden and the penalty was death. God drove the prior inhabitants of the land of Israel out because of their witchcraft and idolatry. Then He strictly warned the children of Israel not to partake in any of these witchcrafts. He did not want His people polluted in the same manner. Witchcraft in any form defiles us mentally, emotionally and spiritually. We should not watch these things on television, or read books that glorify such activities. By so doing we allow ourselves to be tantalized and drawn into the world of the powers of darkness.

Many times and at all hours of the day and night young people would come to my door just to visit. Very often at the door I would welcome them and say something like; "You can come in, but that has to stay outside. You cannot bring that in my house."

"That" most often referred to a book they held, a horror story, a video, an album or C.D. they held in their hand. I welcomed them but made it very clear they could not bring anything into my house that was in any way attached to or glorified the demonic.

Deuteronomy 18:10-12: There shall not be found among you anyone who burns his son or his daughter as an offering, anyone who practices divination or tells fortunes or interprets omens, or a sorcerer or a charmer or a medium or a necromancer or one who inquires of the dead, for whoever does these things is an abomination to the Lord.

An observer of times is an enchanter, a soothsayer or a sorcerer. A charmer is one who uses spells or potions, one who is in league with the powers of darkness. A soothsayer is a fortune teller, a prognosticator, one who tells fortunes or future events through the knowledge and use of evil spirits. This is distinguished from the prophetic gift of the Holy Spirit because it is done with the aid of evil spirits, demonic spirits.

This type of prognostication can be very accurate at times because demons do have certain knowledge of people, their habits, their character and sin, their lifestyle, choices and desires.

Divining is fortune telling. It means to use dice, bones, tea leaves, palm reading, astrology, the zodiac, or any other occult means to determine or divine an answer or solution through the help of demonic entities. In Biblical times divination was done with statues, images, rods, cakes, wine or other food and drink offerings. Also used were pebbles, stones, rods, or the position of the sun, moon or stars, or by observing the entrails of humans or animals. It was most often done through certain rites or rituals. The Old Testament speaks of these types of divining clearly.

All of these activities are certainly ancient black arts, so called, because they rely on the powers of darkness for their success. All of these so called arts are a work of the flesh, an outworking of the carnal nature of man apart from God. Without repentance and a thorough cutting off of all the works of darkness there can be no deliverance. The Bible says the punishment for any witchcraft is death. How then does this affect the succeeding generations of one who has practiced witchcraft without repentance and without a cutting off of the curse?

Isaiah 8:19; And when they say to you, "Inquire of the mediums and the necromancers who chirp and mutter," should not a people inquire of their God? Should they inquire of the dead on behalf of the living?

Galatians 5:19-22; Now the works of the flesh are evident: sexual immorality, impurity, sensuality, idolatry, sorcery, enmity, strife, jealousy, fits of anger, rivalries, dissentions, divisions, envy, drunkenness, orgies, and things like these. I warn you, as I warned you before, that those who do such things will not inherit the kingdom of God.

Sins Of The Fathers

Water witching, which is also witchcraft, was very common in many countries including the United States. Many of our past relatives used this method not only to find water, but gold or minerals buried in the earth as well as oil. This is divination.

CHAPTER EIGHTEEN

YOU SHALL NOT SUFFER A WITCH TO LIVE

Exodus 22:18; Thou shalt not suffer a witch to live.

I will tell you of a woman I knew. Her name was Colleen. I was a young mother with two young children, divorced, and a working woman. Colleen was also divorced and had one son. One day she walked into the office where I worked where she apparently had an appointment for an interview with my boss. I knew right away she would be hired because she was extremely pretty. She was also a practicing witch.

I did not know the Lord at that time. I also did not particularly believe in the supernatural; not in angels, and not in witches, ghosts, mediums or any such thing. However, as I said, I knew she would be hired because she was very attractive and my boss had an eye for the ladies. After a brief interview he brought her to my desk, introduced her to me and told me to take her around, show her where her desk would be, show her the coat room and the lunch room, and brief her on her duties. As my boss turned and walked away from the two of us she stood looking at me and got a big smile on her face. She said, "Oh, my gosh! You are the woman I have seen in my dreams all of my life. I have dreamed about you all of my life and I have seen your face in my dreams over and over again. I knew I would meet you one day. I know all about you, I know everything about your life. Your paternal Grandmother's name was Mary and you were named after your maternal Grandmother. You were raised in a lot of different homes. Let's go to lunch together today and I will tell you how I know all this about you."

Until that moment I did not even know that I was named after my maternal grandmother since I had never known her. Growing up I was strictly forbidden to have any contact with my birth-mother's side of the family and to be honest, I was too afraid to try to find out who they were. I was embarrassed and didn't know what to think. I felt awkward but the hook had already been set in my jaw. I wanted to know how she would know anything at all about me, much less the finer details of my childhood.

Over lunch she told me some amazing facts about my own life, some things no one else knew and things I did not think anyone could ever possibly know. Then she told me that she practiced witchcraft. It unnerved me to be honest. I really did not know what to think about all of this. Even when I was a very little girl living with my grandparents, my grandmother always used to tell me things like,

"Don't ever have anything to do with a witch. Do not play with a Ouija board or have your palm read. Don't allow anyone to read your tea leaves or tell your fortune. These things are witchcraft and they are a terrible sin."

I felt very uncomfortable with her even in broad daylight in a restaurant filled with other people, but at the same time a part of me was also strangely fascinated. She was sociable, had a pleasant personality and was an intelligent, well versed woman, but there was still something about her that gave me the creeps. I tried to shake it off.

She told me that she was able to cast spells, read people's minds, and very obviously knew things about people. It all seemed very eerie to me.

We made it through lunch and I decided that she was odd but probably not dangerous, just a bit strange. She began to call me at home after work and wanted to come over and spend time together. Although something inside of me made me want to avoid her as much as possible and I did not really want to be friends with her, I felt compelled by this strong fear, strangely enough, to continue in relationship with her. I was afraid to tell her how I really felt and to be honest I was actually afraid not to be her friend. I tried over and over to rationalize the whole situation. I kept on telling myself that there were no such things as witches and although I could not explain how she knew all about my personal life, and even though

Sins Of The Fathers

I felt so very uncomfortable around her, yet I agreed to allow her to come over to visit myself and my children in our own home.

One thing the devil commonly uses as a powerful weapon against us is fear. Fear is an open door for attack and for an entrance into our lives. So we must remember that fear and faith are in direct opposition to each other. The devil loves to use fear to pressure us and bend our will.

Colleen told me that she was able to read and write backwards and had a gift for fortune telling. One particular day she told me that she was praying over me and my children. She said she was assigning angels into our house to watch over all of us and keep us safe. I felt really creepy about it. She asked me if that was okay with me. Out of fear I said, "Okay, that's nice," quickly changing the subject to something that didn't make me feel so ill at ease.

Right about this time both of my two small children who slept in separate bedrooms on the second floor began simultaneously to have the same nightmare each night. Each child in a state beyond panic, crying, shaking and saying they each woke up to see a woman standing over their bed staring down at them. They would come screaming down the stairs and hide in bed with me hanging onto me for dear life, terrified out of their wits. It would take me some time to calm them down and comfort them so they could go back to sleep again.

Actually, now I know that it was not a nightmare as I thought, but this was clearly a demonic manifestation of a spirit or spirits that had been conjured by a practicing witch. It was a demonic visitation, what one would call an apparition. My two small children were seeing these spirits because they were being conjured. They were the spirits Colleen channeled and assigned to our house, but it would be many long years before I would have any understanding of this.

Colleen stopped me when I came into work the next morning and told me that she knew about the dreams the children were having. She saw my fear about what was happening and assured me everything was all right.

Night after night the children were terrorized. Then the very next day Colleen would stop me at work and tell me she knew about it. She would even give me details about what the children saw or what had occurred in our house the night before. These were details no one could possibly know. It really worried me and made me so nervous. She kept on reassuring me that the children were being protected from the things that were happening in the house by the very angels she had assigned over them so that nothing bad could ever happen to them. But in fact, the reverse was true. It was the assignments she had placed on me and my children and the spirits she had conjured which were causing all the havoc and terror in our house, not to mention the events that soon followed.

One day my oldest child came into the house from playing outdoors and began to have convulsions. There had been no previous medical history of convulsions in anyone in our family and there had been no injuries that would have caused convulsions. My child screamed and cried as she began to convulse screaming that something was trying to get her.

Since I was not saved I had absolutely no idea what to do. I was terrified but helpless. I had no weapons to use in this vicious war that me and my children were involved in. I held my child in my arms and tried to comfort and help her. She screamed and cried begging me to protect her from what she was seeing. I took my child from doctor to doctor trying to find the origin of the continuing convulsions, but after many tests, the doctors could find no source or reason for the malady.

It was not long after these apparitions began to appear that I began to change having unmistakable personality changes. I began to smoke, drink and curse, frequent bars and nightclubs, and began to do all sorts of things I never did before, things that had never even entered my mind previously. My personality completely changed and I began to manifest various behaviors that were very obviously connected to unclean spirits.

All these things were taking place in our home on a regular basis and we were all scared out of our wits, but I kept telling myself and reassuring the children that everything was all right. Since I did not believe in ghosts, spirits, devils, demons, witches or any such thing, there just had to be some rational explanation. That is what I tried to convince myself.

Spirits appeared on a regular basis, not only to me and the children, but also to those who came to our house to visit. Footsteps in the house, objects being moved around, and people appearing out of thin air and then disappearing again, were common occurrences. Those who came to visit would say things like, "Who was that?" "Who was that person who just walked down the hallway?" "Who was that who stood in the window and watched me pull out of the driveway?"

Many people began to see these spirits manifest physically in our house. They always saw the same woman. I was much too frightened to try to talk to anyone about it and anyway, I had absolutely no idea who I could talk to or even what I could say without sounding like I had lost my mind. It all sounded like craziness and I was certain people would think I was mad and should be locked up. I actually began to question my own sanity. I just kept on hoping it would all somehow go away. Some of my friends (none of them were saved), thought it was really cool to be living in a "haunted" house. One even asked to sleep over in one of the children's bedrooms in order to try to make contact with the spirits. All kinds of demonic manifestations took place in the house. This is called "poltergeist activity" and it is straight from the pit of hell. There were noises, sounds, footsteps, pounding, objects being moved and spirits appearing. One of my friends contacted a well known university which studies paranormal activity and tried to get me to set up an appointment with the university to come and study the activity in the house. I refused because it all terrified me. I had become an absolute nervous wreck afraid to be in my own house.

A neighbor whose house was right next door to mine began to knock on my front door fairly regularly yelling at me about the pounding that he said was going on in the attic all night long. He called the police on several occasions and when the police came, they looked around, inspected the house including the attic, inspected all the bedrooms and found nothing. Over and over the man came and knocked on my door telling me that the pounding that went on all through the night had to end. I certainly never heard it and neither did my children. Yet it tormented him.

I deeply loved my children and up until this time I had been a devoted mother. But soon after these manifestations began taking place in our home, I became very harsh and mean to the children. I abandoned them emotionally first, then taking on the characteristics of an abusive personality, I finally abandoned them altogether.

During this time Colleen gave me some lovely and very expensive gifts. Things you would not want to just throw away. I did not know it at the time but these were gifts that were used as a touch point or a point of contact. I believe she used them when she conjured or channeled spirits.

If you have ever gone to have your palm read or have taken part in some other psychic activity, the person doing the reading will often ask you to give them something. It can be a handkerchief, a coin, a hairclip, or an inexpensive article out of your purse or pocket. It does not have to be expensive it simply has to be a personal item. This is a contact point for them to use when they channel spirits.

Finally, the activity within the house became so strong that I could no longer stand it. I was afraid to go upstairs in my own house, afraid to enter the children's bedrooms, and really afraid to go in the basement alone. I was even afraid to be home alone. I always tried to get someone to go with me into the upstairs or the basement but even then I was still so very afraid. I tried to tell myself that it was silly to be so frightened, but I couldn't help it. Things had gotten so bad with demonic activity and apparitions in the house that as a last resort I went to the local church and talked with a priest about it. He was an older priest whom I did not know. He looked and presented himself in a very dignified manner, yet open and friendly. He was horrified when I began to tell him some of the things that were going on. He told me those manifestations in the house were from demons. That did not help me. I was already scared out of my wits. I was actually hoping he would tell me that there was no such thing and I was imagining it all. I wanted some safe reassuring help from him. But he was emphatic about it and very upset and worried for me and my children. He spoke with me at length about it but I doubt that I heard much of what he was saying because I felt locked into this terror without any escape.

I tried to reason with myself some more, rationalize, and explain these things away, but I could no longer deal with the dread fear. I sold the house and moved away as fast and as far as I could. I lost a lot of money on the house, but I needed to get us out. In a short time I pulled the children out of school, packed up the house and moved across the country hoping to start new life. Even though I did not really believe in God, I prayed that whatever it was in the house, that it would not be able to follow us. I prayed that constantly.

I gave notice at work but did not tell Colleen that I was moving or where I was moving to until the very last minute. Then, when I did tell her, it was because I had no choice because everyone at work knew I was quitting my job. I lied to her about where I was moving and told her I would contact her once I was all unpacked and we would get together. I led her to believe I was staying in the same city, just moving into a different apartment and finding another job. Then I moved to the other side of the country. About two years passed in the new state to which we had moved and one night the telephone rang. I picked up the phone. A cold chill ran up my spine as I heard Colleen on the other end of the line. She told me that she also had moved across the country and now lived quite close by in a neighboring state. Within a short time she began sending small but expensive gifts again and once again I was frightened about the prospect of having this person in my life.

Every now and then she called me and suggested we get together but I always found some excuse not to meet with her. One evening she called and begged me to come and visit her at her home. She told me that her oldest son, who was now fourteen, was going to die. She said he was going to die on the coming Easter Sunday morning. I asked her what was wrong with him that he was going to die and she told me he had leukemia. She said that she had to offer him as a sacrifice for her sins; she said, "the first born for the sins of the parents." I did not understand any of this. It made no sense at all to me. In fact, I was certain she was crazy.

Now I was miserable again. All the old fears were overtaking me again; dogging me and making me look over my shoulder all the time. I was afraid of the dark again, and afraid to be closed in any small space or tight place. For example I was afraid to go in the shower and close the shower curtain, it made me feel trapped. I became very afraid of elevators or any closed in space. I felt like someone was behind me all the time. Even when I went to a restaurant I had to have a corner chair so I could look out on everyone and no one could get behind me. I was always looking over my shoulder feeling like I was being followed or like there was someone right behind me. I became terrified of loud noises, quick movements, shadows, and so many other things. I grew to be very nervous and irritable and began to drink more heavily to dull my fears.

She continued to call and ask me to come and be with her on the day when her son would die. I kept trying to get all this out of my mind but I could not. I was torn between feelings of compassion for her because she believed her son was going to die, and my fear of her. In the end I made the trip and arrived at her home on Easter morning. Her son was propped up in bed. Indeed he was dying. I was shocked to find this was all very real because up until now I still tried to convince myself that none of this was really happening. I thought maybe it was possible that she was making it up; or perhaps she was mentally ill. But no, here was this strapping young man lying in bed dying. That Easter Sunday, in the morning, he did die just as she said he would.

I had no idea how to deal with this. I was mystified about the whole thing but not ready to turn to God yet, so I went back home, packed up my things and moved away once again to yet another state. I was suicidal again. In a very short time I became an alcoholic and no longer controlled drinking, it controlled me. I was introduced to drugs at that time and began doing drugs. Spirits continued to manifest to me on a regular basis. In fact, by this time, it had become a fairly common occurrence once again. By now I had sent both of my own children away to live with relatives. It is interesting to note that this is exactly what my parents did with me. I was abandoned by my parents and now as a parent, I had abandoned my own children. I had no idea how to deal with this. The effects of generational sin are so evident if we just look. All this time I still had no idea that doors in the supernatural realm had been opened up through the practice of witchcraft so many years before in my home so many states away from where I now lived. My life lay in ruins. My sin was destroying the lives of my children and making them extremely difficult. The children suffered severe hardship and were deeply wounded and handicapped by my behavior. Our little family had been completely torn to shreds. I was an unfit mother. I had gotten caught up unwittingly in witchcraft through this hellish relationship and as a result of the spirits operating in and through me, we all suffered tremendously. I got so tangled up in sin and I had no way to get out. I still did not know the Lord.

Eventually I got saved. Soon after I was saved God showed me that those were evil spirits that kept appearing to me and my children. It was such a revelation to me. It was all so clear now. I understood! God helped me recognize that those apparitions were demons manifesting into the natural realm. Our lives had been brutally arrested and cut off from the intents and purposes of God by demons. Our lives were infested and infected and almost completely destroyed by witchcraft and the powers of hell. For all intense purposes our lives lay in desperate ruins.

Now I was completely separated from my own children because of sin. How interesting it is that my own birth-mother was separated from her children when they were very young because of sin. Unfortunately she never got to see her children again until just before her death. I know this grieved her heart and possibly, even literally, made her heart sick. She was never restored in relationship with one of her children although she begged to see her only son. God brought me to her several years before she died and gave me the greatest pleasure and blessing which was to lead her to the Lord in salvation. He restored my relationship with her. But is it not interesting to note that she was separated from her own children all her adult life, from the time her children were very young until the time of her death. Now all these years later I was separated from my own children. Surely this was a generational curse operating in our lives and I knew now that I was the one who opened the door for the attending spirits to operate in my life and the lives of my children when I allowed a practicing witch to be a part of our lives.

After much prayer and intercession my children also came to the Lord. Had each one of us not gotten saved, there is no telling what would have become of us. Our lives were out of control and completely destructive. But God came to seek those who are lost and told us that it is those who are sick who need a physician.

There were curses at work and entrenched in our lives and attending spirits in operation. I believe the devil pursues the anointing at the youngest age possible. That is why we must teach our children well. We must be a true guardian over them, over their mind, their heart and their soul. God gives children parents for a reason. We are commanded to raise them up in order that they may know Him and walk with Him and serve Him all the days of their life. This will keep them from the fires of hell. But many parents fail so miserably. Why? Perhaps we don't understand what God's purpose truly is or what our role is meant to be. Or perhaps we just do not take God seriously and we take our mandate for granted. But the devil is very serious about stealing the soul of our children at the youngest age possible.

The modern Church seems to be built on shifting sand. The foundation is called "Love." However, it is not truly love. It is absolutely not loving to allow our children to rule over us, to run the house, to demand whatever their little hearts desire, to run rampant, to be rude and thoughtless, to practice manipulation and learn deceit, to raise themselves or to choose their own way. We are the ones, the parents, who are supposed to lead and guide them. God, forgive us for failing our children so miserably and heal our land. We pray You would turn the hearts of the parents back to the children and remind parents that it is godly and responsible to correct and yes, even chasten our own children. It is our duty to raise up our own children in godliness. We are not to leave it to the schools or the television or their peers to do the work God has placed in our hands.

It is interesting to note that after I and each one of my children were saved and baptized in the Holy Ghost, each one of us were endowed by the Holy Spirit with very strong prophetic gifts; with dreams and visions, seeing into the spirit realm and with a teaching gift as well. The powers of darkness, knowing the gifting desired to pervert those gifts by bringing them under the control of demonic spirits even before any of us were saved and even while my children were very young. But Jesus redeems to the uttermost.

I and my children will always eagerly testify of God's great mercy to us. Each one of us is very aware that He pulled us from the fires of hell that licked at our heels. He began a great work of healing in each of our lives and He stood us up on our feet again. He is a restorer of the breach; the One Who makes all things new.

I also find it very interesting to note that after I was saved I had the opportunity not only to lead my birth-mother to the Lord in salvation, but also some of her sisters as well. As these relatives (the generation before me), got saved and baptized in the Holy Spirit, they also had very strong prophetic gifts and the gift of teaching as well. So again we see that generational heritage runs along family lines. A godly heritage or an ungodly heritage is what we leave to our own children and our children's children and the choice is ours. We can choose life or death.

How many people die for lack of knowledge? How many die without understanding? How many have their lives wiped out and ripped apart because they do not discern and cannot discern because they have no spiritual understanding? They cannot recognize or differentiate between clean and unclean, between holy and unholy. They cannot perceive the works of darkness because they do not know God. How many people that God created with purpose and intent for His glory and for fellowship with Him will go down into hell because they are deceived?

Hosea 4:6a; My people are destroyed for lack of knowledge ....

CHAPTER NINETEEN

A FORTRESS INSIDE OF ME

I was invited to preach at a very large church of several thousand people in a major city. During my message I got off on a rabbit trail and began to talk about being in bondage to sexual sin. I remember saying something like this; "Some churches have sexaholic groups, which I find to be laughable because it is a demonic bondage which allows an unclean spirit to enter into the individual. This individual cannot be set free by sitting around in a circle and telling others in the group about his or her addiction to uncleanness and sexual perversion. This is a demonic spirit that needs to be cast out. The demonic power must be broken and the assignment must be cancelled. This person is in dire need of immediate deliverance and in danger of hurting someone if he or she is not immediately set free. In fact, by sitting around and talking about it with each other, this increases the power and the effect. It does nothing to alleviate the sinner or cut off the sin. In no way does it advance deliverance or freedom."

Sins Of The Fathers

As I was saying all these things, I remember thinking, "Why am I talking about this? How did I get off on this subject?"

I sold a lot of tapes that night and was invited back to speak again the next month.

The next month on my second visit to this marvelous church, I remember that while I was preaching on a completely different subject than on my first visit, I went off on this same rabbit trail again and began to speak about sexual bondage and sex-aholic groups. As I was saying these things I heard this thought inside my head, "Oh, I just talked about this same thing recently somewhere. I wonder why I am talking about this again!"

Then I remembered that it was here, in this very place that I talked about it last month the last time I preached here. It even seemed to me like I was saying the very same words again. I finished what I was saying on that subject and went right back to the topic at hand. Once again that evening I was warmly received. A lot of people came forward for ministry and I sold lots of tapes again that night. Once again I was invited to come back in one month for the third time in three months, to minister to this group.

Each time I was invited back I taught on a different subject. I waited on the Lord to find out what I was to speak on. The third time I was speaking and once again, right in the midst of my teaching, off I went again onto that same rabbit trail. But this time I recognized it was the same words, the same warnings, and the same pleading for those involved to repent of their sins and seek God's deliverance from the bondage of sexual uncleanness.

I was never invited back again after that. A few months passed and then I learned that the person who selected and invited the speakers was also the head of the "Sex-aholic" group that met in the church bi-weekly. Until then I had no idea that they even had a sex-aholic group and that is a good thing, because if I had known, I would have been very reluctant to speak out what the Holy Spirit was giving me to speak. I learned from someone who had been in the group that they sat around and discussed their afflictions with each other week after week, never coming to freedom. They were being taught and convinced that it was a sickness instead of bondage as a result of their continued sin. These men and women believed they suffered from a sickness which was beyond their control and were taught that what they had to do to survive was to try to keep themselves in check, think positive thoughts, reach out to their sponsors for help, live good lives and try to control themselves. Not very effective without bringing the person into even further bondage by opening the door for a controlling spirit or a religious spirit to enter in the fray.

I do wonder how many ever heard what the Lord was saying during those meetings. I am convinced that was the primary reason God opened the door for me to preach in that church on three separate occasions, each a month apart. I do hope someone heard what

He was speaking to them, believed and sought Him for deliverance from their bondage.

IGNORANCE IS NOT BLISS IT'S JUST IGNORANCE:

Ignorance will not be a protection to you. If you are driving 65 miles per hour on a roadway that is specified as a 35 mile an hour zone, and the policeman stops you for speeding, it won't stop him from giving you a speeding ticket simply because you tell him you were ignorant of the speed limit.

II Corinthians 2:11; Lest Satan should get an advantage of us: for we are not ignorant of his devices.

God tells us that His people die because they lack knowledge. What kind of knowledge? Knowledge of God certainly, but more particularly knowledge and understanding of God's ways. Knowledge of God is not enough. Even the devil knows about God and believes in Him. Knowledge of His Word is key to knowing Him and having knowledge of His attributes and His heart. However, without knowledge of the Word, one cannot begin to understand His ways. He tells us clearly that His ways are high above our ways and unless we draw close to Him, how can we ever begin to understand what is in His heart? Do you remember that in Psalm 103:7, God said that the children of Israel knew God's acts but Moses knew God's ways. What does that mean to us? We are not to be like the children of Israel who only knew of God's great miracles but did not really know Him intimately. We are to have an intense and surrendered relationship with our God and in that, we will begin to have an understanding not only of His acts toward men, but also of His ways. (See Hosea 4:1 and Hosea 4:6).

If we have a real relationship with God, we will know what His pleasure is. We will begin to know how He feels about certain things. We will understand what displeases Him. We have the opportunity to know Him intimately, have His direction in our life, and know His ways by drawing near to Him.

Hosea 4:6; My people are destroyed for lack of knowledge; because you have rejected knowledge, I reject you from being a priest to me. And since you have forgotten the law of your God, I also will forget your children.

We see in the last part of the above verse in Hosea, that this ignorance of the knowledge of God and His ways is passed on to our children and then on to their children because our children learn our ways. It is not so much what we say, but it is how we live that impacts the lives of those around us. Our life speaks so much louder than our words. The book of Job tells us that we are a book written that all men can read. So we are to be very careful how we live our life because others are watching and reading that book. We are each called as believers to be priests before our God. We are called to be the priest in our home, but God says because of ignorance and a lack

Sins Of The Fathers

of knowledge that He rejects those without a true knowledge of Him from being His priests.

II Corinthians 3:2; You yourselves are our letter of recommendation, written on our hearts, to be known and read by all.

We can not use our ignorance of Him and His ways as an excuse if we say that we know and serve Him. Jesus told those who followed after Him to hear what He would say to them, "If you admitted that you were a sinner, you would no longer be guilty, but because you say you are sinless, you sin." (My paraphrase, see John 9:41 and I John 1:8).

CHAPTER TWENTY

MENTAL ILLNESS AND ATTENDING SPIRITS

Many years ago, after returning from a mission trip to South America, I came back to my home town. I had sold everything I owned in order to go and so when I returned I had no apartment, no furniture, no bed and no anything.

Of course I needed a place to stay so when a husband and wife from my church invited me to stay with them I was quick to agree. I considered each person in this small home church to be my brother and sister in Christ. I had not previously had an occasion to visit the home of this couple, but I thought I knew them fairly well and felt blessed that they offered to open their home to me. We had gone out many times after church on Sunday and had lunch together. When we were together we talked about God and what He was doing. We never discussed personal matters so I did not know a lot about their personal life. Now I would have an opportunity to get to know them better and I was looking forward to it.

God has allowed me to come into many difficult situations and had told me early on that if I paid attention to the heat, the cold, the damp, the dirt, the bugs, the gangs, the neighborhood, or any of the circumstances surrounding me, I would never accomplish the things He wanted to do in my life.

I remember the very day He told me this. I was sitting in an outdoor chapel on a very humid day in August in Missouri. There was not even a slight breeze. It was about 105 degrees outside. Only God Himself knows what the temperature was inside that chapel. I have to admit I was not being very spiritual that day. I was not used to the blazing heat and the high humidity. The pastor was no doubt giving an excellent sermon as he always did, however this day I was having great difficulty trying to pay attention. Sweat was dripping everywhere. It was running down my face, my neck, my arms, and my back. My hair had long since fallen and I think perhaps even my makeup was melting. I was squirming and totally miserable. That is when I heard the Lord speak to me about needing to be comfortable or wanting to have things a certain way. He told me then that I was to bypass all the outward circumstances and fix my eyes on Him in every situation. I immediately repented and asked Him to help me get past all the outward conditions and teach me how to count them as unimportant in the whole scheme of things.

I always remembered that day. God did something inside of me on that day and helped me to be able to overlook whatever temporary circumstances I was in the midst of. This played an important part in my ministry from then on. I was no longer afraid to go certain places or meet certain kinds of people, or to be put in circumstances that others might consider very unpleasant.

When my friends from church opened up their home to me where I would take up temporary residence, I arrived with an excitement and anticipation, however, short lived. I found the house quite unclean, actually a real disheveled mess to be honest. The couple owned a cat and the cat apparently had no litter box or else couldn't find it or did not know how to use it. I was shown to the upper bedroom where I would sleep and could hang my clothes. There were cat droppings all over the blanket which covered the bed and all over the linoleum floor. There were mouse droppings in the dresser drawers. I took a deep breath, remembered what God had told me about my surroundings and proceeded to scrub and clean the room as best I could. Even though I stripped all the bedding, thoroughly washed and bleached everything, I remember how uncomfortable I was crawling into bed that night. Prayer is such a good thing! If you just pray until you finally fall asleep, things seem to go so much better!

The coming days and nights became a round of house cleaning. Since my church companion had no desire to clean her house I decided I would do it for her. The cat still had free range of the house and there was cat hair along with all kinds of debris everywhere. I cleaned the stove, the oven, the cupboards, the windows, the floors and even scrubbed the walls. I found it therapeutic and it kept me from thinking about the unclean mess I was temporarily living in.

While in South America I lived in the mountains in a two man tent with no running water and no way to bathe except to trek down the mountainside to a nearby river or to a waterfall about every ten days. Once there we; (which consisted of myself and about twenty other missionaries), were able to bathe and wash our clothes. Sleeping on the ground in two man tents led to all kinds of adventures, none of which were particularly to my liking. There were killer bees, scorpions, tarantulas, and all kinds of strange and nasty looking critters that flew, crawled, hopped or jumped everywhere.

I just tried to keep remembering what God told me and my prayer life no doubt increased at that point.

So back at the ranch, I remember one night we were all sitting in the front room talking when the husband remarked to his wife that something in their bedroom smelled bad. This was not really surprising. They talked back and forth for a while and finally she suggested that he should get a flashlight and look around. It was not long before we heard him frantically calling us to come into the bedroom and help him. I followed behind his wife and poked my head into the bedroom to see what was going on. I saw his body stretched half way under the bed. He had extended one arm as far as he could reach and the flashlight was shining under the bed. As I looked around I saw heaps of clothes stacked and piled and thrown everywhere on furniture, on the bed, and on the floor. The room was

Sins Of The Fathers

a disaster. He strained to reach under the bed with grunts and groans and inaudible sounds and suddenly pulled out a dead cat from somewhere beneath the bed. The cat was as stiff as a board and parts of it had been eaten away by something, (something I did not want to know about). He tossed it away from him. I jumped back completely freaked out. He crawled out from under the bed, brushed away the hair balls and dust and then he and his wife had a long discussion about whose cat this might be. It became clear to both of them that it was not theirs. The cat must have crawled in through the broken screen and open window in their bedroom. I simply left the room and went to pray. I am sure I probably prayed for more grace.

Not long afterwards, I was scrubbing walls in the kitchen and trying very hard to be nice to the cat, (the one still occupying the house), when God spoke to me. He said my friend was mentally ill and there was a generational history of mental illness in her family. Surprise?

Just at that moment she walked out of the bathroom in her slippers and nightgown. I turned to greet her. Much to my chagrin, I saw that she was drinking water out of the dirty soap dish from the bathroom. The soap dish had a thick slimy layer of melted soap in the bottom and the slime was running down the front of her nightgown. I guess I was staring at her. She asked what was wrong and I told her that God had just spoken to me minutes before and told me that there was a history of mental illness in her family. Her response to me? "No, don't be silly!"

Okay, I won't be silly, but do you realize you are standing in the middle of the kitchen drinking water out of a really slimy soap dish?

I took her by the hand and said something like, "Let's just take a minute to pray about this."

As I held her hand in mine sitting at that kitchen table God began to reveal things through a word of knowledge. He told me that some past relatives had been mentally ill and in fact more than one had died in a hospital for the mentally ill. Immediately she remembered and recalled an uncle. Then his wife was added to this list and within only a few minutes several other long since dead relatives were included in our growing list. I had already grabbed a paper and a pen and was writing as fast as I could while she considered her dead relatives. At last she admitted that her son was currently, at that moment, locked away in a local mental ward because he had tried to stab her with a butcher knife while she slept.

Oh joy! What fun to be here! And I thought killer bees and scorpions were nasty!

We prayed in agreement, taking authority in Christ and broke the spirit ties to past generations. We repented for the sins of the past generations even though they were long since dead, and even though we really were not sure what their sins might be. Nonetheless, we prayed a prayer of identificational repentance. Then she prayed and repented for her own sins. We prayed the blood of Jesus over her and her own family, over the house and all her future generations.

We broke the power of the curses that had come on this family and called forth God's blessings in place of the curses.

It is interesting to note that within a few days after our prayer session God gave me another place to stay. No, not because I was complaining. I wasn't! God simply arranged a move for me because He had something else for me to do. I believe I was there in that house for one purpose, to alert her and her husband to the fact that their whole family had been bound by generational sin and generational spirits that brought mental illness and to pray God's freedom over their lives.

We can see several things in her story. First of all we can see how believers can live their whole life and do not understand the demonic influences that are controlling their family. We have gotten so good at surviving that we learn how to adjust to the maladies that come into our lives. We take it for granted that this is all a part of what our life is supposed to be. We may try to get free for a time by using the many and varied methods of the world, but after they fail time and time again, we quietly give up and accept the circumstances of our life as our fate.

One other thing I see is that many generations had been affected by various sorts of mental illness. Some were of an unknown nature and origin, but there were a variety of mental illnesses in her past family history which were identifiable. She was able to identify severe depression, manic behavior, schizophrenic episodes, suicide, and a spirit of murder.

Another interesting thing I see in this example is that so many Christians have no idea that demons can still influence their life, their behavior, their thinking and their character even after they have been saved. They do not understand that they must apprehend what Jesus purchased for them. They must take hold of what has been provided in their behalf. This woman and her husband were so used to living this way and seeing their whole family live like this, that even though they attended church weekly, they had no idea that this was not what God intended for them. Many people use the term "dysfunctional" to describe demonic activity in their homes and their own behavior.

Of course I suppose any psychiatrist worth his salt would probably have to tell me that these are not spiritual matters but physical matters. However let us look at a passage of Scripture to see what God has to say about all this.

I Samuel 16:14-23; But the Spirit of the Lord departed from Saul, and an evil spirit from the Lord troubled him. And Saul's servants said unto him, Behold now, an evil spirit from God troubleth thee. Let our lord now command thy servants, which are before thee, to seek out a man, who is a cunning player on an harp: and it shall come to pass, when the evil spirit from God is upon thee, that he shall play with his hand, and thou shalt be well. And Saul said unto his servants, Provide me now a man that can play well, and bring him to me. Then answered one of the servants, and said, Behold, I have seen a son of Jesse the

Bethlehemite, that is cunning in playing, and a mighty valiant man, and a man of war, and prudent in matters, and a comely person, and the Lord is with him. Wherefore Saul sent messengers unto Jesse, and said, Send me David thy son, which is with the sheep. And Jesse took an ass laden with bread, and a bottle of wine, and a kid, and sent them by David his son unto Saul. And David came to Saul, and stood before him: and he loved him greatly; and he became his armourbearer. And Saul sent to Jesse, saying, Let David, I pray thee, stand before me; for he hath found favour in my sight. And it came to pass, when the evil spirit from God was upon Saul, that David took an harp, and played with his hand: so Saul was refreshed, and was well, and the evil spirit departed from him.

When the Spirit of God left King Saul, then an evil spirit came upon him. This spirit terrified and troubled him. Music in ancient times was believed to have a healing effect on those who were mentally troubled or afflicted. Music therapy is still very widely accepted today to treat mental illness.

But we note that it is the anointing that breaks the yoke. When David took his harp into his hands and played music King Saul was soothed. The evil spirit would depart from him for a time. (See vs. 16 and 23). As a young lad David kept his father's sheep out in the pastures. With so much time under an open heaven, we know that he sang and worshipped the Lord. He had a habit of worship. A habit of worship brings us under the anointing. When he picked up his musical instrument and began to play for King Saul, the anointing came and the devil had to flee in the face of that anointing.

Could King Saul have been freed of this spirit? I don't know the answer to that. The Word tells us that the Spirit of the Lord had already departed from him. He had been given over to the powers of darkness. Yet Jesus delivered other demon possessed men by the power of His word, so I do not know the answer in regard to King Saul.

I Samuel 18:10; And it came to pass on the morrow, that the evil spirit from God came upon Saul, and he prophesied in the midst of the house: and David played with his hand, as at other times: and there was a javelin in Saul's hand.

WE MUST DISCERN:

We see that King Saul **PROPHESIED** under the inspiration of an **EVIL SPIRIT**. This is the same as the instance in Acts when the young girl followed after Paul the Apostle and kept prophesying. She also prophesied by the power and inspiration of an evil spirit. This is where discernment comes in. Paul was so vexed by her prophesying through the inspiration of an evil spirit that finally he cast it out of her.

That is why we must **DISCERN** where the ministry is coming from. We must not just approve every single thing that comes our

Sins Of The Fathers

way. If we are discerning we will know if it is by the Spirit of God or a demonic spirit.

Demonic spirits cannot only prophesy, they can also perform signs and wonders. We can see people and objects levitate, people walk through burning fires without being burned, those who put themself in a trance, divine and tell fortunes, and practice every other form of witchcraft, magic, occult and mysticism. There is much healing going on in the name of New Age which is not of God. People are so eager to allow anyone to lay hands on them and receive from them without even knowing who they are, what they believe, or where the power is coming from. Our culture is rampant with New Age philosophy and techniques. Believers are being drawn in day after day because they do not discern what is from God and what is from hell. Go for a massage and see what happens. I am not saying every masseuse is a New Ager, I am saying **WE MUST LEARN TO DISCERN**. We must learn to discern what is of God and what is from the powers of darkness. It is imperative that we have discernment.

CHAPTER TWENTY ONE

HELP ME!
THERE ARE GIANTS
IN MY LAND!

Sometimes, for reasons only God knows, He just sovereignly sets us free the day we are born again. An alcoholic suddenly stops drinking. A chain smoker quits smoking, and someone is deeply convicted of their heinous sin, repents and never returns to it again. They are totally set free the day they receive Christ as Savior. This is often the case, but there are also times when we must walk through some things even after salvation. We do not necessarily get delivered of every stronghold or bondage in our life the day we get saved.

Isaiah 28:9-10; "To whom will he teach knowledge, and to whom will he explain the message? Those who are weaned from the milk, those taken from the breast? For it is precept upon pre-

cept, precept upon precept, line upon line, line upon line, here a little, there a little."

God gives us our inheritance a little at a time so that we can handle it and grow in it. Just as a baby is weaned from milk and given solid food, God does the same with us. He fills us full of good fresh milk and then the day comes when it is time for us to begin eating solid food. As we begin to partake of solid food our understanding and knowledge of the Word is increased, along with our knowledge of God. We begin to grow more and more because we are being strengthened by the Word of God.

Our New Testament Christian walk is compared to a war. And it is! I remember thinking when I first got saved that my life would be so different ever after. I thought it would be smooth sailing after that. Blessing on the left and blessing on the right, nothing bad ever happening, only blessing from now on. Quite to my surprise I very quickly learned that I had been thrust into the midst of a war not of my making. I did not choose it and in fact I did not want anything to do with it. The last thing on earth I wanted was war. My life before salvation was awful and all I wanted was peace and quiet and some blessing. I wasn't even feeling greedy about the blessing part I just wanted my share of blessing. I was tried of fighting and struggling just to live. Nonetheless, there I was, right smack dab in the midst of a severe, brutal, retaliatory, war.

I can remember the night not too long after I had gotten saved, when I was sitting in my bed reading the Scriptures when God spoke to me. He said, "Now it is time to grow up."

I was a pretty new believer so I had no idea what He was talking about, but I instinctively knew I did not like it. I knew it was going to cost me. He kept giving me the same Scriptures over and over saying; "Count the cost. Unless a grain of wheat falls into the ground and dies it abides alone, but if it dies it will bring forth much fruit. Don't be like the man who decided to build a house and then didn't have what he needed to finish the building."

Luke 14:28; For which of you, desiring to build a tower, does not first sit down and count the cost, whether he has enough to complete it?

John 12:24-25; Truly, truly, I say to you, unless a grain of wheat falls into the earth and dies, it remains alone; but if it dies, it bears much fruit. Whoever loves his life loses it, and whoever hates his life in this world will keep it for eternal life.

God was preparing me and letting me know that there was a price to pay. That price was death to self, death to my own will, death to my own thoughts and my ways of doing things, and death to everything I wanted to hang onto. I was not liking the sound of this at all. When I got saved I was not exactly counting on suffering in the future in any way, it was not a part of my plan. I thought that was all behind me now. I knew this war was now going to become my personal war and the honeymoon period was over. I kind of felt like I was abandoned and could not quite understand why God would thrust me into a war so quickly. I felt like I needed more time with Him all alone, just Him and me enjoying each other. Just Him and me. I just wanted Him to answer all my prayers as soon as I got the words out, let me feel His presence and hear His voice. Just Him and me walking on water together. But that was not to be. He was saying it was time to grow up.

I had a vision. In this vision I was a little girl, very young, perhaps four years old. I had on a beautiful frilly dress, pretty white shoes and sox with ruffles. My hair was fixed really pretty with long curls and made up with a beautiful bow. I was skipping along and holding onto Jesus' hand. I felt very happy being next to Him. He was so big. I remember that I felt so safe next to Him.

As we walked on together it began to grow really dark but with each step we took the step in front of us was lighted. We walked on like that for a while and then all of a sudden I was surrounded by terrible sounds of moaning and groaning. It scared me. Startled I pulled my hand out of His. The moans and groans turned into crying and shrieking. Suddenly I was paralyzed with fear. I couldn't move. Everything was pitch dark. I heard Him say, "Do not let go of My hand. You must hold My hand as you go through because this is war."

I reached around in the pitch black and felt His large hand. I grabbed it as tightly as I could. Even though it was still darker than any dark I had ever known, we continued to walk on. I held His hand so tight! After a little bit it began to grow lighter with each step and I still clung tightly to His hand. As my eyes began to adjust to the dim light I could see people laying everywhere all around me. Some were already dead. Many were dying. Some were in the throws of agony, some were writhing in pain, and there was blood everywhere I looked. I could barely believe what I was seeing. Again He spoke to me and said, "This is a war and you must never let go of My hand as you go through. These are the ones who let go of My hand. They suffered needless agony and many died in the battle unnecessarily because they let go of My hand. You must never let go of My hand."

I have never forgotten that vision. There were times when I was in terrible difficulty, in the midst of real tribulation, and I had no idea how God could ever rescue me. I would remember and then I would pray. I would pray it out loud and tell Him that I was keeping my hand firmly in His hand because I could not make it without Him. I would ask Him to really hold my hand very tightly and not let me go. God kept giving me the Scriptures that say that He will never let go of His inheritance, He will never cast off His people, and those who trust in Him will never be confounded or put to shame. (See Deuteronomy 4:31, Deuteronomy 31:6, 8, I Samuel 12:22, Psalm 94:14, and Isaiah 50:7). I would type up these Scriptures and hang them in my kitchen where I could see them and I would pray them back to Him. By holding onto His hand He would take me past fear into faith. His Word was my sword and His Word had become my safe place.

The wars that the children of Israel fought to clear their land so they could inhabit it in peace is a parallel of our land that God has given to us through Christ. But it must be hard fought and won. Scripture tells us repeatedly that the reward is to the one who overcomes. We each have much to overcome.

I have met some along the way who thought that they were good enough to get to heaven on their own. They lived good lives by all standards. They were people who were kind, just, good and decent. However, we either must repent of our sin or we must recognize and repent of our own self righteousness. Certainly no one is without sin.

At the time when God told me that it was time to grow up, I had already experienced deliverance from actual spirits that had invaded my mind and manifested freely in my life and lifestyle. After being set free I was enjoying this new life and lifestyle in Him. But now this was a new thing. A land that was being given to me as my physical and spiritual inheritance but now I must come into possession of it through warfare.

As I said earlier, when a person accepts Christ as Savior and Lord of their life they may be delivered from some life controlling bondage right on the spot. For example, anger, rage, alcohol, drugs or some other form of addiction or uncleanness may be cut off immediately. However, sometimes they have to walk through some things and take on the giants in their land, just as the saints of old had to battle for their land and their possessions. Even though God promised them a land filled with milk and honey, and He led them through the wilderness to the very land He had promised them, yet, they still had to take up their weapons and go to battle in order to overcome their enemies and take possession of their promised inheritance which was their personal land of promise.

So it is with us. The land is ours. It has been promised to us and secured for us. It was purchased by the blood of Jesus Christ. It was won and paid for in full on our behalf on Calvary. However, we have to put on our armor. We have to stand up, suit up, show up, and go to battle for our inheritance. It has all been bought and paid for, but we must battle to gain entrance into the Promised Land which God has purchased for us because there are giants inhabiting the land of our inheritance and they are not just going to turn it over to us without a fight. God has charged and commanded us to dislodge these giants from our land.

So what are these giants? They can be many different things. They can include objects we have worshipped such as money, reputation, possessions, knowledge, or even other people. The giants can be ambition, pride, status, or any number of other things. These giants who currently possess our land can also be demonic powers who wield an influence on our life because of past generational sin and bondage. These influences can be attitudes, thought patterns that are ingrained deeply in our life, character flaws, or certain habits that are life controlling.

Exodus 23:29-31; I will not drive them out from before thee in one year; lest the land become desolate, and the beast of the field multiply against thee. By little and little I will drive them out from before thee, until thou be increased, and inherit the land. And I will set thy bounds from the Red sea even unto the sea of the Philistines, and from the desert unto the river: for I will deliver the inhabitants of the land into your hand; and thou shalt drive them out before thee.

When we get saved we most likely have some if not many idolatrous habits and life patterns. Self will, selfishness, lack of love, and blatant sin patterns can be compared to the giants that inhabited the Promised Land when the children of Israel went in to possess it. God commanded His children to dispossess those giants. God wanted them driven out of the land and the land cleansed and given over to His children. This was their physical inheritance from Him and it was meant to be a great blessing to them. It is the same with us. God wants our land cleansed because it is meant to be a great spiritual blessing to us. Everything that God gave to the children of Israel was a part of their inheritance. Everything Christ provided for us on Calvary is a part of our spiritual and physical inheritance.

When Christ died on Calvary's hill, He said it is finished! He took back the keys to death and hell and He made a public display the devil. Christ was the Victor. He openly vanquished the enemy and purchased for each one of us all that we would ever need for our life and our godliness.

II Peter 1:3-4; His divine power has granted to us all things that pertain to life and godliness, through the knowledge of him who called us to his own glory and excellence, by which he has granted to us his precious and very great promises, so that through them you may become partakers of the divine nature, having escaped from the corruption that is in the world because of sinful desire.

His divine power has made available to us all that we will ever need to live a godly life. However, it is up to us to take hold of what He provided for us. We do this by faith just as we had to take hold of our salvation by faith. Christ purchased and paid in full for each man's salvation and yet not all are saved. Why? Because each individual must appropriate their own personal salvation through faith. We must appropriate the Baptism of the Holy Spirit individually by faith. We must appropriate our healing individually by faith. Each of these have been purchased and paid for in full by the blood of Jesus Christ. All of it is laid up in heaven where Christ sits at the right hand of the Father in power and majesty. However, we must each lay hold of what is rightfully ours by faith. So there is a battle to be fought. There is a battle to be won. Christ has already promised the victory, but we must be the one to go to battle and take hold of what is rightfully ours. It belongs to us by right of our inheritance in

Him. Even though it has been bequeathed to us in the eternal court of heaven by our heavenly Father, even though it is legally ours, yet the devil will fight to keep us from knowing what is rightfully ours and taking possession of it. He will fight us for control, not only of our very own life, but also our family, our ministry, and all that God has promised and laid up for us in the heavenlies.

Over and over again, God promised His people that He would drive their enemies and all the giants out of the land of their inheritance. However, in most instances, His children had to pick up their weapons and fight the battle. The victory was guaranteed, but they had to battle through and conquer their enemies. Often the battles were long and hard. Many times the saints grew weary in battle, yet the battle continued to rage against them until they were able to take hold of their victory. (See II Samuel 17:29, II Samuel 23:10, Job 10:1, Psalm 6:6).

It wasn't long after that night when God told me it was time to grow up that I realized I had to begin to fight the battle myself. He was still with me, but the battle was mine. I saw it in a vision. I saw myself as an adult now standing next to Him. He was holding my hand and talking to me. He was giving me strategies for battle. My enemy stood facing me prepared in full battle array, but I felt secure because Jesus was standing next to me and directing me. I could feel His strength and power. He urged me to enter the battle arena. I took one step and then another but now He was no longer holding my hand. I turned and saw Him standing behind me smiling and

Sins Of The Fathers

encouraging me to continue into the circle of battle. I could hear His words, "I'm with you. I have given you the victory, now fight the good fight."

I moved forward with fear and trembling looking back again and again to be sure He was still there. Each time I looked back I saw He was still standing there smiling and encouraging me. He did not look nervous but I was getting really nervous. I entered into the battle arena, took this huge sword and swung it around over my head. I took a couple heavy blows myself and stumbled a few times. I got a bit bloodied, but no permanent injuries. As I fought I gained strength and confidence. Somehow I took this nasty giant down. I slew the giant. It was over! I walked away from the battle circle so excited that I had defeated this enemy. Then I heard "Well done!"

I was certain we were finished now. But no, He turned me back again facing away from Him and faced me toward the battle arena once more. There in front of me stood another giant. This one looked a lot bigger and meaner than the last one. I admit I was afraid. But He put His hand on my shoulder and told me, "You can do this! I am with you. I have already given you the victory. Remember the last battle?"

I adjusted my armor with sweaty hands. I picked up the heavy sword and swung it wildly over my head letting out an eerie battle cry. The giant dropped like a sack of flour. I was stunned and elated by my new victory. I turned to face Jesus once again. I was so excited. I could see the joy on His face. I could see He was proud of me.

And so it was that I entered the fray and began to understand that my walk was a battle. I learned that there were many giants who desired to possess the land that was ordained for me. It was always meant to be mine. It was bequeathed to me as my inheritance in God. But I have to fight and win the battles to drive each one of those giants from my land with the weapons, power and the authority He has given me.

We, as believers, have been given weapons to fight our personal war. To us the victory has been guaranteed. Nonetheless, we will have to pick up our weapons and go to war in order to take possession of what is ours by right of inheritance. No one can cower in a corner and think they can escape the battle. The kingdom of heaven is taken by violence and the violent take it by force. (See Matthew 11:12). We must be violent and ruthless regarding the sin in our life and the powers of darkness that have ruled over us in the past.

II Corinthians 10:4; For the weapons of our warfare are not carnal, but mighty through God to the pulling down of strong holds.

Ephesians 6:10; Finally, my brethren, be strong in the Lord, and in the power of his might.

Did you get that? You are to be strong **IN THE POWER OF HIS MIGHT**. Not in the power of your own might, but in the power of His might! That means He is going to go before you, He will come alongside you, and He will come behind you as your rear-guard. You will not go to battle alone. That is how He can guarantee your victory in the battle because He will be with you. He will be fighting for you and He will be standing with you. He already paid for your victory with His death and resurrection. Your victory is assured. It is written in heaven but you must be the one to take hold of it by faith and through battle.

Joshua 1:9; Have I not commanded you? Be strong and coura-geous. Do not be frightened, and do not be dismayed, for the Lord your God is with you wherever you go.

God not only guarantees our victory but He also equips us for the battle. He has given you everything you will ever need to gain your inheritance. It is by faith you will stand and fight. So put on your armor and go into battle to face your own giants knowing that God has already prepared the way for you to come through on the other side in complete triumph. You will vanquish your enemies by faith. You will slay your giants by faith. You will find your deliver-ance by faith. You will cut off generational sin and spirits by faith. You will possess your land by faith.

Ephesians 6:10-18; Finally, be strong in the Lord and in the strength of his might. Put on the whole armor of God, that you may be able to stand against the schemes of the devil. For we do not wrestle against flesh and blood, but against the rulers,

against the authorities, against the cosmic powers over this present darkness, against the spiritual forces of evil in the heavenly places. Therefore take up the whole armor of God, that you may be able to withstand in the evil day, and having done all, to stand firm. Stand therefore, having fastened on the belt of truth, and having put on the breastplate of righteousness, and, as shoes for your feet, having put on the readiness given by the gospel of peace. In all circumstances take up the shield of faith, with which you can extinguish all the flaming darts of the evil one; and take the helmet of salvation, and the sword of the Spirit, which is the word of God, praying at all times in the Spirit, with all prayer and supplication. To that end keep alert with all perseverance, making supplication for all the saints.

Remember, over and over God said that the reward is to the one who overcomes. He told us that the one who overcomes will be given.... What we will be given is what God has stored up for us as our heavenly heritage. God helps us in the fray by giving definite direction and strategy for each battle. He will lay out battle plans for you if you draw close to Him and seek His face.

The children of Israel used many different tactics in battle against their enemies as they were directed by God, strategies which they would not have thought of by themselves. They used lamps and pitchers, a handful of men, tying the tails of foxes end to end with firebrands between them, water in ditches, the sound in the mulberry trees, marching in silence, ambushments, rear attacks, worship, the reflection of the sun on water, and sometimes all they had to do was to stand silently and watch Him work His deliverance in their behalf. (See Joshua 8:2-22, II Samuel 5:23-24, I Chronicles 14:14-15, II Chronicles 13:13, and II Chronicles 20:22).

In the same way that God directed the saints of old, He will direct you in your personal battles with the enemy of your soul.

Exodus 14:13-14; And Moses said to the people, "Fear not, stand firm, and see the salvation of the Lord, which he will work for you today. For the Egyptians whom you see today, you shall never see again. The Lord will fight for you, and you have only to be silent."

The King James Version of the Bible says, "ye shall hold your peace." You aren't going to see them anymore, so just stand still and keep your peace. Don't lose your peace over this, I am going to fight for you. You can just stand there and watch what I can do when you trust me. All you have to do is stand still and keep yourself peaceful while I work in your behalf. When you have done all you can do, then stand still and see the salvation of the Lord, stand still and remain peaceful. I will do the rest!

God also assigns warring angels to battle with us and for us and He will use great signs and wonders in your behalf just as He did for the children of Israel so long ago. He is the same yesterday, today and forever and He is not a respecter of persons.

Exodus 33:2; And I will send an angel before thee; and I will drive out the Canaanite, the Amorite, and the Hittite, and the Perizzite, the Hivite, and the Jebusite.

Deuteronomy 1:30; The Lord your God which goeth before you, he shall fight for you, according to all that he did for you in Egypt before your eyes....

All those "ites" you have been so worried about in your life, those "ites" that have had such strong control over your life and your emotions in the past, God is going to help you drive them out. What He is asking of you is that you do whatever is in your power to in order to fight. Take up your authority and resist them. Then He will do the rest. You will stand and see the glory of the Lord. You will stand in amazement at His power and His great love for you. He will not leave you confounded and confused. You will not be dismayed, because He is a God of Battles and a Man of War.

Exodus 23:28; And I will send hornets before thee, which shall drive out the Hivite, the Canaanite, and the Hittite, from before thee.

God uses natural forces, such as hornets, locusts, frogs, blood, wind, rain, hail, heat, and the sun. He uses signs and wonders. He uses fear, madness, blindness and angels. His indignation, His fury, or His revenge cannot be resisted. The Bible tells us in Job that God has stored up hail for the battle of the last days.

Sins Of The Fathers

As we study the Old Testament we see that upon entering into the Promised Land, the battles were very often long and hard. Even after the children of Israel took possession of their land, they were repeatedly attacked and brought into one battle after another. It was very often the Canaanites who attacked them and not the other way around. As long as there was peace the Israelites left the Canaanites alone. But when the Canaanites assailed them again, the war was on. So it is very often with us. As long as we live in peace and the enemy of our soul seems to be at bay, we leave the battle alone. But then he attacks we are reminded once again that there is a battle to be fought and won and that we still must gain victory over this certain area of our life. Often this is an area of generational sin and bondage.

CHAPTER TWENTY TWO

WHAT KIND OF SPIRIT IS IT?

How can I know what kind of spirit is operating?

You will probably know what kind of spirit it is by its function. In other words the demonic spirit that is operating will demonstrate its powers. That may come in the form of a personality display, a deep character defect, or it can come in the form of an affliction or torment, or the spirit may completely take over the person's will and personality. In this instance it would be possession. No, a Christian cannot be possessed by the devil. He can however be tempted, oppressed, harassed, afflicted and tormented.

Let me make this easy and give you some examples of the manifestations of various spirit beings. A manipulative spirit will manipulate, using lies, deception, treachery, pressure, fear tactics, condemnation and anything else that will back you into a corner and exert pressure on you to accept their will. Whatever the spirit is, that is what the manifestation will be.

A lying spirit will lie and deceive even about small things that would not matter or change anything.

A sexually unclean spirit will manifest in the person's thought life and eventually in their words, dress and outward actions. A sexually unclean spirit can also manifest in a lack of physical hygiene, a dirty home, and even in gluttony. Of course it will manifest also in lustful desires and activity.

A spirit of depression can manifest in oppression, subduing its victim under a lack of emotional display, loss of interest in natural enjoyments, inability to act, depression, and a desire for death. This person may begin to have escape mechanisms such as sleep, food, addictions and alcohol or drugs, or something as simple as television. Escape mechanisms can be anything that will blot out reality and help the person not to think about the circumstances.

I once knew a man who was deeply embittered by the circumstances of his life. He felt that he had been cheated by everyone and everything. Of course he was extremely negative. All his dreams were dead and buried, and he felt weighed down with the burdens of everyday life without much prospect for a different future. Of course he did not know the Lord. He became so bitter and hateful that he would attack people verbally and abuse them without the slightest provocation. Because he often threatened and cursed people he had no friends. People just found it too difficult to deal with him. He had a severe heart condition as well and had been under doctor's care for this condition for many years. I noticed that very often he would clear his throat. He always kept hard candy in his pockets and especially mints. They were always close by in his house and in his vehicle. He would pop them into his mouth regularly and try to clear his throat and he would say that he had such a bad taste in his mouth. One day he was having difficulty with his throat and as he put a hard candy into his mouth to suck on he said; "All this bitterness keeps coming up into my throat and my mouth. The doctor tells me it comes from my heart condition so I need to suck on this hard candy all the time to keep the bitter taste out of my mouth."

I heard the Lord say to me, "Indeed, he does have bitterness in his heart and it does come up into his mouth because of his heart condition."

In his case this was true on two levels, both physical and spiritual. The doctors said he had congestive heart failure. They said that three fourths of his physical heart was dead. His physical heart had become as hard as stone and was hardly functioning. His body was still physically functional to some degree although greatly disabled. He body was trying to survive on less than one quarter of his physical heart. Because his spiritual heart was hard with anger, hatred, bitterness and rejection, it became filled with malice and rancor towards others. Indeed, the bitter taste from his heart came up and filled his mouth. But the bitterness and unforgiveness also damaged his physical heart because of the endless days and years of brooding, resenting and hating.

Sins Of The Fathers

This same man would sit in his easy chair to watch television and all of a sudden he would jump and yell real loud. The first couple of times it scared me, so I began to watch him. I believe that he had a tormenting spirit which no doubt entered in because of his unforgiveness and bitterness. Of course he was not open to any sort of ministry or spiritual discussion. I believe his physical condition was simply a manifestation and outworking of his spiritual condition. Certainly much of our sickness and disease is caused by our spiritual condition or can be passed down into our life through past generational sin and a spirit of torment finds entrance into a heart and life through unforgiveness. (See Matthew 18:34).

Another example of a spirit manifesting follows. I was asked to preach on several occasions in a very small church in a town where I lived. I did not attend that church and do not know how I got to be the one who was asked to preach there, but I was and I did. I decided I should attend the church a couple of times and just sort of check it out so I would know what to do.

The pastor had a small son about two and a half to three years old and a daughter who was just a little older. During a Sunday morning service the youngest child ran down the isle toward the front of the church where his father was preaching. The child began to tear off all his clothes. He would scream and cry as he ran to the front of the church. I have no idea how long this was going on or if it had never happened before. After I saw this happen a second time I gathered up all my courage (and it **DID** take courage), and I made an appointment to speak to the pastor. I had also noticed that his daughter was manifesting signs of an unclean spirit by constantly touching herself inappropriately. I talked with him and told him that his children were being bothered and harassed by an unclean spirit. I wondered if the children had been molested but I did not suggest that to him. The pastor did not receive anything I said and that was the end of that. Of course that was also the end of my preaching in that church. I had no desire to go there ever again.

It was not long after that I heard that the whole family packed up in the middle of the night and left. No one knew quite where. Interesting! I wonder what precipitated that action.

I knew a young married couple who had two little girls. These little girls who were four and five years old at the time would not keep their clothes on. The children also masturbated. I was convinced that parents would always want to be alerted to such behavior so it could be dealt with immediately on a spiritual level. Once again I gathered all my resolve and courage. As gently as I could I talked with the parents. We had just become friends and I really liked them. I informed the parents as tenderly as possible that their little girls were manifesting unclean spirits. They defended the children saying this was normal behavior for such small children, even in public. That was the end of a great friendship with two people I really hoped I would be friends with for a very long time. This was a loss to me.

Whatever happened with the little girls I have no further knowledge. Hopefully they went to their own pastor and talked with him about it and perhaps he was able to minister to them. Or maybe they found someone else they thought might help them. I do hope so. After a time I ran into the husband in a supermarket. I was so pleased to see him. I did not ask any questions, except to ask how the wife and children were. He then told me about the many affairs his wife had throughout their years of marriage. He said that she swore she loved him passionately but she was driven to seek out sexual encounters with other men so often that he did not know if they could hold the marriage together anymore. He said they were being seen by a counselor. But counseling in itself is not sufficient to deal with unclean spirits. There must be deliverance. Obviously the mother had an unclean spirit which now had been passed down to her little girls. I never saw nor heard from them again and have no knowledge of what ever happened to them.

While praying for deliverance over a woman, a certain spirit kept manifesting. This spirit would talk incessantly about anything. Whatever I was praying about at that moment would become the topic of conversation or even questions from her. She would take whoever was praying with her around and around in circles of conversation which led nowhere. I realized quickly that this was a diversionary tactic of the enemy to cause me and others who prayed for her to be distracted and get off track. When she did this, I found it interesting to note that almost everyone who prayed with her got involved in the endless circles of conversation. They did not seem to discern that they were just going around and around while accomplishing nothing. I had to interrupt and tell the others who were praying for her to stop engaging her. Then I took authority and bound the spirit. Immediately she became silent and attentive, and we were able to minister deliverance to her. This was a disrupting spirit.

Whenever I am praying over someone for deliverance, I do not engage the spirits. I see no reason why I should try to get into a conversation with a devil? I know Jesus did on one occasion but He is Jesus, I am not. He asked the demons what their name was and the response was, "Legion, because we are many."

On a gorgeous summer day while I attended a Bible college near St. Louis, a young teenage girl walked into the swimming pool. I was standing beside the fence alongside the pool watching the kids swim and play. I did not know this girl and had never seen her before, but I saw immediately that there was a spirit of rejection that had attached itself to her. She suffered with rejection and great insecurity. Also because of the rejection there was a strong loneliness in her life. This girl wasn't in the pool for a full minute when I saw a young man come around the corner and enter into the pool. He looked as though he was just a little older than she was. I saw a spirit of lust on him and I knew immediately that he would be drawn to her. Sure enough he made his way into the pool and spotted her at the far end of the pool within just a matter of a couple minutes. He was drawn to her, went to her, introduced himself to her and that was that. I knew they would immediately be attracted to one another because a spirit of lust always tries to find a warm friendly recipient in a spirit of rejection.

They became fast friends and of course almost immediately, their young relationship turned sexual. I know this because the mother of the girl came to me seeking counseling regarding this matter.

Someone with a spirit of lust will always be drawn to someone with a spirit of rejection and those spirits will feed off of each other. Someone with a spirit of rejection will also generally manifest behavior that is careless and self destructive because of their own lack of self worth. This behavior will very often be sexually motivated. These behaviors can also include eating disorders, drugs, alcohol or any type of addiction. Depression, oppression and suicidal tendencies may be manifested as well and are very common in people who have a spirit of rejection. Also, there can be a noticeable tendency toward self pity and behavior that draws attention to itself. It is something to pay attention to when you are ministering to someone who has a spirit of rejection. Of course, resentment, unforgiveness and bitterness have an open door in this person, so be sure to minister to those strongholds or spirits as well.

Will there always be a spirit (demon) that you have to cast out? No, that is not always the case. There may just be a stronghold that has to be torn down. Then the one being ministered to needs to have their mind renewed by the washing of the water of the Word of God. But often there will be an attending spirit or spirits, especially in situations when generational sin is involved, and especially when the sin has transferred to more than the succeeding generation.

So how will you know? If the person manifests demonic activity, abnormal behavior, black outs or convulsions while you are ministering to them, obviously there is something at work here, something more than a stronghold. There is a strongman! And the strongman is trying to prevent you from getting to the truth and setting this person free.

WILL THEY TRY TO INTIMIDATE ME?

Demons will recognize you immediately. They will know if you are in the anointing or in the flesh. If you are under the anointing they probably will try to intimidate you right off the bat to keep you from ministering to the person they hold captive to their will. They will try to intimidate you by acting out or by crying out. They may throw the person on the floor or cause the person to scream or manifest in some way that is frightening. Why do they do this? They do it in order to cause you to back off. They want you to turn tail and run.

Luke 8:26-29; Then they sailed to the country of the Gerasenes, which is opposite Galilee. When Jesus had stepped out on land, there met him a man from the city who had demons. For a long time he had worn no clothes, and he had not lived in a house but among the tombs. When He saw Jesus, he cried out and fell down before him and said with a loud voice, "What have you to

do with me, Jesus, Son of the Most High God? I beg you, do not torment me." For he had commanded the unclean spirit to come out of the man. (For many a time it had seized him. He was kept under guard and bound with chains and shackles, but he would break the bonds and be driven by the demon into the desert.)

Also, the demons may try to destroy (kill) the person you are going to minister to because that is their ultimate goal. Kill, steal and destroy.

Mark 9:22; "And it has often cast him into fire and into water, to destroy him. But if you can do anything, have compassion on us and help us."

One time I walked into a church service where a friend of mine was ministering. When he began to lead the congregation in worship, a woman immediately fell to the floor and began screaming and pulling her hair. Everyone got really nervous for just a moment not really feeling sure about what was happening. But finally he went over, took authority and cast the demon out. Then the whole congregation went back to worship.

I ministered to a young woman and her husband for a time until one day God spoke to me and told me I was not to pray for her anymore. She was a pretty young girl. Her husband seemed gentle and soft spoken, really sweet. I really liked both her and her husband. We met at church. She would call me for prayer and she was always in a panic. It seemed there was always a crisis. At first they were general things like noises in the house, shadows, seeing figures darting about the hallways, or something of that nature. I would come and pray through her house and anoint her house with oil, commanding every spirit that was not of God out of the house.

But it did not end there. It actually seemed to intensify. I did not realize it at the time, but that in itself should have been a signal to me. I was still fairly new in all of this and just learning how to deal with spirits. I would always drop whatever I was doing and respond to her emergency. Most often I would run over to her house and with all serious and earnest expectation, I would pray for her current circumstances. I had tremendous compassion for her. It would be one thing and another. I knew that she was being tormented and afflicted by demons and I really wanted to help and see her set free.

This was so many years ago that I do not recall many of the specifics any longer, but I do recall one incident that is burned into my memory. She called me late one afternoon in a great terror begging me to come over immediately. She said she had been raped. I rushed to her apartment and found her lying on the floor with her blouse torn and her clothes disheveled. There was what appeared to be blood all over her clothes. Her face was dirty and her hair messed up.

I cradled her in my arms while she sobbed and begged me to call her husband at work. I said we also needed to call the police but she pleaded for me just to call her husband, get him home by her

Sins Of The Fathers

and they would decide together if they should call the police or not. I honored her wish and called her husband, who of course, rushed right home. I continued to hold her in my arms while waiting for her husband as she sobbed. Her husband rushed through the door and was terrified by what he saw. He took her in his arms and held her talking quietly trying to calm her down while questioning her as to the actual events that had taken place.

I asked if I should stay or leave and he motioned for me to go, which I did. I very quietly exited and left them alone to make their decisions and begin healing. Several days later she called me on the phone and it seemed as though nothing had ever happened. She had a new crisis and never even mentioned what had gone on earlier. In fact, she seemed quite chipper. She spoke in a singsong voice and told me that her husband was back at work. She said they decided not to call the police but that they had spent several wonderful days together after that.

Some time passed and her husband called me asking if we could meet. He wanted me to pray with him but would not tell me what it was about. I met with him at some coffee shop and he proceeded to tell me that the earlier incident of rape never happened. She smeared her blouse with some concoction she made up, ripped her own clothes, and made herself appear as though she had been raped, when all along, nothing at all had happened. He continued to tell me that she wanted and needed his constant, every second, undivided attention. He said that he didn't know how to please her or care for her anymore because of her lying, controlling, divisive tactics. He said he loved her but he was so worn out and frustrated with the constant trauma in their life due to her spirit manifestations. She was driven by a need to control and an insecurity and rejection so deep that she needed constant affirmation and affection from him, not to mention the constant attention which she felt deepened his love and commitment to her, but never solved the problem. The next time she called me, God told me I was not to talk with her anymore. I directed her to her pastor and asked her to be very open and honest with him about all the things that were going on in her life. I did assure her that God desired to set her free and heal her wounds.

Again, when I was still very young in the things of the Spirit of God and did not have a great understanding yet, another incident occurred.

I had an opportunity to meet a wonderful lady who was gracious and generous. She had a magnificent heart of giving and love. On one occasion I and my son had opportunity to stay at her home. She was a believer with a wonderful gift of hospitality. She loved everyone she met and treated them as though they were a royal guest who graced her home.

One night while sleeping in one of the bedrooms a spirit woke me. It was standing over my bed looking at me. I was terrified but I commanded it to leave in the name of Jesus. It did leave immediately upon my command, but I was shaken, to say the least. After a bit I prayed and asked God to show me what kind of spirit that was. I heard Him say it was a spirit of insanity. I went into the next room, woke my son and told him what had just happened and that we needed to pray and take authority.

The next morning I was trying to decide if I should say anything or not. I did not know this woman prior to our having occasion to stay in her home, so I knew nothing of her or her family. However, upon observing her I could see that she seemed quite stable mentally and emotionally, even more so than most. So, although troubled, I tried to dismiss it. Just then the doorbell rang and she opened the door with a grand flourish. She welcomed another guest into her home. It was a gentleman. She introduced us and made him feel as though he were the most important person in the world. I saw her treat each person she met in that manner. She was a most gracious woman.

She explained that she was in the midst of finishing up breakfast, requiring him to stay and partake of course, and leaving the two of us to each other for the remaining moments before breakfast would be served. He talked and talked and talked and to be honest, I kind of wished he would be quiet. I was not used to hearing someone talk on incessantly and I found it quite bothersome actually. But he asked me a million and one questions about myself and told me a million and one things about himself, that to be truthful, I really didn't care about one way or another. Oh well! Finally, he began to go around the room and tell me about the picture of each person which adorned the very large living room. There was grandma and grandpa, each one of the children, each one of the grandchildren and so on. Then he came to one picture and asked me, "Do you know who this is?"

Of course I did not, how could I? He proceeded to tell me that this was a picture of the mother of our gracious hostess. He mentioned her name. Then he told me that she had died within the last few months and explained that she was not in her right mind when she died, she was insane. So obviously, this spirit of insanity had left her mother and was now looking for a new host in the family line.

Unclean spirits want to inhabit human bodies because that is how they can do the most damage to the kingdom of God. Very obviously, it was a generational spirit. I have no idea where, when or in whom the habitation began but this spirit was now roaming through a dry place looking for another habitation in the same family line.

Luke 11:24; "When the unclean spirit has gone out of a person, it passes through waterless places seeking rest, and finding none it says, 'I will return to my house from which I came.' And when it comes, it finds the house swept and put in order. Then it goes and brings seven other spirits more evil than itself, and they enter and dwell there. And the last state of that person is worse than the first."

This Scripture refers to waterless places. The King James refers to the same as "dry places." What are these dry places? Is it a physical place the demons are relegated to when they are cast out? I often hear people pray that way and have wondered about it. But I do not believe that is correct. I believe they live in and prefer dry places. These are the places that are absent of the presence of God and the presence of the Holy Spirit. The Holy Spirit, the freshness of a relationship with Father God through Jesus is what waters our soul. The word washes us (water), cleanses us (water), and refreshes us (water). Dry places are arid places without the word and without the presence of God. Where else could a demon dwell?

I believe there are desert places in the human heart, possibly in your heart and soul. Examine yourself. Do you have desert places in your heart and soul? If you don't spend time with the Lord, if you don't spend time before Him talking to Him, time in prayer, time in worship of Him, if you don't spend time in His word, then you have dry or waterless places in your heart and soul, (mind, will and emotions). When the house is swept clean and in order but is empty, that means that there was a shallow confession, an outward confession, which allowed surface things to be dealt with, but all the while knowing there was so much more. Just below the surface there is a myriad of hidden sin still remaining and covered over. Things that are known about, but the person thinks it is okay to just leave them there for the time being, perhaps even thinking they would deal with them later. Do not allow the enemy to be cast out and come back only to find you have not changed and you have not filled your house with His presence and His Word. Scripture tells us that the enemy will come back with a vengeance and the last state of this person will be far worse than the first.

Sins Of The Fathers

And this is true in the case of generational sin and affliction. An unclean spirit always wants to continue in the same family line because it can cause terrible damage and bring fear on family members, even destroying whole families through its habitation from one generation to the next.

I used to be a member of a ministry team that ministered in the local jails and prisons. It was during these times that I saw the destruction of generational spirits at work in family lines. First one family member went to juvenile hall or jail for a petty crime. Then his or her son or daughter ended up in jail. One after another the family members down the line went to jail or prison. Each time another new member of the family went to jail or prison, it was for a worse crime than the one before. So with each generation there was increase. The things that the first generation thought of in sin but did not do, the second generation did boldly. There was a great increase in the type and ferocity of the sin as the generations went on. One family member after another was being affected. Often members of the family became so hardened that they did not even consider another way of life. Their circumstances seemed normal because it was what they had known for so long. Short of God's salvation and deliverance, they were doomed to continue their life of crime and incarceration and so it would be also for their children after them.

After that I worked for a time in a safe house in Hollywood, California. This was a huge house set up for the care and protection of prostitutes who wanted to get off the streets. I would roam

Hollywood Boulevard at night looking for girls and young woman I could talk to. Most of them would be too frightened to talk to me and would warn me to not come close to them because their pimp was watching from very nearby. On a couple of occasions I was actually able to talk with the pimps as well and would share the gospel message. They would sometimes listen, sometimes not. But they would be eager to have me move on because I was restricting traffic from their girls. Also, they did not want any of their girls rescued or getting any idea about trying to run.

As I went out into the streets night after night for a period of weeks I greeted the young girls and women and soon they began to greet me back. Then one by one I was able to have a minute or two to talk with them and to slip them the address and phone number of the safe house or at least tell them what street it was on and what it looked like in case they ever decided to try to make a run for safety and get out of the life on the streets.

Over and over again I heard the same story. They ran away from home because they were either molested and raped (even violently) by their fathers, brothers, uncles and cousins, by the man who was a family friend, by the mother's new boyfriend, their teacher, their coach or some other trusted adult. Often they were passed around and abused sexually by many family members. Finally, they came to the breaking point and decided it was better to run than to remain in that situation. So one by one, both boys and girls, boarded a bus or a train, or thumbed their way to Hollywood, California, thinking they would be able to make something of their life there. Most often they were met at the bus or train station by the most unscrupulous vultures of our society, who immediately spotted the vulnerable ones. They were approached, often flirted with by a good looking young man. They made quick friends. Because these young kids were alone and needed a friend and a safe place to stay, they were easy to befriend. A tour of the city and introductions to those who would be able to help them make it in modeling or show business, which is what they hoped for, was very welcome. Sometimes they were approached by a young female about the same age, a prostitute who was dressed very conservatively and would be able to make friends with the new person. Convincing her or him to come along, they were offered a safe place to stay and new friendships. It all sounded very inviting to one who had been so abused and wanted so desperately to escape the past and make something different out of their life.

Some of the kids were already drug users, but if they weren't when they arrived, it was only a matter of days until they were offered drugs. Rounds of sitting on the floor cross legged and eating pizza with a bunch of new friends, trading clothes, receiving money for their immediate needs, and soon the drugs were introduced. Being assured that this would not harm them, it would be fun and their new friends would watch over them to make sure nothing bad happened. That was it!

Often these young people were injected with heroine or hallucinatory drugs while they slept, and it was not long before they were

Sins Of The Fathers

so desperate for their drug they would do anything. Also, at this time, their new friends changed and began to threaten them, beat them, abuse them and pass them around sexually; all the while continuing to supply the drugs they were now addicted to. It was not uncommon to hear of a young prostitute who was found by the police after being thrown off the top of one of the buildings along the boulevard. Or ending up slumped against a dumpster in an alleyway, dead from an overdose, or even murdered for no doubt trying to escape an even harder life than she or he had tried to escape in the first place.

Almost all of these young girls and women displayed the same personalities. They were filled with self loathing, anger, bitterness, a sense of revenge, wanting to punish the ones who trapped them in the first place. They had sexually unclean spirits and very often displayed eating disorders; anorexia, bulimia and food addictions. Many of the girls practiced cutting themselves and were disfigured to some degree by their scars. Besides being addicted to drugs, each of them had hardened their hearts to the point that they no longer felt much. That's the way they wanted it. They felt that was the only way they could survive.

But when they ran and got away to our safe-house, they were taken in, loved, clothed (with sensible clothing), fed and told about Jesus Christ and His love for them. They were told this love was clean, pure and holy, not like what they had been promised and known in the past. They were taught that they were accepted by Christ and that He had died for all their pain and sorrow and grief.

It was an ongoing process, teaching them to respect themselves and to expect to be treated with respect. Eventually, most of the girls received Jesus as Savior and Lord, and many received the Baptism of the Holy Spirit. They had classes every day where they learned about His grace and mercy, and learned that they could forgive those who had sinned against them. In this place they were delivered from their hatred and bitterness, the deep roots of rejection they suffered from and the unclean spirits that tormented and ruled over them with an iron fist.

It was interesting that often quite late at night there would be a knock on my bedroom door. When I opened the door I would see a young girl or woman standing there with something in her hand. I would invite her into my room where she would sit on the edge of my bed and hand me a g-string, some see through shirt, or some leather thing, saying she would no longer need this. This was always a sign of tremendous progress because it was a breakthrough. It spelled out the breaking of the ways of the past and a sense of the girl or young woman wanting to go on in her new life. Every once in a while one of them would run back to the streets. That was always such a heartache, whenever one of them would choose their old life again.

Another instance I can relate to you is this. In a church I attended right after I was saved, an elderly woman would sit down next to me on Sunday mornings. During the service she would begin to wiggle and then suddenly her tongue would begin to dart in and out of her mouth and she would start to hiss like a snake. Why she chose to sit

Sins Of The Fathers

next to me I have no idea. But perhaps the spirits that operated in and through her knew that I was a novice; that I didn't understand all of this yet and wanted to intimidate me. It worked!

Every once in a while she would slip onto the floor at my feet and begin to move like a snake slithering under the pews. One day someone grabbed her by the feet, pulled her out the door and took her to another building where they prayed deliverance over her. I don't know whatever happened because I never saw her again. Did she get free? Or did the demons just know their time there was up? I am believing she was delivered. Perhaps she was too embarrassed to come back. But once we have been delivered we need to come back to give testimony and give God the glory.

A few years later I moved into a lovely apartment after returning from a mission trip abroad. When I first looked at the apartment I didn't pay much attention to the two men who lived there. But shortly after moving in I would be visited in the night by a spirit that terrified me. In the beginning I would be too afraid to even open my eyes. The presence was so strong and so evil that I would not even dare to move. I was actually paralyzed with fear. With my heart pounding I would try to speak the name of Jesus but could not, at least not out loud. Finally, under my breath I would be able to say His name and the spirit would leave.

Night after night this went on. Out of a sound sleep I would awake terrified with the presence in my room. Night after night I struggled to say the name of Jesus and command it out, but failed.

Sins Of The Fathers

Finally over a period of time I got stronger and was able to open my eyes. Then after a while I was able to reach for the lamp next to my bed and turn it on. Then I gained enough intestinal fortitude to sit up in bed with the light on. Still I was afraid, but at least now I could pray and when I called on Jesus, the spirit left immediately. Finally, after months of being harassed in this way, I had graduated. The spirit would enter the room while I slept. I would feel his evil presence in my sleep and it would wake me. But now within a split second after feeling the presence I would be on my feet shouting, "In the name of Jesus I demand you leave now!"

I'm sure my neighbors loved this at two o'clock in the morning when my feet hit the floor and I was shouting at the devil! But God was trying to teach me about warfare and the operation of spirits. He was teaching me about the use and the effects of that power which is in His name and in His blood which was shed for us on Calvary.

CHAPTER TWENTY THREE

JEZEBEL IS IN THE HOUSE

Most often when one thinks or talks about Jezebel we use the word "she." We generally think of a Jezebel spirit operating in a woman. Very often that is so. It seems that a woman is a softer target because of her natural ability to be a people person, to be more open, her desire to give and be involved. Even a woman's ability to serve can be targeted by the devil. Also a woman has a natural nurturing spirit and character which makes room for her. But men can also have a Jezebel spirit operating in and through them.

If Jezebel is operating in and through a woman, this Jezebel will most often set her sights on a weak willed man whom she can manipulate easily and use as her voice of authority. She will make friends with him, flatter him and pay the utmost attention to him trying to build him up at every turn. All of this is simply groundwork. She is building a platform from which she can work. When the Jezebel spirit is operating in and through a man, that man is often mean, harsh and abusive. In either case, control is the general mode of operation.

MANIFESTATIONS OF A JEZEBEL SPIRIT:

Just for the sake of making this simple, I will use the female gender when outlining these Jezebel traits. But as I said, a Jezebel spirit can operate through either a male or female.

- Idolatrous
- Lying, cheating and deceitful
- Manipulative, crafty, scheming and calculating
- Divisive, in constant conflict with others
- Will always cast blame refusing to accept responsibility for her part.
- Controlling
- Vengeful
- Not trustworthy, speaks out of two wells (good and evil), whatever suits the moment.
- If Jezebel is a part of the Church, she probably has a religious spirit.
- Will be full of pretense. Will do things in the name of God in order to further her own cause or career.
- Backbiting to bring someone down.
- Spiteful, anything that Jezebel perceives as a threat will be the current target of wrath.

Sins Of The Fathers

- Jezebel has a seducing nature. That may be displayed in her style of dress or even speech, but more often than not it will be more subtle. If Jezebel is male, the seduction may be sexual. It will often come from either male or female in the form of flattery.

- Jezebel will flatter and lift someone up, to cause them to relax and trust, so she can gain their confidence in order to find out secrets. Any dirt is good dirt to Jezebel.

- Jezebel loves secrets and gossip. Anything you say can and will be used against you at a future date. Jezebel is always looking for a way to get something against the person she is dealing with, always looking for leverage and an upper hand. Always looking for tools to do the work perceived as needed to get to the top, pull rank and get attention. Anything Jezebel can use in a pinch to back you in a corner or to shame you into obedience.

- Will try to annihilate you publicly through shame and con-demnation if given the opportunity.

- Whatever you say will be filtered through Jezebel's lenses and changed to suit her current need.

- Jezebel wants all the attention and limelight.

- Jezebel will often say things like "we" when she was not involved in any way. She will often take credit for your work and effort. She will publicly proclaim it as her own work.

Sins Of The Fathers

- If you object or defend yourself or your work you will find yourself in a deceitful battle carried to all fronts in order to bring you down.
- Will do whatever it takes to discredit you if you are receiving attention or under the anointing.
- Nothing you say or do will ever be sacred to Jezebel. It's all future ammunition for a time when you are either in a weakened state or least likely to be expecting it.
- If you confide in a Jezebel you will rue the day.
- Jezebel works out of the flesh but proclaims it to be a work of the Spirit of God.
- Jezebel will even use God as a prop for grandstanding or to get her way. Jezebel will say things like; "Well, God told me...." Who can argue with that? Who can say what God said or did not say to someone else? Unless it goes against the Word. Jezebel will use God to manipulate others into a position to get whatever she is after.
- Will play mind games with anyone and everyone.
- Will use control tactics even such things as mind-control.
- Often privately in league with the powers of darkness to deceive, practicing witchcraft, using new age mind control tactics, or some form of dark arts.
- Always high profile. Needs to be seen and heard.
- Unable to be a faithful friend or companion because it won't always suit her most immediate need.

- Pretends to be a people person, but is need driven and goal oriented.
- The need is to be in total and complete control and have her way in every circumstance.
- While the goal is to be recognized and applauded as number one top dog.
- Jezebel cannot tolerate competition of any sort.
- If you want to be in relationship with a Jezebel you will have to be willing to compromise your own beliefs, character and standards on her behalf on a regular basis. Jezebel will not tolerate disagreement. You will always have to take a subordinate position with her.
- Jezebel can turn all emotions including tears on and off like a faucet. A drama queen extraordinaire.

If Jezebel is in the house it will not take long for you to know it. You will feel her looking over your shoulder and breathing down your neck to see if there is anything you are doing that she can get in on or take credit for. She will try within a very short time to rule over you with an iron fist. If you are weak willed you will succumb to the charm and manipulation. If you are strong willed you will most likely clash. If you are a godly person you will discern what is at work and you will ask God to give you wisdom and guide you through the alligator infested waters.

SPIRIT OF FEAR:

Fear can manifest in many forms. It would be very interesting to know exactly how many people in this country are on anti-anxiety medication or tranquilizers of any sort. Anxiety, worry and tension, fear, torment, phobias and paranoia, seem to be very common among the general population and even in the church. Fear is a tormenting spirit. It leaves one without rest and without peace. At one time I was driven by fear. Fear occupied and ruled over so much of my life. Finally I sat down with the Bible and wrote out every Scripture I could find that spoke about fear and which commanded us not to fear. There are hundreds of Scriptures relating to fear and yet we do fear. Like any other spirit, a spirit of fear can be cut off and cast out. We are to fear no one except the Lord.

This spirit can manifest is so many different ways, but one of the chief ways is that it causes a great fear of displeasing others. This is a man pleasing spirit. The words "man pleasing" are used in the universal sense meaning either a man or woman. Some of the signs of a man pleasing spirit follow.

- A fear of what others might think or say in any given situation. It is someone who is always struggling to keep everyone happy. Never wanting anyone to be upset for fear of rejection.
- Becoming a perfectionist who wants to do everything right so there would be no blame or criticism. Trying to present themself as perfect in every situation. Never a hair out of place, the

house impeccably spotless at all times, clothes and jewelry have to be the best.

- May become an overachiever because of fear of criticism.
- Puts on airs because they want others to think highly of them.
- Fear of the unknown.
- Fear of the future.
- Fear of failure.
- Secretive. Fear that someone would know or discover something unpleasant or something that would put them in a bad light.
- Constant worry and anxiety.
- May be given to exaggeration because of fear of not measuring up.
- Can become aggressive and competitive in their effort to gain attention.

SPIRIT OF DEATH:

A spirit of death can operate in many different ways. This spirit often gains entrance to a life through depression and rejection.

- Constant oppression.
- Depression.
- Self hatred.
- Unforgiveness

- A spirit of death may also manifest itself in certain styles of dress like Goth.

- One with a spirit of death may have odd habits such as a preference to visit cemeteries and dark lonely places instead of bright sunshiny places full of fresh air. I knew someone who used to travel a lot. Whenever they traveled they would go to a drive through restaurant, pick up their lunch or dinner and then find a deserted cemetery in which they would sit all alone and eat. They said they found it peaceful, but in truth, a spirit of death was manifesting in them and drawing them to the cemetery on a regular basis creating a bond with a spirit of death. They admitted to me that their constant thoughts spoke to them about how peaceful life would be if they were dead.

- Thoughts of death can cloud a person's mind all the time no matter what they are doing. Thoughts of death will never be far from them.

- This person can develop an intense desire for death and they may begin to speak of death or write about it on a regular basis.

- They may talk about suicide. People often say that if someone is talking about suicide they will not do it. I strongly disagree.

- This person can become very reckless in their behavior because they begin to tempt death. They are testing their limits to see how they really feel deep inside; to see if they really have what they need to actually commit suicide.

Sins Of The Fathers

- They might have very extreme enjoyments, (very extreme sports), always pushing the limits.
- This person does not care if they live or die. They may vacillate between wanting to live and see change and a strong desire for death.
- A spirit of death can begin to manifest in various illnesses of short or long duration.
- This person may enjoy music that glorifies death, suicide or murder.
- This spirit can also manifest itself through torture or murder, getting involved in crimes of this sort.
- Murder brings a curse (See Genesis 4:11).

It is interesting to note that my father was suicidal for many years before he died. He would tell me often that he wanted to kill himself. My grandfather also was suicidal at one time in his life and perhaps for the rest of his life, I don't really know. Was my real mother suicidal as well? I do not know, perhaps she was. But it was definitely a generational spirit of death coming down from my father and grandfather.

If God had not intervened in my circumstances and I had died when that demon appeared to me as an angel of light and told me God required my death, (before going to the seminary), would I still have gone to heaven? Yes, I would have because I belonged to Him! But my life would have been cut off because of being deceived by this unclean spirit. I would never have fulfilled His ministry for me and through me. I would have been cut off in the midst of my days.

Remember, that the devil and his cohorts come to **STEAL, KILL,** and to **DESTROY** and God's people die because they have a lack of knowledge.

HOPELESSNESS:

- Hopelessness will be another manifestation of the same spirit. One who suffers from the torment of this spirit will see no purpose in their life.
- This person is oppressed and depressed most of the time.
- They will try to block everything out one way or another.
- They may have many escape modes, one of which is often sleep.
- Other escapes are of course, drugs, alcohol, food, shopping or any other type of addiction.

SPIRIT OF INFIRMITY:

This spirit goes along with a spirit of death.

- Various symptoms without the illness.
- Various illnesses of a very serious nature.
- Diverse complaints and symptoms in various parts of the body at the same time.

Sins Of The Fathers

- Pain inside the body that moves from place to place. This is a spirit that afflicts and or torments one with pain.

- Desperate emotional pain inside where no one can touch it opens the door for a spirit of infirmity to begin to manifest.

- Resentment, unforgiveness and bitterness.

- I got very strange illnesses, like blood poisoning, food poisoning, pernicious anemia, cysts and tumors, and then very serious diseases like scleroderma, malaria (the kind that affects your brain and kills you), swollen liver and spleen, and many varied viruses.) One thing after another.

- Hearing doctors proclaim over me while they examined or treated me, "You are going to die, there is nothing we can do." This increased my desire for death because I felt like it was inevitable anyway, so we might as well get it over with.

SPIRIT OF REJECTION:

- Depression is a major sign.
- Feeling a deep sense of sorrow and grief.
- Despair.
- Feeling like their personal life has absolutely no value, no future and no direction. A sense of hopelessness.
- Believing no one loves them.
- Self centered and constantly introspective.
- Feeling like there is no place to belong.

Sins Of The Fathers

- Thinking something is dramatically wrong with them and constantly questioning themself about what it could be.
- Compares themselves with others.
- A problem with envy and jealousy.
- Anger, resentment unforgiveness and bitterness.
- Unwilling to recognize and accept responsibility for their own sin but wanting to blame others.
- Cannot let go of the past.
- Self hatred.
- Fear of man and fear of rejection.

ADDICTION:

- A person can become addicted to anything.
- Addiction may manifest in the form of alcoholism or drugs.
- Food, overeating or anorexia or bulimia.
- Shopping, hoarding.
- Smoking.
- Gambling or other games especially computer games.
- Sports of any type.
- I once knew a woman who was addicted to chewing coffee beans. She would get out of bed in the middle of the night and go into the kitchen to sit and eat coffee beans by the handful.

When I refer to a person as a "host" to a demonic spirit I am not necessarily saying that person is possessed, although they certainly can be. But most generally I am saying that a spirit or spirits are operating through this person by exerting influence or control over a particular area of their life. Therefore I refer to that person as the host. The demon(s) need a person or animal to operate through, most generally a human being.

SEXUALLY UNCLEAN SPIRIT:

Spirits will operate through the family lines in various ways. Any unclean (demonic) spirit can have many varied manifestations. Rejection brings a longing to be loved and accepted. One who is suffering from rejection does not know what it feels like to be loved and will often mistake sex for love. Sexually unclean spirits can manifest in every form of uncleanness and activity imaginable.

There is always a progression of sin. Just as an example, let's say that the first person of the family line where the bondage begins has had a problem with lustful thoughts that he does not take control of. This person gives themself to their sin and bondage is created. This same spirit being passed on may now manifest in another family member in the form of a lust for food becoming a glutton, or a lust for things as a shopaholic or a hoarder. In the next generation this same spirit will try to find a likely host and bring that person even further into bondage, causing the next host to become more deeply involved in sexual uncleanness. Now this spirit takes on a more sinister role and can be acted out in the form of molestation, incest, pedophilia or rape. Soon that spirit has full sway over its host and at least several members of the same family line and may begin to manifest sexual uncleanness in other ways as well. It may manifest in other forms such as homosexuality, bestiality or prostitution, and so on down the family line. With each successive generation the sin becomes more entrenched and is practiced in an even greater measure than the previous generation. In other words, what grandpa or grandma only thought about, their children actually practiced, at least in secret. Then their children took that sin to a greater measure and what had previously been practiced in secret was now practiced openly. The following generation always takes it to new and greater lengths. It is always progressive and it is always a downward spiral unless it is dealt with.

As these spirits travel down through the generations they gain strength because they are fed continually by sin. The gain a stronger hold on the family line and become more destructive with each generation. The sin that was only considered in one generation becomes a strong iron clad hold on the next generation.

Often it will skip one generation only to reappear in the next generation.

A spirit will always work in two directions at the same time. The spirit of lust for example will not only cause the person under bondage to lust after others, but it will also draw others to its host by lust.

Another example is this; a spirit of rejection will not only feel and manifest traits of rejection, but that same spirit will also cause

Sins Of The Fathers

others to feel rejected by its host. Also, it will draw others with a spirit of rejection to them. A demonic spirit will always be drawing someone to it but it will also be operating against others through its host at the same time.

CHAPTER TWENTY FOUR

TEARING DOWN STRONGHOLDS AND BREAKING CURSES

If you will read Deuteronomy chapter 28 and Leviticus chapter 26 you will see that curses are conditional. They cannot come on someone without an underlying cause. The curse causeless cannot come upon us. This cause is always sin. Sin is the sowing part and the curse is the reaping part. The solution is sincere repentance. That means a deep hearted desire to turn from sin and have a lifestyle change in this area. If it is a matter of generational sin, then there must be an identificational repentance. Identificational repentance is putting ourselves in the place of the one who has sinned and asking God's forgiveness for the sin or sins that were committed which brought the curse in the first place.

Galatians 6:7-8: Do not be deceived: God is not mocked, for whatever one sows, that will he also reap. For the one who sows

to his own flesh will from the flesh reap corruption, but the one who sows to the Spirit will from the Spirit reap eternal life.

To have a head-knowledge of God and His ways is not sufficient. We must come to a place of understanding where we know that we are His people and He is our God. We must come to the place in our walk with Him that we have a working knowledge and comprehension of what is ours through salvation. We must be aware and knowledgeable of what is ours by right of inheritance through the finished work of Calvary.

YOU CAN BREAK THESE CURSES:

Ask the Spirit of God to search your heart and soul to show you if there is any wicked way in you. The first step is always repentance. We must come before God, humble ourself, admit our sin and ask His forgiveness. God is faithful and just to forgive our sins when we confess them to Him.

I John 1:9: If we confess our sins, he is faithful and just to forgive us our sins, and to cleanse us from all unrighteousness.

You can break curses on your life or in your family line because Jesus wore the crown of thorns on Calvary. Thorns are a symbol of the curse. (See Genesis 3:15-19). When the crown of thorns was placed on His head He took the curses we deserved. Therefore we can be freed because He already paid the price in our behalf.

Here is what you can do to break a curse that is operating in your life:

- Renounce all the works of darkness.
- Renounce every known curse on your life or your generational line.
- If it is generational, pray a prayer of identificational repentance asking God to forgive the sins of your past generations that initiated the curse or curses. If you know who the people are who committed particular sins pertaining to this bondage, name them specifically, name their sins and ask for God's forgiveness for their sins.
- Break all spiritual ties you have with anyone in the past generations or currently have that would be displeasing to God in any way.
- Renounce any allegiance or alliance you have made with the powers of darkness by coming into agreement through oaths, vows, verbal agreements, mental assent or unrepented sin.
- Renounce and repent for any participation in idolatry of any sort.
- Renounce and repent for any part you have had in witchcraft, mysticism, or the occult, including New Age practices.
- Renounce any attending spirits and their activity in your life, the life of your family and the previous generations.
- Ask Father God to begin to give you a really clear understanding of what was purchased for you on Calvary. Ask Him

to show you what is yours by right of redemption through Jesus Christ. You cannot walk in it if you do not know what is yours. II Peter 1:3-4.

- Contend in prayer for what is rightfully yours.

- Break the curse by an act of faith in God and an act of your will.

- Choose the fullness of salvation.

- In your own words pray and reverse the curse.

- Ask God's blessing to come on you and your family including your future generations according to His word, to overtake and replace the curses that were destroying you and your family.

- Now stand firm in the promises of God in the Word. Bury the Word in your heart.

- Resist further temptation and refuse any further agreement with the powers of darkness.

- Walk in faith believing God is true to His Word and the curses are broken.

I think it is real important for you to pray in your own words. God will honor your words if they come from a sincere heart. After you have prayed in your own words, remember to thank God for His great faithfulness to you and for the blood of Jesus Christ that delivers you and sets you and your family free from all bondage. Remember that you must turn from all the past behavior patterns that would reinforce or encourage this type of behavior again. By choosing the same old behavior patterns, you will allow the enemy to reestablish the same strongholds and bondages once again. If you choose your sin again, you will fling the door in the spirit realm wide open to invite those same spirits right back into your life to operate in the same manner as before. However, this time it will be with a greater vengeance. You will bring the same curses right back down on your head. You are now the gatekeeper. Guard your heart and choose wisely. Choose to live a holy life and stay under the protection of the Almighty.

A HERITAGE OF GENERATIONAL BLESSING:

Just as there can be a heritage which comes to us of generational sin and generational curses, there can also be a heritage of generational blessing passed on to us and our children after us. God said He would **BLESS** the generations of the righteous to a thousand generations. That is a heritage of blessing being passed down upon our children and our children's children for one thousand generations. There is an inheritance to the saints of God which is ours if we choose it. Just as there is a harvest of sin and curses that is passed down through the generations of the unrighteous there is also a harvest of tremendous blessings which can be passed down through all our future generations. We are the ones who can choose what kind of heritage we desire to leave our children, our grandchildren, our great grandchildren and all our future generations. That is exciting!

Sins Of The Fathers

You have an enemy. It is his mission, his desire and his plan to destroy you and your loved ones, even through future generations. You have a choice now. Truth is a weapon. Choose life.

Numbers 33:55; But if you do not drive out the inhabitants of the land from before you, then those of them whom you let remain shall be as barbs in your eyes and thorns in your sides, and they shall trouble you in the land where you dwell.

Breinigsville, PA USA
14 March 2011
257573BV00003B/2/P